The Hellenistic Kingdoms

PORTRAIT COINS AND HISTORY

Norman Davis and Colin M. Kraay

Photographs by P. Frank Purvey

with 212 illustrations
2 maps
and 1 plan

THAMES AND HUDSON

Contents

Chapters 2, 3, 5 and 6 are written by Norman Davis; chapters 1, 4, 7 and the numismatic descriptions by Colin M. Kraay.

Introduction

The three centuries of the Hellenistic Age were inaugurated by Alexander the Great's invasion of the Persian Empire in 334 BC. We present here, dynasty by dynasty, successive accounts of the kings and queens of that age, illustrated by their portrait coins. Though all these monarchs were overshadowed by Alexander's gigantic personality many were remarkable personages in their own right, and some of their names still linger in common memory; Ptolemy of Egypt, Perseus of Macedon, Seleucus Nicator and Antiochus Epiphanes of Syria and Cleopatra, the last of the Ptolemies.

Their coin portraits rarely flatter these strong-willed men and women. Most were of Macedonian descent, well featured and ruddy complexioned, handsome as a king should be, and some of their queens were beautiful. But where the face was unimpressive it appeared so on the coins, 'warts and all'. Even Cleopatra, with all her charms, looks on her coins the plain and heavy featured woman she was. Although most of these monarchs inherited their thrones, generally they were fully possessed of the attributes essential to kingship in their turbulent times; military prowess, a shrewd ruthlessness and that ability to inspire personal loyalty which is the very essence of leadership.

Be they kings, presidents or dictators, in our time rulers are ever present, the familiar face and voice inescapably with us. But in antiquity the king was remote, clothed in majesty, seen rarely and then only at a distance. 'There's a divinity doth hedge a king'. If he were deified during his lifetime there would be cult statues in the temples, but for the mass of his people it was only on his coins that the likeness of the king could be seen.

Thus over and above their value as money, these royal portrait coins, bearing the king's head, name, dignities and titles, were a necessary communication between the king and his subjects, a continuing proclamation of his royalty and his rule. Otherwise, word of the king and his doings reached the provinces rarely and belatedly as traveller's tales. Such news as did come was of the greatest interest, to be long and eagerly discussed, for the careers of many of these Hellenistic monarchs were stranger and made more romantic telling than imagination could well invent.

The Hellenistic Age, during which the light of Greek civilization, its art, philosophy, literature and science (and the Greeks themselves) spread over and transformed much of the world, was 'grandfathered' by Philip II of Macedon, the father of Alexander the Great. At the battle of Chaeronea in 338 BC, Philip's professional army decisively defeated the combined forces of Athens and Thebes, and at last the endlessly warring Greek states were united—with Philip as master. Then at a congress at Corinth in the following year he tied all the states except Sparta in a political and military league, the ultimate purpose of which was to join with him in a war to free the Greek cities of Asia Minor from the Persian yoke, his long cherished ambition.

Philip would, of course, have been well informed of Persia's weakness in her western satrapies, and confident that with a Greek army added to his own Macedonians he could overcome any force that might be brought against him. He proceeded to organize men and supplies. When he was assassinated two years later, ten thousand of his troops were already across the Hellespont into Asia Minor in preparation for the coming of the main army.

Alexander succeeded to his father's kingdom, he succeeded also to his father's war, but his vision and ambitions were wider and greater. Philip's aim had been no more than to free the Greek cities of Asia Minor from the Persian yoke; that would be glory enough. Alexander wanted to conquer the empire of the Great King, he who declared 'I am the Lord of all the world from the rising to setting of sun'. He wanted not only to conquer the Persian Empire but to Hellenize it. Aristotle had been his schoolmaster and from childhood he had steeped himself in Greek literature, sleeping with a volume of Homer beneath his pillow; he believed himself descended from Heracles, predestined for the task. With his army went scientists, historians and philosophers.

Thirteen years later, as he lay dying at Babylon, Alexander must have realized that his generals would soon abandon his concept of a Graeco-Persian state; that being the men they were they would fight among themselves for power, quite heedless of his hopes and plans. He had begun the Hellenization of his empire with the founding of dozens of cities strategically placed within the lands of his conquest, Alexandrias which were to be centres of Greek culture. The early Seleucids did indeed follow him in this, building many Seleucias, Antiochs and the like, but their purpose was no more than to create foci of military power with which to hold down their subject peoples.

Yet much of Alexander's dream did come to pass. The Hellenistic kings were immensely proud of their Greek heritage, and once firmly established they lavished money and effort on the Hellenization of their realms. Alexandria, Antioch and Pergamum especially became centres of Greek art and scholarship, beautiful cities which came to rival Athens herself, 'the school of Hellas'. For all her power and pride Rome too became Hellenized, and familiarity with Greek culture and the Greek tongue was essential to the education of a gentleman. Two centuries after the death of Cleopatra of Egypt, the last of the Hellenistic monarchs, the Emperor Marcus Aurelius wrote his *Meditations* of a Stoic philosopher in Greek.

Like other Ages created by historians the Hellenistic Age is a sector cut from the continuum of History; it developed out of previous Ages and with them became the joint foundation of those that were to follow. Yet despite the inevitable dependence on what had gone before, the beginning of the Hellenistic Age is unusually clearly marked and the political character of the Age itself is decisively different from those of preceding periods.

Philip II of Macedon had already exhibited the weakness of the city-state, but it was Alexander who firmly changed the course of political development into the direction of much larger units, even though the single great empire which he envisioned and momentarily created was not to be lastingly realized for another three centuries. The end of the Hellenistic Age is much less clearly defined. The death of Cleopatra in 30 BC and the absorption of the last major Hellenistic kingdom into the Roman Empire marks its final disappearance, but the beginning of the end is perhaps nearly two centuries earlier when Rome first conquered a Hellenistic state, Syracuse, in 212 BC. From this point of view the greater part of the three centuries usually called the Hellenistic Age could equally well be called the Age of Republican Rome; in fact, it is often their contacts with Rome that form the best documented episodes of the history of the Hellenistic Kingdoms.

Against the menace of Rome the Hellenistic kingdoms failed
to combine exactly as the Greek city-states had failed to combine against Philip II and both succumbed piecemeal to their
more powerful adversaries. Yet the military record of the
Hellenistic Age should not be allowed to obscure its achievements in other fields. In warfare the Greeks could teach the
Romans little except in a few technical fields such as artillery;
in more peaceful pursuits the Romans had everything to learn.
'Graecia capta ferum victorem cepit': in the famous line of Horace
Greece was not the Athens of Pericles but the Greek civilization
of the Hellenistic Age. The conquest of the Persian Empire by
Alexander had opened vast territories to Greek activity whether
by trade or government or scientific study; Greek thought in
all fields was enlivened and reinvigorated by contact with other
civilizations. The kingdoms into which Alexander's empire
dissolved each possessed far greater resources with which to
foster these new tendencies than any Greek city-state, except
perhaps Athens, had ever previously had.

These resources were used to promote scholarship, art and
architecture. A few examples only need be quoted of that
intellectual spirit upon which the Romans eagerly seized, realizing that their own native culture provided nothing comparable.
Both the Attalids and the Ptolemies founded great libraries,
and the Ptolemies in addition maintained a body of scholars
in the Museum at Alexandria; at these institutions the texts of
the literary works of the past were collated and edited, and
the chronological co-ordination of ancient history was attempted. In this climate the geometrical works of Euclid were
composed, and the chronological, astronomical and geographical studies of Eratosthenes. In poetry the writings of Apollonius
Rhodius, Aratus, Callimachus, and Theocritus all had their
influence on Roman literature and, in particular, on Virgil in
the Augustan Age.

Perhaps a more original contribution of the Hellenistic Age
which was to be developed on a tremendous scale throughout
the Roman Empire was in monumental architecture. At
Alexandria and Antioch all traces of the great competitive
complexes of buildings which once existed have disappeared,
but at Pergamum enough remains for its scale to be appreciated.
High up on the hillside, where its marble fan could be seen from
afar, was cut the precipitous theatre as the central feature of
the group of monuments which crowned the hill—the royal
palace, the library, the great altar of Zeus and other buildings.

Elsewhere, huge temples were erected at Sardis and Didyma, both of which survive in part, and at Ephesus, which has wholly perished; more practical works which directly inspired copies were the great theatres, as at Ephesus, and the famous lighthouse of Alexandria. In the course of time cities throughout the Roman Empire were to be equipped with similar buildings which in a single complex can today best be seen at Leptis Magna in North Africa.

Such features and ideas will always be inherited by one civilization from another, but sometimes the Romans inherited territories in the most literal manner, as when Attalus III bequeathed his kingdom in Asia Minor in 133 BC, and Ptolemy Apion bequeathed Cyrene in 96 BC to the Roman people. Such bequests tended to be received at short notice and without preparation, so that the territories in question, which might be settled and highly organized, were often left to govern themselves. The results were sometimes unhappy, for in the absence of an effective controlling power piracy and other disorders so developed that soon drastic and prolonged action was called for; but such cases do show very clearly how non-Roman systems of administration could be taken over wholesale with a change only at the very apex of the administrative pyramid.

The clearest example, because it is the best documented, is Egypt. The country and its inhabitants had always been in the full sense the property of its divine ruler, the Pharaoh; following the Macedonian conquest the Ptolemies, and then the Roman emperors, in turn occupied the exalted position of their predecessors. Though we cannot always tell how much was adopted from Pharaonic practice, and how much was Ptolemaic innovation, it is clear from surviving papyrus documents that under the Ptolemies the whole economic life of the country was regulated down to its last detail by royal officials with the sole object of securing the maximum income for the royal Treasury. This elaborate organization was inherited by the Roman emperors who, as absentee Pharaohs, had to install a prefect with vice-regal powers to administer a country which was virtually a private imperial state. In eastern Sicily, too, the tax system regulated by Hiero II seems to have long remained in force in the Roman province. In the western half of her empire Rome normally acquired territories which had no higher form of organization than that of minor competing tribes; in such areas a deliberate policy of Romanization was required, the creation of towns as administrative centres with their equipment of public buildings, the recruitment of officials, and the education of at least the upper class in the Latin language and Roman practices.

In the eastern half little of this was needed; great cities had long existed as centres of settled population; Greek was everywhere used as a common language; elaborate legal, financial and administrative systems were in operation. In short the whole organization of the Hellenistic world was available to be taken over, requiring only slight adaptation to serve the new masters. Alexander's empire had been too varied in race, culture and language to survive; but over the areas which were to be incorporated in the Roman Empire the Hellenistic Age had diffused a common Greek culture, much of which was also absorbed by the paramount power, Rome. The Roman state was represented by a number of senior officials changed at frequent intervals, and by a military garrison in frontier provinces; loyalty was focussed on the emperor in Rome not only by certain administrative procedures whereby addresses, appeals and petitions could be sent direct to the emperor, but by the development of the imperial cult.

The Roman emperor was the successor of the various rulers, kings and dynasts of the Hellenistic Age, and at least in Egypt continued to be invested with the titles and trappings of his predecessors, the Pharaohs. But even in Rome the emperor was not a native growth; his prototype was not the ancient kings of Rome who had been expelled with ignominy in the sixth century BC, but the much more recent Hellenistic king, whom he had replaced. Apart from occasional experiments in adoption, the Roman emperor was a hereditary monarch like the Hellenistic king and, like him too, was the object of state cult. Already in the civil wars following the assassination of Julius Caesar the triumvirs are identified with deities, Antony with Dionysus, Octavian with Apollo, and Sextus Pompey with Neptune; on cistophori struck in Asia Antony is portrayed wearing the ivy wreath of Dionysus like a Hellenistic king. Early in the empire first the deceased Augustus, but from Nero onwards the living emperor as well, is frequently portrayed on his coinage wearing the rays of the sun-god like Antiochus VI of Syria. But these are only selected outward signs of the fact that the Roman emperor, as Antiochus IV and other Hellenistic rulers, was a Θεὸς ἐπιφανής, a god visible in human form, whose powers enabled him to be the saviour and benefactor of his subjects and the victor over their enemies. As such the Roman emperors followed Hellenistic precedent in regularly displaying their portraits upon their coins.

Finally, to end where we began, with Alexander himself. The Romans remained very conscious that in their empire they had recreated something which Alexander had already created before them, 'and the shining example of Alexander himself remained vividly before them. Until the western provinces of Spain, Gaul, Germany and Britain had been fully integrated into the Roman empire the Greek East appeared to some to be its natural centre, and both Julius Caesar and Caligula are said to have contemplated transferring its capital to Alexander's greatest foundation, Alexandria in Egypt. Augustus used a portrait of Alexander as his personal seal, which suggests that he saw some parallel between Alexander's youthful rise to world power and his own. Less worthily, Caracalla in gesture, dress and bearing modelled himself on Alexander of whom he claimed to be a reincarnation; and one of his near successors ruled as Alexander, dropping his many other imperial names. Even at the very end of antiquity on those coin-like pieces, known as contorniates, which seem to be connected with heathen propaganda around AD 400, Alexander Magnus still appears in that gallery of the great men of the past, whose portraits were transmitted to the medieval world.

CHAPTER ONE

Alexander the Great 336–323 BC

When, in 336 BC, Alexander the Great succeeded his father   *1–9*
Philip II of Macedon, his life had already been varied and
eventful. Three years of tuition from Aristotle had opened his
mind to Greek literature and political theory; at the age of
sixteen he had acted as regent in the absence of his father, and
in this capacity had conducted a successful campaign against a
rebellious Thracian tribe; at eighteen he had commanded the
heavy cavalry on the left of the Macedonian line at the battle
of Chaeronea against the combined forces of Athens and
Thebes. These activities had no doubt been conducted under
the eyes of experienced administrators and generals, but if any
doubted the calibre of the new king, the first two years of his
reign showed that he was no more to be trifled with than his
father had been. On his succession to the throne he eliminated
all possible rivals with a ruthlessness which was to show itself
time and again whenever he detected any threat to his own
supremacy.

By the winter of 335/4 BC Alexander was ready to prepare for
the great project initiated by his father, the invasion of Persia.
The bridgehead across the Hellespont into Asia Minor established by Philip in 336 BC with the landing of 10,000 men under
Parmenio and Attalus still held, for in the absence of decisive
direction from King Darius, who was newly established on
the throne, only the inadequate and piecemeal forces of the
local Persian governors had been brought against it.

Alexander's main striking force was the phalanx, a formidable body of heavily armoured infantry equipped with the
sarissa, an eighteen-foot long pike. Philip had learned the order
of the phalanx from Epaminondas at Thebes, when in his youth
he had been held hostage there, and with it he disciplined the
wild Macedonian tribesmen into a powerful weapon which
he and Alexander used with almost unfailing success. The
phalanx, a Greek word which meant originally 'heavy infantry

in order of battle', was organized in battalions of a thousand men, who fought shoulder to shoulder seven to nine ranks deep. Later the sarissa was shortened to fourteen feet for the first rank and lengthened to twenty-two feet for the third, so that in battle the phalanx front presented a triple row of pike points.

There were also contingents of heavy infantry (hoplites) contributed by the Greek allies and light armed and specialist troops such as the Cretan archers. The total infantry force numbered about 30,000 men. The 5000 cavalry were partly Macedonian and partly Thessalian, with smaller units drawn from Greek and native allies.

In race and language Alexander's army had a homogeneity that could never be matched on the Persian side, for Persian armies were recruited from all the many peoples of their vast empire, with bodies of Greek mercenaries enrolled to stiffen the local levies. In cavalry the Persians far outnumbered Alexander's but this advantage could be neutralized by a skilled tactician so that, in general, the superiority of Alexander's army could be safely predicted.

At sea the position was different, for Macedon was not a maritime power and Alexander had to rely upon a fleet of only 160 triremes assembled from his Greek allies. Though adequate for guarding his link across the Hellespont, which was far from Persian waters, and for occasional operations off the coast in conjunction with the army, it was no match for the far larger Persian fleet, which was based on Phoenicia. But whatever assessment of relative strength is made, the decisive factor was that though there were many brave and loyal commanders on the Persian side, there was no one commander of genius with a dynamic singleness of purpose comparable to Alexander's.

But despite all this, one may well ask why Alexander and his generals believed that an army of thirty-five to forty thousand men, half of them Greeks who had neither admiration nor loyalty for Macedonia, and with whom until recently they had been at war, should be thought strong enough to challenge successfully the Persian King, with his enormous reserves of manpower and great wealth.

Their belief arose from their knowledge of the Persian Empire's weakness, especially in Asia Minor, where the Greek cities of the Aegean coast provided the west with a continuing flow of information as to conditions there. Persia was no longer the empire of Cyrus the Great or even of the days when Macedon, a century and a half before and herself then a vassal of the Great King, had seen the enormous armies of Xerxes march across her land to the invasion of Greece. Now Persia was in disarray, its king Darius III a weak and amiable man, who in the event was to panic in the face of danger during the crucial battles of Issus and Gaugamela. Most of the far eastern provinces had been lost, and in the west several satraps had either seceded or lapsed into semi-autonomy.

Leaving his father's general Antipater as Viceroy in Macedonia, in the spring of 334 BC Alexander crossed the Hellespont with the main body of his army. As his ship approached the far shore he is said to have jumped down in full armour after casting his spear into the beach, thus manifesting his intention of conquering Asia by force of arms.

At the start the local Persian commanders certainly underestimated their opponent, their fears having been allayed by the Macedonian failure to extend the bridgehead established by Philip two years before. With an army of about ten thousand cavalry and a contingent of 5000 Greek mercenaries they attempted to check Alexander's advance at the river Granicus, about forty miles east of the Hellespont. Alexander forced the river crossing, dispersed the Persian cavalry, and surrounded and massacred all but 2000 of the Greek mercenaries. His losses were small and his victory decisive, but it had nearly ended the invasion, for at one moment Alexander in great danger was saved only by the intervention of Cleitus, one of his closest companions.

The way into Asia Minor was now open, for it would be some time before a new and more effective Persian army could be assembled. But this did not mean that Asia Minor could be simply 'occupied', for it was a vast and varied area, some parts of which had never submitted even to Persian rule, while others belonged to princes who, though nominally Persian vassals, were in effect independent.

Mindful of the need of securing his line of communication and of his role as leader of a Panhellenic crusade, Alexander first liberated the Greek cities of the west coast. He or his representatives were welcomed with enthusiasm except at Miletus and Halicarnassus, whose garrisons, with the aid of contingents of the Persian fleet, stood siege until they were taken by assault. Elsewhere less purely Greek or wholly non-Greek areas such as Caria, Lycia and Pisidia proved more troublesome, and the task of pacification was left to subordinates.

In this way Alexander passed some eighteen months, moving first to Lycia in the south-west and then to Gordium in central Anatolia, where he dealt with the famous knot. This knot, the ends of which were concealed within it, tied the yoke to the pole of King Gordius' wagon. Legend said that whoever untied it would rule Asia; Alexander cut it with his sword. Finally, in the summer of 333 BC, he passed through east Anatolia to force the narrow pass through the Taurus mountains into Cilicia, and by a dramatic cavalry dash saved Tarsus from destruction by the local Persian satrap Arsames. He left Asia Minor imperfectly subdued, but it was an area too heterogeneous to constitute any serious military threat to his rear; also it was the most highly organized part of the Persian Empire, requiring comparatively little administrative attention.

It was now urgent that Alexander should press on to Phoenicia, for in the absence of an adequate Greek fleet the cities of the coasts and islands of the Aegean lay open to Persian naval power, which could only be neutralized by the capture of its home bases, the cities of the coast of Phoenicia. Another reason was strategic; the Persian Empire would have to be fought for, but the further east the decisive battles could be staged, the more of the Empire would automatically fall to Alexander as the fruit of victory. An army under Darius himself was now on the way to recover the western satrapies, and the coastal plain around the Gulf of Alexandretta, on the confines of Cilicia and Syria, was the only convenient link by land between these satrapies and the rest of the empire. Somewhere in this area would be fought the battle which would decide the fate of at least the western half of the Persian Empire.

THE BATTLE OF ISSUS

The battle of Issus, on the north Syrian border, was fought early in November 333 BC in a way which neither side had planned. Alexander had pushed on into Syria believing Darius to be still in front of him whereas Darius had meanwhile, by a different pass, crossed into Cilicia, where he supposed Alexander to be still encamped. With the Persians entrenched across his communications on the narrow plain between the hills and the sea, Alexander was forced to retrace his steps to meet them.

At Issus Alexander had less than the 35,000 man army with which he had fought at the Granicus eighteen months before, for garrisons and fighting units had been detached at various points in Asia Minor. Against him Darius had assembled the regular Persian army. It included 30,000 cavalry, both men and horses armoured in link chain mail, 60,000 Cardaces, young Persians trained in the use of bows and javelins, 10,000 Greek mercenaries and a number of other foot and light troops. Though this was not the huge horde which Greek propaganda alleged, it was the principal fighting force of the Persian Empire and was accompanied by the court and the royal family.

The main infantry action was fought between the Greek mercenaries on the Persian side and the Macedonian infantry, the phalanx; the decisive moment came when Alexander himself led his right wing in a furious cavalry charge which overwhelmed the Persian left and fell upon the flank of the infantry at the centre. It was here that Darius in his chariot, surrounded by his personal bodyguard, was stationed. At the sight of this charge Darius turned and fled, a moment brilliantly portrayed in the great mosaic from the House of the Faun at Pompeii, probably based on a painting by a contemporary artist. When the going became too rough for his chariot he mounted a horse and continued his panicky flight. Though most of the Persian army, including the main body of the Greek mercenaries, escaped from the field of battle, Darius' family and much royal equipment were captured by Alexander's troops.

The months following the battle of Issus form a turning point in Alexander's career. Having fulfilled the *declared* objective, the liberation of the Greeks of Asia Minor, he could have stopped in Cilicia and there maintained a defensive frontier for his already considerable conquests. He certainly rejected this limited objective, if only because its adoption would have left the Persian naval bases in Phoenicia untouched, and thus the Aegean still open to attack.

The second alternative, to which Alexander immediately proceeded, was the occupation of Syria, Phoenicia and Egypt, an area to which the Euphrates to the north and the desert to the south provide natural frontiers. There is an indication that in his initial negotiations with Darius after Issus, Alexander was prepared to stop on this line provided that Darius were to recognize him as overlord of all Asia. But his attitude soon hardened, perhaps under the influence of the long resistance of Tyre, so that Darius' offer to cede all territory west of the Euphrates was flatly rejected. It was on this occasion that Parmenio, one of Alexander's senior generals, is reported to have said that if he were Alexander, he would accept the offer, to which Alexander replied that so would he, if he were Parmenio. Thus with little hesitation, and perhaps with little consideration of any but the strictly military factors, the third alternative of the total conquest of the Persian Empire was decided on.

In the confidence that it would be many months before Darius could assemble a fresh army, Alexander sent a force under Parmenio which captured Darius' war-chest at Damascus, so relieving Alexander of his financial embarrassments. Meanwhile Alexander himself advanced down the Phoenician coast to Sidon and Tyre. Most of the Phoenician cities welcomed him, and their adherence brought him naval squadrons and harbour facilities which permitted the re-opening of maritime communications with Macedonia and mainland Greece.

Tyre, however, the principal Phoenician city, declared its neutrality and refused to admit Alexander within its walls, so that he was compelled to take it by force. This proved difficult, for the city lay upon an offshore island and the Tyrian fleet was still at large. For seven months Alexander strove to drive a mole across the half mile from the shore to the city, while the Tyrians used every device to delay and dismantle the work completed. In July 332, after he had assembled a fleet from Cyprus, the other Phoenician cities and elsewhere, Tyre was taken by assault and most of the population massacred or sold into slavery.

After Tyre, Alexander was delayed for two more months in besieging Gaza on the Palestinian coast, where he was wounded in the shoulder, before reaching Egypt in November 332. This visit to Egypt might appear to be an unnecessary diversion from his main objective, yet it could be justified on practical grounds. Egypt was geographically isolated and easily defended, so that in the hands of an aggressive ruler it could become a secure base for attacks by land and sea on Alexander's conquests. Politically, Egypt had been for nearly two centuries part of the Persian Empire, and if Alexander was to enter fully into the inheritance of the Persian kings, he would have to be crowned at Memphis with the ancient religious ceremonial of the Pharaohs.

Fortunately, after the delay and hardship of the sieges of Tyre and Gaza, Egypt gave him no trouble, for Persian rule had been unpopular and Alexander was hailed as a deliverer. He appears to have been crowned with due ceremony at Memphis. As the accepted Pharaoh of Egypt he made an expedition to the oracle of Ammon in the oasis of Siwa, and was there duly greeted by the priest as the son of Ammon, as had been all his predecessors on the throne of the Pharaohs of dynastic Egypt.

But his most significant act during his four months' stay in Egypt was the foundation of his name city, Alexandria, destined very quickly to become and thereafter to remain, one of the great cities of the world. This first of many Alexandrias stands apart from its successors, which were mostly intended as garrisons and nuclei of settled Greek life among alien peoples; it was planted in one of the world's oldest civilizations which, though not readily receptive of foreigners and their ideas, had nonetheless for long had dealings with Greeks and had given them facilities for settling in the country. Indeed, in the interior of the Delta only twenty miles from Alexandria there had stood for some two and a half centuries the fully-Greek town of Naucratis, which Alexandria was intended to supplant. Doubtless Alexandria was founded primarily as a commercial centre and as a focus for the Greeks in Egypt; in the context of Alexander's career its greatest interest is as evidence for non-military planning in his empire.

In spring 331 BC Alexander returned from Egypt to Tyre, where he delayed until he joined his main army on the Euphrates in July. Activity had been intense on both sides during his absence in Egypt, for the final battle for the Persian Empire was about to be fought in Mesopotamia.

To get there the only route practicable for the invading army was across the upper course of the Euphrates where it approaches Syria. Darius accordingly held a covering force in that area under an experienced Persian commander, Mazaeus, while he himself marshalled the main imperial army further to the east, beyond the river Tigris. This time it was drawn almost wholly from the various races that made up the Persian Empire. Arrian notes that there were bodies of Greek mercenaries on either side of the centre of the Persian line, where Darius was stationed, but they appear to have numbered far less than at Issus. He states also that Darius had 40,000 cavalry and 1,000,000 infantry, a quite preposterous figure. Nevertheless the Persian army was far larger than that of Alexander. Against him Alexander had assembled 40,000 infantry and 7000 cavalry, a larger force than at either the Granicus or Issus. Reinforcements were coming through from Macedonia, and troops left behind to reduce and garrison troublesome areas in the rear had been called up.

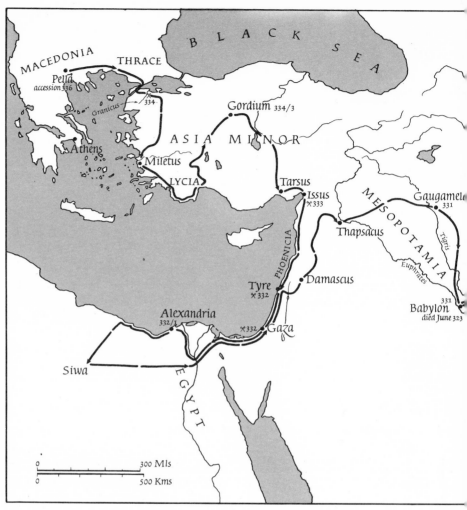

1   *Alexander's empire and his journeys*

In the summer heat of 331 BC Alexander marched from
Syria across the desert to the Euphrates, crossing the river at
Thapsacus over bridges built by his engineers. Mazaeus, the
Persian commander, was waiting for him with a substantial
force, but he fell back before Alexander's advance, drawing
him north across the Tigris and then east to Gaugamela, where
the main Persian army was encamped. Here, about three hundred miles north of Babylon, was to be fought the battle which
would decide the fate of the Persian Empire.

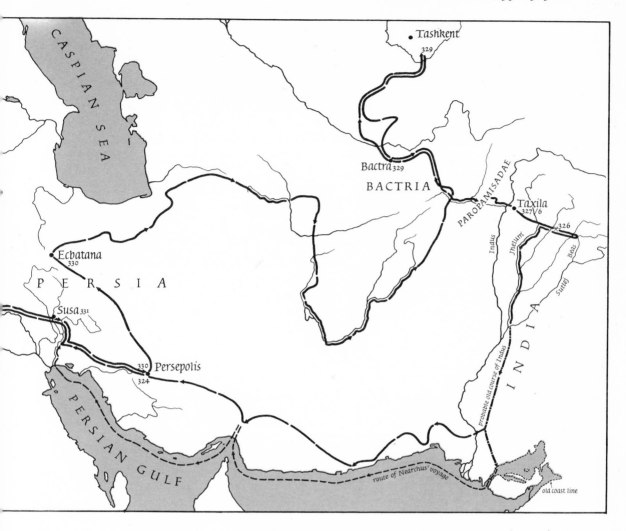

THE BATTLE OF GAUGAMELA

The battle of Gaugamela was fought on 1 October, 331 BC. It was an untidy affair; in the centre the Persians, lacking an adequate force of heavy infantry, used scythed chariots as their main assault weapon, but these proved almost wholly ineffective, being overturned or dispersed before they could come to grips with Alexander's phalanx. On the right wing, after several hard-fought cavalry actions Alexander observed a gap in the Persian line into which he charged with his personal bodyguard, followed by some infantry battalions. The Persian line broke and Darius once again fled prematurely from the field. On the left wing, however, Mazaeus got the better of Parmenio, for the Persian cavalry broke right through the Macedonian infantry lines, but instead of then turning to attack the phalanx in the rear where it was vulnerable, they followed Darius' orders to attempt a rescue of the Persian royal family and made for Alexander's baggage train. In the meantime the news of Darius' flight had spread and the whole Persian line disintegrated, to be hotly pursued for many miles by Alexander's cavalry.

The heart of the Persian Empire now lay open to invasion, but speed was necessary, for Darius was still at large and might yet succeed in transporting the imperial treasury from Susa and Persepolis to some remote eastern stronghold at which he might rally support. Babylon was handed over by Mazaeus without a fight, and Alexander thereupon made his former opponent satrap of Babylonia. Susa and Persepolis with their vast treasures were secured before the end of the year, and in Persepolis Alexander at last came to rest for four months until the early summer of 330 BC. In four years he had progressed more or less directly from Pella to Persepolis with a kind of simple inevitability; in these years his representatives and subordinates must have usually had a reasonably clear idea of where he was to be found, so that decisions taken at this time can be attributed to Alexander himself or to his immediate staff in close consultation with him. In the following years the pattern becomes much more confused, for he was to be marching and counter-marching in areas ever more remote from the Greek world, so that his control over the western half of his empire must inevitably have become looser.

This then is the moment to say something of Alexander's imperial administration. Two fundamental facts must be remembered. One is that he retained the basic satrapal organization of the Persian empire, the other, that whatever the claims of Panhellenic propaganda, Alexander's army was essentially Macedonian, and it was therefore Macedonians to whom most of the principal appointments were given and who later formed the rival dynasties who partitioned his empire.

Since Gaugamela, Alexander was no longer merely king of Macedon and Hegemon of the Greek League. He was now the Great King of Persia as well, and the royal title *basileus* begins to appear on his coinage. Hitherto he had normally appointed

Macedonians to take charge of conquered satrapies, but this was a matter of convenience rather than principle as was early shown by his elevation of the Sidonian Abdalonymus to the throne of Sidon.

Further east again, no doubt because of familiarity with local language and customs, Alexander commonly appointed Persians as civil governors of satrapies, the first being Mazaeus to the satrapy of Babylonia; military and financial functions, however, were always kept separate and entrusted to Macedonians. His secretariate was in the charge of Eumenes of Cardia, a Greek who had been private secretary to Alexander's father Philip and who attained some political prominence in the years after Alexander's death.

It is in the field of finance that we have clear evidence of a strong central administration, namely Alexander's coinage. From the years 332–330 a whole series of new mints came into operation – Tarsus, Myriandrus, Ake, Damascus, Alexandria and Babylon are reasonably certain. Few of these cities had ever coined before, and when they had there had been no uniformity in their productions. But under Alexander coin designs and technique were uniform at all centres, reproducing official patterns circulated with royal approval. Coinage on this scale was previously unknown in the ancient world.

1–3

THE FIGHTING IN THE EAST

About May 330 BC Alexander moved from Persepolis to Ecbatana, where he received news that Darius had assembled a number of still loyal satraps with their troops near the southeast corner of the Caspian Sea. This threat required to be stifled quickly, and Alexander set off in hot pursuit. On word of his approach the Persians fled, but when Alexander was found to be pressing on their heels Darius was murdered and the satraps dispersed to their various dominions.

For the next three years Alexander was engaged in a series of battles, marches and counter-marches through east Iran, Afghanistan and Turkestan, from Kandahar in the south to Tashkent, Samarkand and Bokhara in the north. In its duration and intensity this fighting was certainly as costly and wearing as the battles of the Granicus, Issus and Gaugamela, for time and again areas apparently subdued flared into revolt. Because no substantial towns existed as centres of control and administration, a whole series of new Alexandrias was founded to fulfill this role.

But the strain of these years was beginning to tell on both Alexander and his followers. In the summer of 330 BC a conspiracy had been unmasked in which a number of highly placed Macedonians were implicated, including Parmenio's son Philotas, who was executed. Parmenio, who had been one of Philip's and Alexander's trusted generals and against whom there was not a shred of evidence, was murdered on the instruction of Alexander.

One cause of the trouble was that as king of Persia, Alexander inherited an elaborate court ceremonial which involved prostration by anyone approaching the King's person. For political reasons he determined that this ceremonial should be practised, at least in his Persian dominions, by Macedonians and Greeks alike, and in this decision he was supported by some of his closest advisers. Yet Greek and Macedonian opposition proved too strong, for prostration of man before man had long been ridiculed as a sign of barbarian slavery. Alexander was forced to drop the practice, but one of the principal opponents of prostration, Callisthenes, Alexander's official historian, was shortly afterwards found to be involved in a conspiracy, was arrested and later executed. The strain under which Alexander himself was living at the time is illustrated by an ugly incident. In the course of a drunken argument he speared to death Cleitus, one of his oldest comrades, the man who had saved his life at the Granicus – and was then totally distraught with remorse for several days.

ALEXANDER'S INDIAN CAMPAIGN

By the summer of 327 BC Alexander was ready to invade India: his army was probably less than 30,000 fighting men, for though reinforcements had arrived from Antipater in Macedonia, Bactria had to be heavily garrisoned in his rear.

Why did Alexander continue to drive ever eastward, when the mountains of Afghanistan could well now have formed the frontier of his already vast Empire? It may be that he and his staff supposed that a little more effort would bring them literally to the 'River of Ocean' which they believed flowed around the world. It was with the idea of some such limited objective, to be quickly attained, that the army set out on the final phase of its advance.

The passage from Bactria to India involved much mountain fighting, and beyond there were the successive river barriers of the Punjab, the 'Land of the Five Rivers'. The crossing of the Indus was easy and the local king, Taxiles, offered his capital city as a base against his enemy King Porus, beyond the Jhelum river. But the hard fought battle against Porus in the following year, which was preceded by a difficult river crossing, made a deep impression on Alexander's men. It was the first time they had had to face elephants in war; they were victorious, but the casualties were heavy.

The special character of the battle is underlined by its commemoration on a coin which shows Alexander on horseback pursuing King Porus on an elephant – an almost unique representation in Greek numismatic art of two historical personages engaged in an historical act.

10–12

After confirming Porus in his kingdom and reconciling him with his neighbour King Taxiles, Alexander pushed on eastward to the River Beas, where at last his army refused to follow him further, and he was forced to retrace his steps.

Alexander, however, was not the man to take the same road home when an alternative was available. Returning to the Jhelum, he enlarged the fleet which he had built for the river-crossing against Porus with the idea that it should sail down the Indus and then follow the coasts of the Indian Ocean and the Persian Gulf back to the mouth of the Euphrates. At the same time the army would follow a parallel course on land, establishing depots to supply the fleet. The purpose was to visit parts of the former Persian Empire which had not yet seen Greek arms, and to survey the sea route from Babylonia to the mouth of the Indus.

Before the joint force left the Punjab there was more fighting of a particularly bitter and desperate character; in one action Alexander with three companions was cut off in a citadel, and in the ensuing fight was seriously wounded in the chest before the army broke in to rescue him. This last and probably most serious of a number of wounds no doubt contributed to his early death.

The long journey down the Indus was comparatively uneventful; the channels near the Indus' mouth were explored, cities were planned and harbour works put in hand, and in late summer 325 BC the army, with the fleet under command of Nearchus, a Cretan who was one of Alexander's trusted generals, set out on their respective journeys. Unfortunately the plan for the army to form depots of water and provisions for the fleet proved impossible to realize. The scarcity of water and food, the heat of the season and the rugged nature of the country compelled the army to concentrate on its own survival. Many died of thirst and hunger, and the fleet was left to fend for itself. It had the benefit of the monsoon; otherwise it had to scavenge daily along the coast for the little food and water that could be found. At last, after a voyage of eleven weeks and with the loss of only four ships, to Alexander's great relief both fleet and army were reunited near the mouth of the Persian Gulf.

THE FINAL YEARS

It was about two and a half years since Alexander had left Bactria to invade India, and he had been largely out of touch with the rest of his empire. During his absence many satraps had committed acts of oppression, had enrolled private armies and had otherwise exceeded their powers, and in some areas disorder was rife. Alexander removed the unsatisfactory satraps, but as he progressed from Susa there were signs of deep-seated discontent in the army, particularly among the Macedonians.

Basically this was because Alexander was no longer just King of Macedonia but Great King of Persia as well, and the Persians could not be treated as a subject race; they had to be given some share in the running of their country. The attempted introduction of prostration had been designed to secure Persian co-operation, but now other less obvious but nonetheless resented steps were taken. For example, the necessary enrolment of Persians in the army was felt to be a dilution of Macedonian influence, and when to this was added a proposal to send a large number of veterans back to Macedonia a serious mutiny broke out. Alexander could not deal with a mutinous army as easily as with disobedient satraps; there were emotional scenes before the army and its commander were reconciled – but a large contingent of veterans was sent home nonetheless.

One other incident from this time illustrates Alexander's policy towards Persians; this was the great feast at Susa in 324 BC at which Alexander and eighty of his officers married daughters of the Persian aristocracy, Alexander himself taking as wife Barsine, a daughter of Darius. At the same time some ten thousand of his Macedonians married their native mistresses. There is here no doubt some attempt to encourage the creation of a Graeco-Persian governing class, but the large number of more humble marriages was also intended to introduce an element of stability into the many new Alexandrias, which were to be the centres of settled life in backward areas.

When Alexander arrived in Babylon in the spring of 323 BC it must have seemed that a new phase of his reign was about to begin. The main work of conquest had been achieved, re-organization and integration lay still in the future. Problems were numerous and many envoys, particularly from the Greek world, were awaiting his decisions. But most of them were destined to remain unsatisfied, for during the summer Alexander caught a fever, probably malaria, to which he succumbed on 13 June 323 BC in his thirty-third year.

At the moment of Alexander's death his authority was acknowledged, apart from a few pockets of resistance, from Epirus to the Punjab, and it is a tribute to the force of his personality that though no heir had been designated, it was nearly twenty years before the fiction of a unified empire was finally abandoned by his successors. The Diadochi ('Successors'; the term used to describe the heirs of Alexander's Empire) were confronted with a world very different from that into which they had been born. The most obvious change was that of geographical scale, for the Greek world, hitherto confined to the area between Sicily and the eastern shores of the Mediterranean, was now extended to the confines of India.

Naturally this great area was not all equally Hellenized, but the persistence of Greek dynasties in Bactria and India, and the Greek language and culture of the Parthian empire are sufficient to show that there was a very real extension of Greek civilization into Asia, which could not have taken root there without the settlement of many Greeks. This extension involved a shift of political and cultural centres from Mainland Greece to the new Hellenistic capitals of Pergamum, Antioch and Alexandria, where the Diadochi, as absolute rulers of wide kingdoms, deployed resources far greater than any single Greek city had ever had at its command.

Politically too, Alexander changed the world. Great as had been the merits of the city-states, their fatal defect was an inability to combine into larger units. The monarchy of Alexander, oriental in origin but modified by contact with Greek ideas, provided the model for the smaller kingdoms of his successors, and ultimately for the Roman Empire.

1 ALEXANDER THE GREAT 336–323 BC

ALEXANDER THE GREAT

1, 2, 3 ALEXANDER THE GREAT 336–323 BC
The head of Heracles wearing the scalp of the Nemean lion (*Ill. 1*), the prize of his first and most famous Labour, was an appropriate design for a Macedonian imperial coinage, for the Macedonian kings traced their descent from the hero. Soon after Alexander's death the head was regarded as a portrait of the conqueror himself, and already in his lifetime his features may have been imposed upon the head of Heracles, though there is no evidence that this was ever official policy. The enthroned Zeus holding eagle and sceptre perhaps expresses the same claim to the hegemony of Greece as had been expressed by the head of Zeus on the coinage of Alexander's father, Philip II; but in the context of Alexander's empire the figure could also be interpreted as the Baal worshipped by many of Alexander's subjects in the Persian Empire.

4, 5, 6 ALEXANDER THE GREAT *posthumous portrait, minted by Lysimachus*
Lysimachus had taken the title of king in 306/5 but not until 297 BC did he abandon the imperial coin types of Alexander in favour of new designs peculiar to his kingdom. On the obverse the head of Alexander is diademed and wears the ram's horn of Zeus Ammon (*Ill. 6*); in the tousled hair there is a hint of the frenzy of Dionysus whose mythical exploits Alexander had emulated by his conquest of India. On the reverse a seated Athena holds Nike who seems to be crowning the name of Lysimachus; Athena wears a crested Corinthian helmet, her spear is laid aside, and her shield embossed with what may be Lysimachus' own device, a lion's head, leans against her throne. The name Lysimachus means 'one who ends strife', and this seems to be the character of the seated Athena, her weapons laid aside and Victory in her hand.

6   ALEXANDER THE GREAT 336–323 BC

7, 8, 9   ALEXANDER THE GREAT *minted by Ptolemy I*

Alexander here appears wearing the attributes of several deities. The elephant scalp belongs to Dionysus, the mythical conqueror of India; below the edge of the scalp is seen the tip of the ram's horn of Zeus Ammon, the god who had hailed Alexander as his son; round his neck are knotted the snaky terminals of the aegis of Zeus. Beneath all, the presence of the Persian royal diadem may be assumed, for it is shown in other versions of this type. The type expresses unified dominion over Greece, Egypt, Persia and India, and belongs to a time (318 BC) before Alexander's generals and associates had seized the opportunity of creating kingdoms for themselves. On the reverse the coinage is still minted in the name of the dead Alexander, and his imperial reverse type of the seated eagle-bearing Zeus is retained.

10, 11, 12 ALEXANDER THE GREAT 336–323 BC

From ancient accounts of the battle between Alexander and Porus it
is known that the former was mounted on a horse and the latter on
an elephant. On the obverse Alexander with lance levelled is charg-
ing in pursuit of the retreating elephant; on its back are mounted
King Porus, who was repeatedly wounded in the battle, and his
driver who turns to throw his spear at Alexander. On the reverse
stands Alexander in the dress of a general wearing a cloak, a cuirass
and a sword, and holding a spear; above, Victory flies to crown him.
But he is more than just a successful general, for he wears a strange
high head-dress. This is the Persian tiara, which only the Great King
himself could wear in its erect form, as here; on the heads of nobles
and satraps the ends were shown folded down. In his outstretched
hand Alexander holds a thunderbolt, showing that he wields not only
the power of the greatest earthly king, but the divine power of Zeus
as well. This very rare decadrachm may have been struck at Babylon.

THE PTOLEMIES OF EGYPT

13, 14, 17   PTOLEMY I 323–283 BC

From about 300 until his death in 283 BC Ptolemy minted coins bearing his own name and portrait. Like many contemporary rulers he represented himself with the attributes of a deity – in this case Zeus. In addition to the royal diadem he wears the aegis of Zeus over his shoulders (*Ill. 17*), and adopts the eagle and thunderbolt of Zeus as his personal device on the reverse. The portrait of Ptolemy I and his reverse type were repeated by his successors as the normal types of the Ptolemaic coinage until the end of the dynasty.

15, 16, 18, 19   PTOLEMY II AND ARSINOE II/PTOLEMY I AND BERENICE I
Gold octadrachm minted by Ptolemy III, 246–221 BC

This coin graphically expresses the Ptolemaic preoccupation with dynastic continuity. Minted by Ptolemy III, it shows on the obverse the diademed portraits of his parents, Ptolemy II and Arsinoe II (*Ill 18*), who were in fact brother and sister (*adelphon*); on the reverse are the diademed portraits of his deceased and deified (*theon*) grandparents, Ptolemy I and Berenice I (*Ill. 19*). Even in the case of the latter no divine attributes are included.

17 PTOLEMY I 323–283 BC

18 Ptolemy II and Arsinoe II

19 PTOLEMY I AND BERENICE I

20, 21, 22   ARSINOE II *minted by Ptolemy III, 246–221* BC

Arsinoe II died in 270 BC, and was honoured thereafter for many years by a dated coinage issued in her name by her husband and her son; this example is dated 29 and was therefore struck in 242 BC. The queen wears an elaborate head-band and her hair is coiled at the back of her head; the veil indicates that she is no longer living (*Ill. 20*). Below the ear is seen the tip of a horn and above her head there projects the end of a sceptre; these hint at her deification, possibly as the Egyptian cow-goddess Hathor. On the reverse a double cornucopiae, bound with a royal diadem, overflows with the fruits of the earth, symbolizing the fertility of the queen in producing an heir to the throne and, as a goddess, her care for the fruitfulness of Egypt. The legend describes her as 'brother-loving', and indeed her brother, Ptolemy II, was also her husband.

23, 24, 27   PTOLEMY III 246–221 BC

The king is shown with the attributes of three Greek deities, the rays of Helios, the aegis of Zeus, and the trident of Poseidon (*Ill. 27*). Is this simply a casual assemblage of cults with which Ptolemy was associated or is there a definite political message? The co-operation between the Ptolemies (Zeus – *cf. Ill. 9*) and Rhodes (Helios) secures control of the sea (Poseidon). Ptolemaic maritime power was at its greatest extent during the third century. On the reverse the cornu-copiae bound with the royal diadem is surmounted by the rays of the sun. The meaning is that the king, identified with the sun-god, assures the fertility of the earth. The iconography throughout is purely Greek, and the only possible native Egyptian element is the association of the king with the Sun-god (Ra).

25, 26, 28   BERENICE II *wife of Ptolemy III*

The queen's head is veiled and diademed (*Ill. 28*); on the reverse the horn of plenty is bound with a royal diadem, and flanked by the wreathed caps of Castor and Pollux.

27   PTOLEMY III 246–221 BC

28   BERENICE II

29, 30, 33   PTOLEMY IV 221–203 BC

Only rarely do the Ptolemies replace the traditional portrait of
Ptolemy I with contemporary likenesses. Ptolemy IV's features suggest that he may indeed have been idle and self-indulgent (*Ill. 33* and
p. 162). The reverse type is the usual dynastic badge of an eagle on a
thunderbolt inherited from the first Ptolemy but, exceptionally, the
honorific title Philopator ('father-loving') is included.

31, 32, 34   ARSINOE III *wife of Ptolemy IV*, 221–203 BC

The queen wears a coronet, no doubt of precious metal, an ear-ring,
necklace and a diadem; her robe is secured on the shoulder by a
brooch, and the tip of a sceptre is seen behind her head (*Ill. 34*). On
the reverse a cornucopiae, bound with a diadem, contains barley, a
poppy-head and grapes, and is surmounted by a star.

33 PTOLEMY IV 221–203 BC

34　Arsinoe III

35, 36, 39 PTOLEMY V 203–181 BC
The king is diademed and wears a cloak (*Ill. 39*). On the reverse his
name and royal title accompany the eagle of Zeus, the badge of the
dynasty.

37, 38, 40 PTOLEMY XII *Auletes* 80–51 BC
This young diademed head (*Ill. 40*) cannot be intended to represent
the aged Ptolemy I, Soter, whose head had long remained on the
obverse of the Ptolemaic coinage. The reverse is the usual Ptolemaic
eagle on thunderbolt, here carrying the palm branch of victory.

39   PTOLEMY V 203–181 BC

40   PTOLEMY XII 80–51 BC

41, 42, 46 CLEOPATRA VII (*and Ptolemy XV*)

On this bronze coin, probably minted in Cyprus, Cleopatra holds her
infant son by Julius Caesar, Ptolemy Caesar, nick-named Caesarion
(*Ill. 46*). He was born in 47 BC and put to death by Octavian in 30 BC;
from 44 BC he was nominal ruler of Egypt with his mother. By
Egyptian subjects who identified the queen of Egypt with the goddess Isis, the type could be interpreted as Isis and Harpocrates, by
Greeks as Aphrodite and Eros; the royal sceptre is seen in the background. As for other Ptolemaic queens (*cf. Ills. 22, 26, 32*) the reverse
type is the double cornucopiae; Cleopatra was, however, the only
queen of Egypt to mint coins in her own right.

43 JULIUS CAESAR

Caesar was the first Roman to be portrayed on coinage during his
lifetime, and this portrait is taken from a denarius minted very shortly
before his assassination on the Ides of March, 44 BC. He wears a
peculiar wreath which projects far out beyond his forehead; its rigid
metallic structure is proved by the absence of the usual wreath ties at
the nape of the neck. This crown, derived from the early kings of
Rome, became the ritual head-dress of the *triumphator*.

44, 45, 47 CLEOPATRA VII (*and Antony*) 51–30 BC

By 36 BC Antony and Cleopatra were married, and the Roman world
was divided between Antony in the east and Octavian in the west.
Here the bareheaded Antony proudly describes himself as *autokrator*
(=*imperator*) for the third time, and as triumvir. Cleopatra is 'queen'
and wears the royal diadem (*Ill. 47*); she is also entitled 'Thea, the
younger', a title that distinguishes her cult from that of her ancestress
Cleopatra Thea. Minted in 36 BC at Antioch in Syria where Antony
and Cleopatra spent the winter of 37/6 BC.

46   CLEOPATRA VII AND PTOLEMY XV 51–30 BC

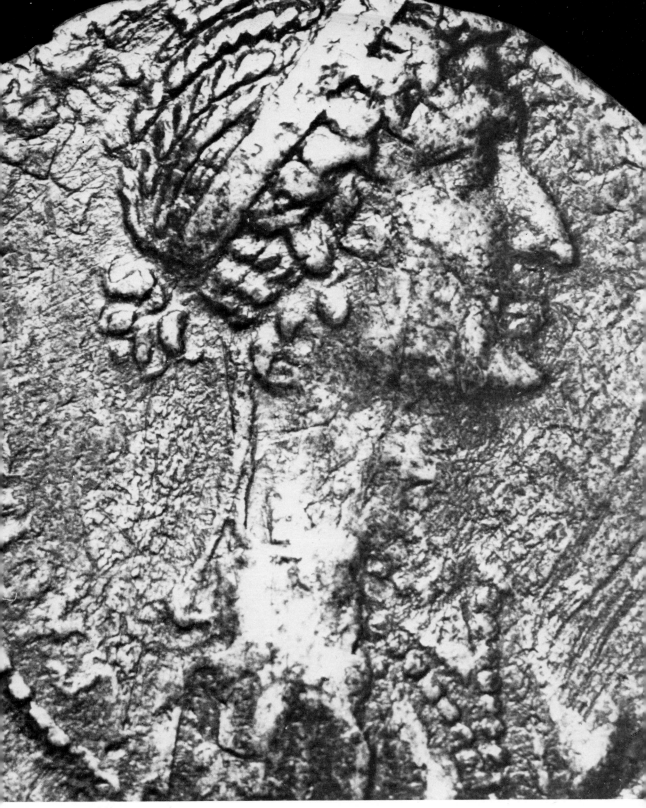

47   CLEOPATRA VII 51–30 BC

48, 49, 52   SELEUCUS I 321–280 BC

The helmeted warrior is usually taken to be Seleucus himself, though a posthumous portrait of Alexander has also been suggested (*Ill. 52*). As with the bull's horn of Demetrius Poliorcetes (*Ill. 121*), so here the helmet of Seleucus, incorporating a bull's horn and ear and covered with panther skin denotes superhuman strength, and the panther's skin, again knotted round his neck, perhaps alludes to Dionysus, the conqueror of India in whose steps first Alexander and then Seleucus followed. On the reverse Nike crowns a trophy of arms symbolizing the secure establishment of Seleucus' kingdom by his decisive victory over Antigonus I at Ipsus in 301; this design is an unskilful adaptation of an almost contemporary type of Agathocles of Syracuse. Like his rivals Seleucus too took the title of 'king', which had once belonged pre-eminently to Alexander. Minted at Persepolis soon after 300 BC:

50, 51, 53   SELEUCUS I 312–280 BC

This portrait (*Ill. 53*) was minted by Philetaerus, who in 281 BC deserted Lysimachus for Seleucus. The name Philetaerus appears on the reverse together with Lysimachus' type of the seated Athena (*Ill. 5*), which was retained as the distinctive reverse of the Attalid dynasty (*Ill. 181*). Minted at Pergamum, *c.* 280 BC.

52   SELEUCUS I 321–280 BC

53　Seleucus I 321–280 BC

54, 55, 60 ANTIOCHUS I 280–261 BC

It was Antiochus' father, Seleucus Nicator, who had established Apollo as the patron deity of the Seleucid dynasty, and built for the god an impressive shrine at Daphne, near Antioch. Though Apollo had never appeared on Seleucus' own coinage, from now on he becomes the commonest Seleucid reverse type. The god is shown seated upon the *omphalos*, the sacred stone of his shrine at Delphi, which marked the centre of the earth; the omphalos is criss-crossed by sacred ribbons. Apollo is testing an arrow for straightness, and his bow, his special weapon, is at his side. This is a conventional representation, not the cult-statue of Daphne, which was a draped figure by the sculptor Bryaxis.

56, 57, 61 ANTIOCHUS II 261–246 BC

The youthful portrait of Antiochus II in his twenties (*Ill. 61*) is in striking contrast to the drawn features of his aged father (*Ill. 60*). The reverse type of Apollo remains unchanged.

58, 59, 62 SELEUCUS II 246–226 BC

On the obverse is the diademed head of the young king (*Ill. 62*). The reverse shows Apollo, naked, leaning upon a tripod and examining an arrow, the god's special weapon with which he had slain the serpent Python to win the Delphic tripod and with which he had slaughtered the children of Niobe. The coin was minted at Nisibis in Mesopotamia.

60 ANTIOCHUS I 280–261 BC

61 ANTIOCHUS II 261–246 BC

62   Seleucus II 246–226 BC

63, 64, 69 ANTIOCHUS HIERAX 246–227 BC

The types are the now traditional ones inaugurated by Antiochus I (*Ill. 55*). The owl in the exergue of the reverse is a mark of the mint of Sigeum in the Troad, a town, which, because of its position controlling the trade of the Hellespont, had long had a connection with Athens and a cult of Athena.

65, 66, 70 SELEUCUS III 226–223 BC

The diademed head (*Ill. 70*) and the seated Apollo maintain the now established dynastic types (*cf. Ill. 55*).

67, 68, 71 ACHAEUS 220–214 BC

The very rare portrait coins of Achaeus resemble closely those of his contemporary Philip V of Macedon (*Ill. 127*). He departs from the usual Seleucid model in being portrayed with bust and drapery instead of as a head alone (*Ill. 71*). Athena's shield is emblazoned with an anchor (of the Seleucids) and an eagle (of the Ptolemies), for Achaeus claimed the Seleucid throne with Ptolemaic support; the horse's head may be his personal device. Minted at Sardis, Achaeus' base for his revolt against Antiochus III.

69   ANTIOCHUS HIERAX 246–227 BC

70 SELEUCUS III 226–223 BC

71 ACHAEUS 220–214 BC

72, 73, 76   ANTIOCHUS III (*the Great*) 223–187 BC
The diademed head of the king is surrounded by the bead and reel
border which is common on Seleucid coins (*Ill. 76*). The dynastic god
Apollo (see *Ill. 55*) here examines his arrow while seated on the
omphalos of Delphi, the centre of the world; his bow is at his side. The
seated type is more usual than the standing version of *Ill. 59*. The
mint is the Syrian capital, Antioch-on-the-Orontes, and the date
c. 208–200 BC.

74, 75, 77   ANTIOCHUS III (*the Great*) 223–187 BC
For most of his coinage Antiochus employed the traditional Apolline
type; the elephant on the reverse of this tetradrachm is exceptional.
It refers to his great eastern campaign, and the tribute of war elephants
received from Euthydemus of Bactria and from Sophagesenus in the
Punjab. The same type had been used a hundred years before by
Seleucus Nicator to celebrate the acquisition of war elephants from
Chandragupta (p. 186). Minted at Ecbatana.

76   ANTIOCHUS III 223–187 BC

77   ANTIOCHUS III 223–187 BC

78, 79, 84 SELEUCUS IV 187–175 BC

Antiochus III's son once again employed the traditional type of the seated Apollo.

80, 81, 85 ANTIOCHUS IV 175–164 BC

The observe (*Ill. 85*) shows a youthful and somewhat idealized portrait of the king, who was in his middle forties when it was minted. The reverse represents a revolutionary change, for after the first issue of the reign the traditional seated Apollo was abandoned in favour of a seated Zeus holding Victory. Though the type had been Alexander's (*Ill. 3*), its last appearance on the Seleucid coinage had been about a century earlier and its re-introduction now was due to Antiochus' predilection for this deity, another sign of which was his resumption of work on the unfinished temple of Olympian Zeus at Athens. Another new feature of the reverse is the first use of honorific titles, for hitherto coins had been inscribed with the title 'King' only. Antiochus here declares himself to be 'God Manifest' (*ΘΕΟΥ ΕΠΙΦΑΝΟΥΣ*), and it is as a god that his idealized portrait was presented to his subjects. Outside his kingdom, however, he was entitled only Epiphanes in the vaguer sense of 'Illustrious'. The title *NIKHIOPOY* ('Bearer of Victory') was adopted after his successful Egyptian campaign in 169.

82, 83, 86 ANTIOCHUS V 164–162 BC

This head of the nine-year-old son of Antiochus IV (*Ill. 86*) is recognizably a younger version of his father's portrait (*Ill. 85*). On his reverse he naturally retained the seated Zeus. His honorary title Eupator ('of a noble father') is unusual in the Seleucid dynasty for it is confined to Antiochus V and to some of the coins of Alexander I Balas who likewise claimed to be a son of Antiochus IV (*Ill. 90*).

84 SELEUCUS IV 187–175 BC

85 ANTIOCHUS IV 175–164 BC

86 ANTIOCHUS V 164–162 BC

87, 88, 91   DEMETRIUS I 162–150 BC
The diademed head of the king is enclosed within a wreath of laurel, sacred to Apollo (*Ill. 91*). On the reverse the seated female figure holding short sceptre and cornucopiae is Tyche (or Fortune); the side of her throne is adorned with a female winged monster, whose lower limbs end in fishy or serpentine coils. The type of Tyche at this time is peculiar to Demetrius; his distinctive title is Soter, 'Saviour'. The mint is Antioch.

89, 90, 92   ALEXANDER I BALAS 150–146 BC
Alexander's coinage was employed to bolster his claim to be a son of Antiochus IV; he used the seated Zeus of Antiochus V, whose brother he claimed to be, as his reverse type (*cf. Ill. 83*), and his honorary title Theopator ('of a divine father') recalls the Theos Epiphanes of Antiochus IV (*Ill. 81*).

91 DEMETRIUS I 162–150 BC

92　Alexander I Balas 150–146 BC

93, 94, 97 DEMETRIUS II, *First Reign* 146–140 BC

This elder son of Demetrius I won his throne by overcoming the
usurper Alexander I Balas (*Ill. 89*) and taking over his wife, Cleopatra,
thus earning the title Nicator ('Conqueror'), which had previously
been borne with more reason by Seleucus I. The brother whom he
loves (*ΦΙΛΑΔΕΛΦΟΥ*) was he who as Antiochus VII (*Ill. 107*) occupied his throne and married his wife during Demetrius' captivity in
Parthia, with which his first reign ended. He retains as reverse type
the Tyche which his father had introduced to the Seleucid coinage
(*Ill. 88*).

95, 96, 98 DEMETRIUS II, *Second Reign* 129–125 BC

During his years of captivity in Parthia Demetrius had adopted the
Parthian fashion of wearing the beard long, and is so represented on
coinage minted after his release (*Ill. 98*). The reverse type of the seated
Zeus holding Victory was taken over from Alexander I, whom
Demetrius had displaced. The coin was minted at Antioch and is
dated year 183 (129 BC).

97   DEMETRIUS II *First Reign* 146–140 BC

98   DEMETRIUS II *Second Reign* 129–125 BC

99, 100, 105 ANTIOCHUS VI 145–142 BC

The childish features of Alexander I Balas' son, who was only seven years old when he became king, are well portrayed (*Ill. 105*). The rays rising from his head suggest an identification with Helios, the sun-god, but are perhaps simply a translation in pictorial terms of the epithet Epiphanes; the rays spring from the head itself, and are not part of the diadem as was the case with the radiate crown of the Roman emperors. On the reverse Antiochus is called Epiphanes Dionysus; Epiphanes ('illustrious') recalls Antiochus IV, whose grandson Antiochus VI was, according to the claim of his father, Alexander, but the adjective can also be combined closely with Dionysus to mean 'Dionysus in visible form'. No doubt both meanings were intended. Despite the surname Dionysus the reverse types shows the Dioscuri galloping into battle. The 'sons of Zeus' provided a suitable type for one whose father and supposed grandfather had both used Zeus himself, but it was also a popular design of the period. Only shortly before it had been chosen by Eucratides in Bactria (*Ill. 145*), and it was one of the commonest reverses of the denarii of Rome.

101, 102, 106 TRYPHON 142–139 BC

Originally called Diodotus, this usurper, having arranged the murder of Antiochus VI, adopted the name Tryphon, meaning 'the magnicent'. His honorary title is also a remarkable departure from precedent, for instead of the usual complimentary Benefactor or Saviour, it describes factually his position in the state, for Autokrator means 'absolute ruler'; the term was later used to translate the Latin *imperator*. Tryphon was clearly at pains not to represent himself as yet another ineffective Seleucid. His reverse type also is a departure from the sequence of deities favoured by the Seleucids. The strange helmet, fitted with a goat's horn (perhaps the horn of the goat Amalthea, who suckled Zeus), and with a thunderbolt on the cheek-piece is thought to be an attribute of Zeus at Apamea, whence Tryphon started his revolt; the royal diadem hangs down from within the helmet. The surrounding oak wreath also is an attribute of Zeus. Minted at Antioch.

103, 104, 107 ANTIOCHUS VII 139–129 BC

This younger son of Demetrius I had spent his youth at Side in Pamphylia whence he was known as Sidetes. During his elder brother's captivity in Parthia he overthrew the usurper Tryphon and established himself as king. His type of the standing Athena perhaps alludes to the important cult of that goddess at Side. His title Euergetes was not unjustified for his reign did bring some stability to a kingdom long rent by rival claimants to the throne. Minted at Antioch.

105 ANTIOCHUS VI 145–142 BC

106 TRYPHON 142–139 BC

107 ANTIOCHUS VII 139–129 BC

108, 109, 114   CLEOPATRA THEA 125 BC
For a short while after the execution of Demetrius II Cleopatra ruled
alone and placed her portrait on the coinage (*Ill. 114*) like the Ptolemaic queens of her homeland, Egypt (*cf Ills. 20, 25, 31, 41*). The reverse
too is Egyptian; the legend makes explicit the idea of fertility represented by the cornucopiae for Cleopatra is described as the 'goddess of
fertility' (*ΘΗΑΣ ΕΥΕΤΗΡΙΑΣ*). For the wife of three kings to whom
she had borne nine children, the compliment was not unearned.
Minted at Antioch and dated 187 (=125 BC).

110, 111, 115   CLEOPATRA THEA AND ANTIOCHUS VIII 125–121 BC
After a short period as sole ruler (*Ill. 108*) Cleopatra decided or was
compelled to share the throne with her son by Demetrius II, Antiochus
VIII (Grypus). As senior partner her head appears in the foreground
(*Ill. 115*); both wear the royal diadem and both names are given
equal prominence on the reverse. The Zeus on the reverse (*Ill. 111*)
is interesting because Antiochus, descended from Seleucus IV, might
have been expected to use the traditional Apollo. But here too Cleopatra seems to have prevailed, for the Zeus type descends from Antiochus IV, through Alexander Balas, his supposed son and Cleopatra's
first husband; Zeus had also become the type of the second reign of
her second husband Demetrius II (*Ill. 94*).

112, 113, 116   ANTIOCHUS VIII 121–96 BC
The portrait of Antiochus (*Ill. 116*) fully justifies his nickname Grypus
(hook-nosed). On the reverse the usual type of seated Zeus is enclosed
within a laurel wreath. The king's distinctive title is Epiphanes
('illustrious'). Minted at Antioch.

114   CLEOPATRA THEA 125 BC

115　Cleopatra Thea and Antiochus VIII 125–121 BC

116 ANTIOCHUS VIII 121–96 BC

117, 118, 121   DEMETRIUS POLIORCETES 306–283 BC
The lively head of the young Demetrius (*Ill. 121*) wears the trappings
of both royalty and divinity; the blue diadem of the Persian kings
binds his hair and asserts his kingship of Asia, and the little bull's horn
hints at his superhuman strength (*cf* Seleucus I, *Ill. 52*). As Alexander
had been hailed as the son of Zeus Ammon, so Demetrius presented
himself as the son of Poseidon. The god himself, who had given him
mastery of the seas by his victory over Ptolemy at Salamis in 306,
appears on the reverse, holding a trident, his foot upon one of the
islands of the sea. Like his contemporaries and rivals Demetrius took
the title of King in 306, a step which marked a stage in the frag-
mentation of Alexander's empire. Minted at Amphipolis, *c.* 290 BC.

119, 120, 122   ANTIGONUS GONATAS 277–240/39 BC
Antigonus Gonatas ('knock-kneed') owed his throne to his victory
over the Gauls at Lysimachia; he himself attributed his victory to
the god Pan, who spread panic among his enemies, and it is his horned
head which forms the blazon of the Macedonian shield on the obverse
of Antigonus' tetradrachms. The unique specimen in Berlin shown
here has the words 'of king Antigonus' inscribed round the head,
making it probable that Pan is here given the features of the king
(*Ill. 122*). On the reverse Athena, the goddess of Pella, the Macedonian capital, strides into battle armed with the thunderbolt of her
father Zeus and a shield charged with the petrifying Gorgon's head.

121   DEMETRIUS POLIORCETES 306–283 BC

122   ANTIGONUS GONATAS 277–240/39 BC

123, 124, 127   PHILIP V 221–179 BC

The fighting Athena of the reverse is the deity of Pella, the capital of Macedonia, and was repeated by Philip from the coinage of his grandfather, Antigonus Gonatas. She carries a shield emblazoned with a star, and brandishes the thunderbolt of her father Zeus.

125, 126, 128   PERSEUS 179–168 BC

The lightly bearded head of the king wears the usual diadem (*Ill. 128*). The oak wreath of Zeus of Dodona on the reverse was inherited from his father Philip V, whose coinage had done much to establish a fashion for wreathed reverse types. The eagle on thunderbolt, also belonging to Zeus, can be interpreted as the personal device of Perseus himself (*cf.* Ptolemy I, *Ill. 14*).

127   PHILIP V 221–179 BC

128 PERSEUS 179–168 BC

129, 130, 133   DIODOTUS *c.* 250 BC

By his diademed portrait on this coin (*Ill. 133*), Diodotus claims
kingship, though on the reverse he retains the name of Antiochus II
of Syria as his overlord. In view of his name, 'Zeus-given', his choice
of Zeus as a patron deity was an obvious one. The type of the
thundering god seen from behind is perhaps copied from the earlier
Poseidon of Demetrius Poliorcetes, seen from an angle, and is related
to the contemporary Athena Alkis of Antigonus Gonatas (*Ill. 120*).
The naked god carries the protective aegis over his outstretched left
arm and brandishes his thunderbolt in his raised right hand; his eagle
stands before him ready to join in the fray.

131, 132, 134   EUTHYDEMUS I *c.* 235–200 BC

Euthydemus chose for his reverse type a rather elderly Heracles seated
upon a rock resting from his Labours. The type was perhaps intended
to suggest a sense of achievement or success.

133   Diodotus c. 250 BC

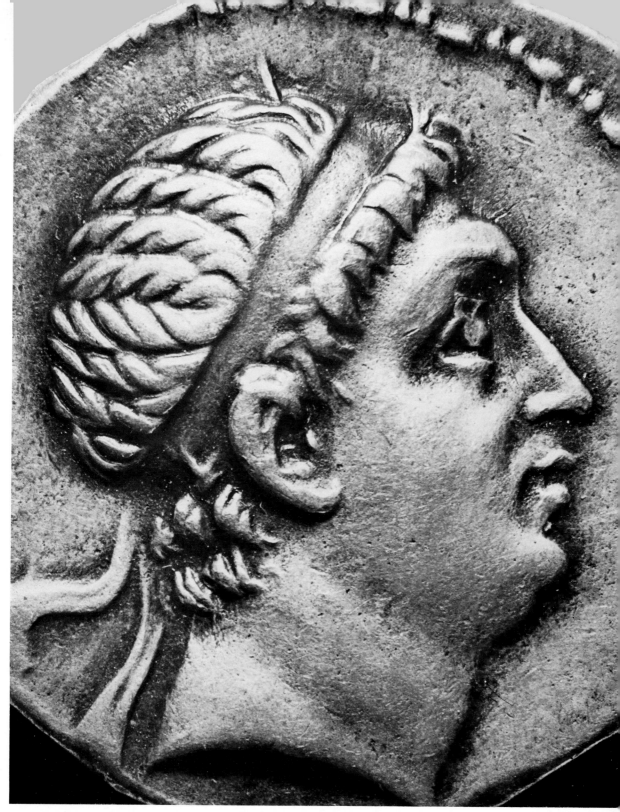

134 EUTHYDEMUS I *c.* 235–200 BC

135, 136, 141   DEMETRIUS OF BACTRIA *c*. 200–185 BC
The draped bust and diadem (*Ill. 141*) appear designed to underline
the peaceful character of Demetrius' rule; on the reverse the static, as
opposed to fighting, Athena carries the same message.

137, 138, 142   EUTHYDEMUS II
The reverse type of Heracles seems to be the badge of the Euthydemid
dynasty. The spread, thin flans of these coins are related more closely
to those of his father Demetrius I, than to the thicker flans of Euthydemus I. Euthydemus II seems not to have reigned for long, for his
coins are rare and the portraits are always youthful (*Ill. 142*).

139, 140, 143   ANTIMACHUS *c*. 190–180 BC
On one of the most attractive of Hellenistic portraits the diademed
head of the king unusually wears the felt Macedonian *kausia* or sun-
hat (*Ill. 143*). On the reverse Poseidon, half-draped, holds a trident
and a beribboned palm. The choice of the god of the sea as a type in
land-locked Bactria is rather surprising.

141 DEMETRIUS OF BACTRIA *c.* 200–185 BC

142 EUTHYDEMUS II

143   ANTIMACHUS *c.* 190–180 BC

144, 145, 148   EUCRATIDES *c.* 171–155 BC

The king is equipped for war; he wears a crested bronze cavalry helmet adorned with a bull's horn and ear like the helmet of Seleucus I (*Ill. 52*); beneath his helmet he wears the usual diadem; at his shoulder can be detected the plates of his cuirass. On the reverse the disposition of the legend suggests that 'megalon' ('great') qualifies not the individual but the office of king, implying that Eucratides was an overlord, of whom other kings were vassals. The mounted Dioscuri, Castor and Polydeuces, were warlike deities appropriate to a warrior king (*cf.* Antiochus VI, *Ill. 100*).

146, 147, 149   EUCRATIDES I (*with Heliocles and Laodice*)

On this exceptional tetradrachm the normal portrait and titles of Eucratides are relegated to the reverse, thus emphasizing the obverse portraits named Heliocles and Laodice (*Ill. 149*). The fact that their names are in the genitive, while that of Eucratides is in the nominative shows that they are his parents, and they are given this prominence because they evidently constituted Eucratides' claim to the throne – though in a way which we no longer exactly understand. While Heliocles is bareheaded (and therefore not a king), Laodice wears a royal diadem; she may have been a Seleucid princess or the widow of one of Eucratides' predecessors.

148 Eucratides *c.* 171–155 BC

149 HELIOCLES AND LAODICE

150, 151, 154   HELIOCLES *c.* 155–140 BC

This coin comes from an Indian mint, and carries the royal titulature repeated on the reverse in the local Kharoshti script. On the obverse the head of Heliocles is diademed (*Ill. 154*), his bust is draped with the aegis of Zeus, and he thrusts with a spear; on the reverse Zeus holds a sceptre and a winged thunderbolt.

152, 153, 155   DEMETRIUS I 200–185 BC

Like Alexander the Great before him (*Ill. 9*) Demetrius here wears an elephant's scalp over his royal diadem signifying that he is a conqueror of India, the land of the elephant (*Ill. 155*). On the reverse Heracles is crowning himself, implying that the labours of conquest are over.

154 HELIOCLES *c.* 155–140 BC

155 DEMETRIUS I 200–185 BC

156, 157, 160   PANTALEON *c.* 185–175 BC
He may well have been a brother of Agathocles, for he too has as reverse type the unusual Zeus carrying a figure of Hecate, though here Zeus is seated.

158, 159, 161   AGATHOCLES *c.* 180–165 BC
His coins are so similar to those of Euthydemus II (*Ill. 137*) that the two must be close in date. They also share the same monograms on the reverse. As reverse type Zeus here holds in his hand Hecate, carrying two torches, instead of the more usual Nike.

160 PANTALEON *c.* 185–175 BC

161 AGATHOCLES *c.* 180–165 BC

162, 163, 166 MENANDER *c.* 165–130 BC
The head is diademed and the bust draped. The honorary title is Soter ('Saviour'). The fighting Athena of Pella on the reverse perhaps alludes to the Macedonian descent of Menander.

164, 165, 167 MENANDER *c.* 165–130 BC
The owner of the austere and intellectual features on this unique Greek tetradrachm could well have engaged in debate with a Buddhist sage. The drapery and diadem present the ruler in his civil aspect. On the reverse again is the fighting Athena of Pella in Macedonia, armed with her father's thunderbolt, with her allusion to Menander's descent. His honorary title is Soter ('Saviour').

166　MENANDER *c.* 165–130 BC

167 MENANDER *c.* 165–130 BC

168, 169, 172   STRATO AND AGATHOCLEA *c.* 130–75 BC

On this coin Strato, in the nearer plane, takes precedence over his mother who had been regent during his minority. He follows Menander (*Ill. 166*), who may have been his father, in taking the title Soter ('Saviour') and in using the fighting Athena as a reverse type.

170, 171, 173   APOLLODOTUS II *c.* 115–100 BC

Apollodotus is shown diademed and with draped bust (*Ill. 173*). In his titulature he calls himself 'great king', which implies the existence of a number of subordinate kings; he also has the titles 'Saviour' (Soter) and 'father-loving' (Philopator). Surprisingly, in view of his name, his chosen reverse type is not Apollo, but a fighting Athena, carrying a shield and brandishing a thunderbolt. Since this type had been used by the great Menander on his coinage (*Ills. 163, 165*), it may therefore indicate kingship inherited from him.

172   STRATO AND AGATHOCLEA *c.* 130–75 BC

173 APOLLODOTUS II *c.* 115–100 BC

174, 175, 178   AMYNTAS c. 100–75 BC

Apart from his coins Amyntas is unknown, but he has the distinction
of having minted the largest surviving silver coins of the ancient
world. These double decadrachms bear a handsome portrait of the
king as commander-in-chief, wearing cloak and cuirass, and a crested
cavalry helmet decorated with the ear and horn of a bull as symbols
of strength (*Ill. 178*); from beneath the helmet fall the ends of the
royal diadem. On the reverse is an enthroned Zeus holding a sceptre
and palm-branch in one hand and Athena in the other. Whether
Amyntas had won a specific victory to justify the title Nicator
('Conqueror') is unknown.

176, 177, 179   HERMAEUS AND CALLIOPE c. 75–55 BC

Both the king and the queen are diademed and have draped busts (*Ill.
179*). Hermaeus is entitled Soter ('Saviour'). The horseman on the
reverse wears a helmet and cuirass and attached to his saddle is a large
quiver for bow and arrows; he is probably not Hermaeus himself,
who is represented with his wife in a pacific role, but Alexander the
Great, still revered as the founder of Greek rule in India.

178 AMYNTAS *c.* 100–75 BC

179 HERMAEUS AND CALLIOPE c. 75–55 BC

THE ATTALIDS OF PERGAMUM

180, 181, 184 PHILETAERUS 282–263 BC

The head of the heavy-jowled, tough, Philetaerus is one of the most individual in the whole Hellenistic series; it is not, however, a strictly contemporary portrait, for Philetaerus himself never put his own head on his coinage, though it was regularly used in preference to their own heads by succeeding members of the Attalid dynasty. The seated Athena of the reverse is a slight variation of the type of Lysimachus (*Ill. 5*) to whom Philetaerus had owed the foundation of his fortune as commander of the fortress of Pergamum; the wreath which had been in the hand of Nike is now held by Athena herself. It is to be noted that the title 'king' is never attached to the name Philetaerus, for until his death, despite almost complete independence, he still regarded himself as a vassal of the Seleucids. This portrait of Philetaerus (*Ill. 184*) was minted in the reign of Attalus I, 241–197 BC.

182, 183, 185 EUMENES II 197–160 BC

The Attalids of Pergamum were normally reticent in the matter of personal propaganda, featuring only the head of Philetaerus, the founder of the dynasty, on the coins of reign after reign (*Ill. 184*). Exceptionally Eumenes II here uses his own portrait (*Ill. 185*) on a tetradrachm which probably belongs early in his reign and may be an accession issue. On the reverse are the Dioscuri, Castor and Polydeuces, standing. This too is a departure from previous practice, for the dynastic type had hitherto been the seated Athena (*Ill. 181*). Conceivably the reference is to Pergamum's close ally Rome, for the Dioscuri (mounted) had also provided the reverse type of Rome's recently instituted denarius coinage.

184 PHILETAERUS 282–263 BC

185 EUMENES II 197–160 BC

186, 187, 190   NICOMEDES I *c.* 279–255 BC
The rugged portrait of the king wears the usual diadem (*Ill. 190*). On
the reverse a warrior goddess, perhaps the Thracian Bendis, sits upon
a rock holding two spears and a heavy sword in its scabbard; her
shield strengthened with rings of rivets rests by her side. In the background is a stump of a tree, perhaps prepared to support the spoils of
her adversaries.

188, 189, 191   PRUSIAS I 228–185 BC
The king is a handsome bearded man wearing the simple diadem
(*Ill. 191*). The reverse establishes the unchanging type of the
dynasty – Zeus half-draped holding wreath and sceptre; the immediate juxtaposition of the wreath of Zeus and the personal name of
the king is perhaps a claim to divine support. Zeus' thunderbolt is
placed in the field.

190 NICOMEDES I *c.* 279–255 BC

191 PRUSIAS I 228–185 BC

192, 193, 196 PRUSIAS II 185–149 BC

This son of Prusias I exceptionally wears a winged diadem (*Ill. 196*). This has been interpreted as a sign of the connection between the Bithynian royal house and the hero Perseus, for Prusias married a sister of the Macedonian king Perseus, who claimed descent from this hero; others have seen the wings as a mark of the mint of Alexandria Troas, where kings may have been identified with some deity to whom such wings were appropriate. Otherwise there is little but the portrait to distinguish the coins of Prusias II from those of his father. On the reverse Zeus' eagle now carries his thunderbolt.

194, 195, 197 NICOMEDES II 149–128 BC

Nicomedes, son of Prusias II, made little change in the appearance of the coinage. The epithet Epiphanes ('illustrious') may have been borrowed from the Seleucids, but the usage here appears to be different. Among the Seleucids the adjective follows the personal name, and thus qualifies the particular ruler; here it precedes the name and thus qualifies the royal title itself, and is so used constantly throughout the remaining coinage of the dynasty – 'illustrious king, Nicomedes', rather than 'King Nicomedes, the illustrious'. From now on Bithynian coins were dated annually from the foundation of the dynasty in 298 BC, and the portrait of Nicomedes II (*Ill. 197*) was retained unchanged by his successors. This coin is dated to the year 166 (= 132 BC).

196   PRUSIAS II 185–149 BC

197   NICOMEDES II 149–128 BC

198, 199, 202 MITHRADATES III *c.* 220–185 BC

The head is diademed and the bust draped. The bucolic features of
Mithradates (*Ill. 202*) have distinct family traits which were transmitted to his successors. The reverse type of the seated Zeus holding
an eagle is that of Alexander the Great, which was still being widely
used a century after his death. Beneath Zeus' right arm are to be seen
the sun and moon, a dynastic badge which occurs frequently on Pontic
coins.

200, 201, 203 PHARNACES I *c.* 185–169 BC

The puzzling draped male deity of the reverse has not been satisfac-
torily explained; in his left hand he holds a cornucopiae and a cadu-
ceus, and in his right a vine branch at which a doe nibbles. In the field
once more appears the dynastic badge of sun and moon.

202   MITHRADATES III *c.* 220–185 BC

203 PHARNACES I *c.* 185–169 BC

204, 205, 206 MITHRADATES IV AND LAODICE *c.* 169–150 BC
The heads of both are diademed, and their busts draped (*Ill. 206*). On the reverse Zeus and Hera holding sceptres stand side by side. The placing of the names, Mithradates against the figure of Zeus and Laodice by Hera, indicates that the royal pair are here seen in the guise of deities. Both are entitled Philadelphus ('brother/sister-loving') and they were in fact brother and sister as well as husband and wife. The usual sun and moon device is missing, but since Zeus, the sky-god, is radiate, it may be that Hera here represents the moon, and that the two deities stand in place of the symbol.

206　MITHRADATES IV AND LAODICE *c.* 169–150 BC

207, 208, 209 MITHRADATES VI 126–63 BC

The forward thrust of the head, the streaming locks, the snaky ties of the diadem all convey Mithradates' assumed character as the god Dionysus, whose name he took as a surname. The same theme is reiterated in the wreath of ivy leaves and berries of the reverse. But this had a second purpose for it relates his coinage to the obverse type of the cistophori which had long been the standard currency of the kingdom of Pergamum and of the Roman province of Asia, which by now belonged to Mithradates by right of conquest. The grazing stag is perhaps the mint-mark of Ephesus, the sun and moon a dynastic badge of the kings of Pontus. Eupator is an honorary epithet which serves to distinguish Mithradates VI from his predecessors of the same name. This coin is precisely dated to the ninth month of the year 223 (=75/4 BC).

209 MITHRADATES VI 126–63 BC

THE KINGDOM OF CAPPADOCIA

210, 211, 212 Orophernes 158–157 BC

The coins of Orophernes are so different from the usual regal coins of Cappadocia that they were probably minted at Priene, where Orophernes deposited his treasure in the temple of Athena, in the ruins of which all the surviving specimens of his coinage have been found; the owl on altar in the field of the reverse may be an allusion to this temple. Orophernes adopts Victory as his reverse type, and the same theme is repeated in his honorary title Nicephorus, 'Victory-bearing'. This title is particularly appropriate in the cases of men like Orophernes, or Antiochus IV and Alexander I of Syria, who owed their thrones to their personal initiative rather than to the rights of succession.

212 OROPHERNES 158–157 BC

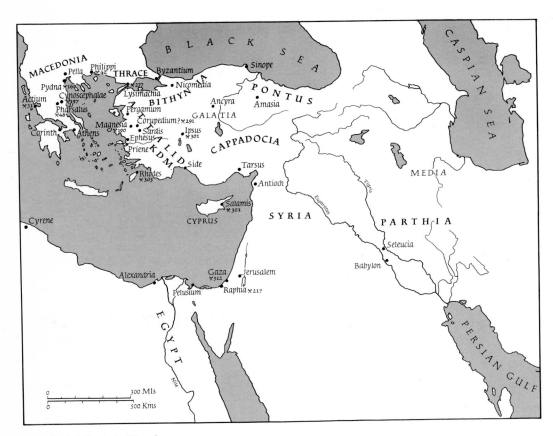

BLACK SEA

CASPIAN SEA

MACEDONIA
Pella
Pydna ×168
Philippi ×42
THRACE
Byzantium
Sinope
Nicomedia
Lysimachia
BITHYNIA
PONTUS
Actium ×31
Cynoscephalae ×197
Pharsalus ×48
Pergamum
Ancyra
Amasia
GALATIA
Corupedium? ×291
Corinth
Athens
Magnesia ×190
Ipsus ×301
Sardis
Ephesus
CAPPADOCIA
Priene
KDM.
LID.
Side
Tarsus
Rhodes ×305
Antioch
MEDIA
Salamis ×306
SYRIA
PARTHIA
Cyrene
CYPRUS
Seleucia
Babylon
Alexandria
Gaza ×312
Jerusalem
Pelusium
Raphia ×217
EGYPT
Nile
Euphrates
Tigris
PERSIAN GULF

0   300 Mls
0   500 Kms

2   *The Hellenistic Kingdoms*

The Ptolemies of Egypt

THE PARTITION OF ALEXANDER'S EMPIRE
AND THE WARS OF THE DIADOCHI

The calamity of Alexander's early death bared the weakness of the political structure of his vast empire; worse yet, there was no heir competent to take the throne nor any will or personal testament. And so there followed the 'Wars of the Diadochi' (the Successors), the generals who had been closest to Alexander and who by reason of their military commands and personal authority were now men of power. Alexander had taught them that to the audacious nothing is impossible, and for the next forty years and more they fought among themselves for dominance, dividing and redividing his empire between them.

Though the revolt at the river Beas (p. 29) had compelled Alexander to abandon the march to the 'River of Ocean' at the eastern edge of the world, being the man he was his mind had turned to the west, to Carthage and the unknown lands beyond the Pillars of Hercules. Alexander's memoranda of plans and projects included the building of a thousand warships for a campaign against the Carthaginians and a road to be constructed along the African coast, together with harbours and docks along the route. These plans were formally put to the Army Assembly and rejected; his generals were lesser men. With their great leader gone, most of them were intent only to seize, each for himself, some part or some one of the many countries of his conquest. Few remained loyal to his memory or to the heirs to his throne.

Soon after Alexander's death at Babylon on 13 June 323 BC those of his generals who were with him there formed themselves into a Council of State, the first purpose of which was to decide the succession to the throne. The senior was Perdiccas son of Orontes to whom Alexander, lying speechless on his deathbed, had handed his signet ring. Of the princely house of

Orestis, Perdiccas was an older man of Philip's time, proud, harsh and capable.

Another was Ptolemy son of Lagus, to be the founder of the Ptolemaic dynasty of Egypt which ended with the death of Cleopatra in 30 BC. He was an able field commander, even-tempered and shrewd, popular with the army. Also at Babylon was Seleucus son of Antiochus, the boyhood friend of Alexander who succeeded to the greater part of his empire. Another was Lysimachus who ruled in Thrace for almost forty years; a fine officer, cautious and tenacious, a hard man and very strong; he was said to have overcome a lion with his bare hands. In his eightieth year he was killed on the field of battle fighting against Seleucus.

4, 5, 6

Three leading generals were absent from the deliberations of the Council of State at Babylon, of whom the most prominent was Antipater, for the past eleven years Alexander's regent of Macedonia. Antipater was unswervingly loyal to the royal house, but by this time his regency had almost the authority of a monarchy, the more so since Alexander's death. Another was Craterus, Alexander's second in command of the army, who at the time was on the march to Macedonia with ten thousand veterans, with orders that he himself should replace Antipater as regent there. Craterus had reached Cilicia when the news of Alexander's death reached him and after some hesitation he joined forces with Antipater, to be killed two years later fighting against Eumenes.

The most important of the three was Antigonus Monophthalmos, the One-eyed. Aged about fifty, he had commanded under Philip and had marched with Alexander on the Persian expedition in 334 BC. After the battle of Issus (p. 20) Alexander had posted him to the satrapy of Phrygia Major, to guard his rear while the army continued its eastward march. From 321 until his death at the battle of Ipsus twenty years later Antigonus the One-eyed was the strongest power in Asia. His son Demetrius, then a boy of thirteen, was to be king of Macedon and founder of the Antigonid dynasty there.

In the Macedonian tradition it was the army assembly, representing the nation in arms, which elected the king. Since Alexander had left no heir but had passed his signet ring to Perdiccas, the Army Assembly offered the kingship to him. But he declined it; Alexander's queen Roxane, the Persian princess he had married four years before was with child, and he proposed and the Council of State agreed that the decision on the monarchy should wait until the child was born. If it was a boy, he should be king. Meanwhile, and in any case, the army and the empire must have an effective head, and Perdiccas was determined that that head should be himself.

Meleager, an officer who was popular with the army rank and file, was sent to tell them of the Council of State's decision to wait on the birth of Roxane's child, but there was violent opposition. Perdiccas was a nobleman of distinction, the senior of the generals at Babylon, and it was quite consonant with Macedonian tradition to make him king; but the child of a Persian woman – never. Meanwhile, and how or why is not known, there was present in the camp a youth who was a half-brother of Alexander, one of Philip's bastards named Arrhidaeus. He was epileptic and half-witted, despite which the infantry would now have him as king. With the aim of making a place for himself, Meleager had him dressed up in Alexander's robes, and the men acclaimed Arrhidaeus. Later Perdiccas had Meleager executed.

Tension between the infantry and the cavalry, representing the nobility, had reached the point of open mutiny before a compromise was reached. It was agreed that should Roxane's child be a boy, he and Arrhidaeus, renamed Philip, should rule jointly. A few weeks later Roxane was indeed delivered of a man-child, who was named Alexander.

The Council of State now decided on the government of the empire during the minority of the boy kings, that is to say, the division of the spoils. Perdiccas, the strongest and most senior of the generals, was to be commander of the Grand Army in Asia and to be *chiliarch* (vizier) of Alexander's kingdom. Craterus was to be joint regent with Antipater in Macedon and Greece and, in return for their support of Perdiccas, the generals were allocated or reconfirmed in the various satrapies; the best to the most important. Doubtless there was much hard bargaining. All appointments were made in the name of the king, or kings.

Antigonus the One-eyed was confirmed in his satrapy of Phrygia Major and also given Lycia and Pamphylia. Leonnatus, who like Ptolemy was related to the royal family and a member of the 'Bodyguard', got the key satrapy of Hellespontine Phrygia. He was killed in 321, fighting Greek insurgents in Thessaly. Menander was confirmed as satrap of Lydia and later was Antigonus' second in command of the army. Lysimachus was awarded Thrace – he had to fight for it – and Philotas was confirmed in Cilicia. Laomedon, a Greek, got Syria and another Greek, Eumenes of Cardia, was awarded Cappadocia and Paphlagonia, as yet unconquered. Eumenes had been Alexander's Chief of Secretariat, and he is the prime source of our knowledge of Alexander's wars (p. 151). He became a first-rate field commander and was completely loyal to the royal house. Six years later his Macedonian troops betrayed him to Antigonus, who had him executed. Peithon, another ambitious member of the Bodyguard, was given the satrapy of Media. He was killed by Seleucus in 312 BC (p. 184). Archon, an unknown, was named to Babylonia. Perhaps Perdiccas intended later to make Babylon his capital as, it was said, Alexander had planned to do.

Seleucus stood aside. He may have wanted Babylonia, but it was not then available, though he got it later. Meanwhile, foreseeing trouble to come, he decided to remain with the army, in the centre. He was appointed Perdiccas' first lieutenant, in command of the élite Companion cavalry corps.

Ptolemy got Egypt, the richest prize of all. Egypt had no satrap, having been left by Alexander under the administration of one Cleomenes, a Greek banker from Naucratis on the Nile.

PTOLEMY I SOTER 323–283 BC

Nine years before, during his four months in Egypt with Alexander, Ptolemy had taken full note of that ancient land, of how easily its borders could be defended and with what little force its people held subject. At the far end of the Mediterranean, away from the main currents of its traffic and its wars, Egypt was shielded from invasion by the marshes of the Nile delta and the deserts of Arabia and Libya. The one practicable road of entry was along the Palestine coast with thirty miles of easily defensible desert to cross. This was indeed a kingdom.

Little was known of the farther reaches of the Persian Empire, but Egypt was familiar to the Greeks. For several centuries they had had a city there, Naucratis (Mistress of Ships) on the Nile, where there were temples to Zeus and Hera, Apollo and Aphrodite, and a great Hellenium built jointly by many cities whose nationals traded at Naucratis. Greek mercenaries had served in Egyptian armies, and travellers, including Herodotus, had brought back tales of its millennias old civilization.

Ptolemy son of Lagus had grown up with Alexander at Pella; his mother was said to have been related to the royal family. Though several years older than the prince he was a

13, 17

close friend, and along with him was banished from the court when Alexander quarrelled with his father, Philip II. Ptolemy was with Alexander when he set out on the expedition to Asia, and although he did not figure prominently in the early years, with time he moved up in command as a competent if not a dashing general. He was one of the seven 'Companion Body-guards' of Alexander, one of the most important honours in his gift.

All this called for qualities of character and intelligence of a high order, and as his long and extraordinary career was to prove, Ptolemy had them, together with a most uncommon prudence. He was in fact the only one of the first round of the Hellenistic kings to die in his bed, and that in his eighty-fifth year and after securing a peaceful succession to his throne.

With his satrapy agreed Ptolemy left Babylon without delay. Perdiccas gave him a little money and two thousand men, and to help him to a welcome to Egypt, Ptolemy took possession of the idols and sacred objects which had been looted from there years ago by the Persians.

7—9

He went directly to Memphis, where he was given an account of the years of Cleomenes' stewardship: temple robbings, extortionate taxation, embezzlement of soldiers' pay and the like; all of course in the name of Alexander but actually for his own enrichment. The country was in a sad state. The irrigation canals upon which agriculture depended had been long neglected, while commerce and industry languished. The misery of the peasants and the disaffection of the nobility and the priesthood had been but worsened by the activities of Cleomenes, the 'honourable banker from Naucratis'. The relief, the hopes with which the Egyptians had welcomed Alexander had been wholly disappointed.

Ptolemy took stock. He had only a handful of men and little money, and it had been decided at Babylon that Cleomenes should continue in office as Ptolemy's first assistant (*hyparchos*), probably with instructions to report privately to Perdiccas. But regardless of the regent, Ptolemy had come to Egypt determined to be his own man, and thus had no choice but to deal promptly with Cleomenes. A trial was held and Cleomenes was sentenced to death for his betrayals of trust and executed. His treasury of more than eight thousand talents was thus at Ptolemy's disposal.

Ptolemy was a soldier and his first consideration was the army. Most of the troops left in Egypt by Alexander had run to seed in idleness and indiscipline, but in Greece there were mercenaries needing employment. Ptolemy let it be known there that he was in the market and before long his recruits, together with those soldiers in Egypt still fit to serve, were being trained under his own eye into a strong and efficient fighting force.

About a year after Ptolemy's arrival in Egypt, word came that the body of Alexander the Great had left Babylon on its way to interment at Aegae in Macedonia, the ancient burial place of its kings. The funeral cortège, with its golden coffin and splendid bier drawn by sixty-eight mules was in charge of an officer named Arrhidaeus. It was intercepted at Damascus by Ptolemy, who had with him an armed force; he claimed that Alexander's expressed wish was to be buried at the shrine of Zeus Ammon in the Oasis of Siwa in the western desert of Egypt, and that Perdiccas had no right to order otherwise.

Taking over from Arrhidaeus in the greatest body-snatch in history, Ptolemy escorted the cortège with all due ceremony to Memphis, there to await, he proclaimed, the building of a suitable shrine at Siwa. In the event the shrine was built at Alexandria, although it is not clear whether it was completed by Ptolemy Soter or his son Philadelphus.

For Ptolemy the possession of Alexander's mortal remains was of great importance. The Conqueror's aura was powerful, not only with the Macedonians and Greeks but also with the Egyptians. In the temple of Ptah at Memphis he had been received as a king, and thus in the eyes of the people he was the son and heir of the god and sovereign of the two lands of Egypt. With Alexander's body actually in Egypt, Ptolemy could claim that he now ruled by right of the conqueror himself, rather than that of a council of satraps, and were he some day to proclaim himself king, he could do so as Alexander's heir; he was triumphant.

Then came an appeal for help from Cyrene, the ancient Greek colony which was Egypt's western neighbour. When Alexander had arrived in Egypt, Cyrene had sent submission and gifts, but after his death civil war had broken out, and the country was now torn between the forces of the oligarchs and the democracy.

For Ptolemy this was an opportunity. It was little more than a year since his arrival in Egypt, but he had worked hard at the building of an army, and now he had one. Without a thought of asking permission of Perdiccas he marched it across the desert under command of his general Ophellas, who quickly quelled the civil war. When later Ptolemy himself arrived he took Cyrenaica as a prize of war, installing a garrison there with Ophellas in command. But Ptolemy was not to be left long undisturbed. The regent, Perdiccas, was no man to brook a show of independence by any of the satraps, yet here in open defiance of his authority Ptolemy had executed Cleomenes, had seized Alexander's precious remains and had now taken possession of Cyrenaica. In the spring of 321 BC he marched on Egypt with an army of 20,000 foot and 5000 horse, determined to put an end to Ptolemy and his presumptions.

Perdiccas reached the Nile at a point near Memphis where the river was fordable and where there was an island in the middle large enough for the army to camp. But by the time half the men and animals had got across to it the fine sand of the river bed had been so disturbed that it had washed away downstream. Many were drowned trying to reach the island, while those already there could not get back. In the rear all was confusion, which was resolved in the spirit of the time. Three of Perdiccas' senior officers, Seleucus, Peithon and Antigenes, came to his tent and killed him.

At a loss for leadership, the army offered Perdiccas' place and authority to Ptolemy, but he declined. His one ambition was a secure Egypt. On his advice Peithon and Arrhidaeus were appointed stop-gap regents for the boy-kings, and the army marched back to Syria. There at Triparadisus, on the arrival of Antipater and Antigonus the One-eyed, a second conference of the Council of State was held. Antipater was elected sole Regent of the Empire, and Antigonus commander in chief of the Grand Army in Asia. Among other changes Seleucus was made satrap of Babylonia and Ptolemy was confirmed in his possession of Egypt and Cyrenaica; to seal the new arrangement he thereupon married Antipater's daughter Eurydice.

With the reconfirmation of his satrapy of Egypt and his marriage to Antipater's daughter, Ptolemy might well have reckoned himself secure, but it was soon apparent that Antigonus the One-eyed, the new commander-in-chief of the Grand Army, was as formidable a threat as ever Perdiccas had been.

Like his friend Antipater, Antigonus was an older man of Philip's time. Of great height and commanding presence, he had the aristocratic virtues of courage, honesty and generosity. But he was overbearing, 'holding most men in contempt', though his rule in the satrapies was reputed to be mild. He was very good at war and politics, perhaps the only one of the Diadochi who might have reunited Alexander's empire in whose name he claimed the right so to do.

Once firmly in control of the bulk of Alexander's empire, Antigonus proceeded on a circuit of the eastern satrapies, reviewing their administration and evicting or killing off any satrap whose complete loyalty to himself might be doubted. He reached Babylon in 316 BC, to be received with due ceremony, but when after a few days he demanded an accounting of Seleucus' five years of satrapy and brushed aside a protest that he was not entitled to one, Seleucus realized that his head was next for the block. He fled for his life in the night, heading for refuge with his friend Ptolemy in Egypt.

Of the Diadochi opposing Antigonus there now remained only Ptolemy in Egypt, Lysimachus in Thrace and Cassander son of Antipater in Macedon. All were able generals, trained and hardened in Alexander's wars, and shrewd politicians to boot. But Antigonus towered above any of them, only in combination could they survive. So, willy nilly, jealous and suspicious of each other as they were, the three were compelled into alliance. In 315 BC they sent a joint embassy to Antigonus, demanding a further share of the spoils of Alexander's conquests. Seleucus was with Ptolemy, and his reinstatement at Babylon was one of the demands. Antigonus scornfully rejected the embassy, and both sides prepared for war.

THE BATTLE
OF GAZA

Three years later the alliance came into action. Antigonus was preparing an attack on Cassander in Macedon, and to guard his vulnerable southern flank against Ptolemy he sent his son Demetrius with a strong army to Syria. But for almost ten years now Ptolemy had been free to consolidate his kingdom and above all to build a first rate army, and early in 312 BC, probably urged by Seleucus, he marched against Demetrius, who on the news hurried south. He came up with Ptolemy at Gaza in Palestine, where he was wholly defeated, and with Demetrius in flight and Ptolemy in Palestine and Syria, Antigonus perforce abandoned his projected attack on Cassander.

In return for the part he had played in the victory at Gaza, Ptolemy gave Seleucus a small force with which to regain his satrapy of Babylonia. He did so (p. 183) and then advanced into Media, threatening Antigonus' eastern provinces. In counter action Demetrius, in 311 BC, appeared before Babylon with an army of 20,000 men, but there was no one to fight. Seleucus was away in Media and the small garrison he had left at Babylon hid in the desert. Antigonus had put a time limit on Demetrius' expedition so that he could not follow Seleucus, and with only loot to show for his trouble he marched back to Syria.

The fiasco at Babylon left Antigonus and his enemies about evenly matched, and in the same year, 311 BC, a treaty of peace was made. It ended the pretence of a united empire, for foremost of its terms was that Antigonus was now General of Asia. He had lost the eastern satrapies to Seleucus, to whom he refused to concede Babylonia and who was excluded from the treaty, but had gained Syria, Phoenicia and Caria. Lysimachus was now formally ruler of Thrace and Ptolemy of Egypt; the form of 'satrapy' was gone. Ptolemy had lost Syria and Cyrenaica but had gained Cyprus. Cassander was to be General of Europe until the thirteen-year-old Alexander IV was old enough to rule, which meant that sooner or later Cassander would do away with him. This he did in the same year, murdering both the boy and his mother Roxane. At sea neither side had the advantage.

Peace treaty or no, the wars of the Diadochi continued. With their powerful armies, central position and great wealth Antigonus and Demetrius probed and prodded at Cassander, Lysimachus, Ptolemy and Seleucus alike. In 310 Antigonus descended on Babylonia but failed to bring Seleucus to battle, though he did lay waste half of Babylon and ravaged the countryside. Two years later Demetrius sailed unopposed into the Piraeus, the port of Athens, with a fleet of 250 warships and transports – the harbour booms were up. Cassander's garrison retired to the citadel of Munychia and his governor of Athens, Demetrius of Phaleron, surrendered the city. Later he went off to Alexandria to assist Ptolemy in the building and organization of the Museum (p. 150). Demetrius then took and razed the citadel and declared the freedom of Athens, claiming that he had come only as a liberator of the Greeks. Antigonus sent 150,000 bushels of corn and timber for the building of 100 warships. He and Demetrius were hailed by the Athenians as kings, and worshipped as 'Saviour Gods'.

Also in 306 BC Demetrius sailed for Cyprus with over a hundred warships and transports carrying 15,000 mercenaries. Ptolemy's brother Menelaus was governor of the island, with 60 warships and 12,000 men. Demetrius landed and defeated Menelaus, shutting him up in the fortress of Salamis and

THE BATTLE
OF SALAMIS

bottling up his sixty warships in the harbour. As expected, Ptolemy sailed to his brother's relief with his main fleet and ten thousand men. In the ensuing sea battle Demetrius was out-numbered in ships, but his were mostly bigger and stronger, and his tactics better; Ptolemy lost the bulk of his fleet and men. Menelaus and his officers surrendered, their men went over to Demetrius. It was a major victory; his coins show a statue of Victory standing on the prow of his ship.

With this defeat Ptolemy lost his command of the Aegean and of his possessions there, and the Antigonids were again far and away the strongest of the Diadochi, dominating and threatening all. To celebrate their triumph Antigonus and Demetrius now took the title of king and assumed the royal diadem. A year later Ptolemy, Seleucus, Lysimachus and Cassander followed suit. Alexander's line was extinct. His mother Olympias had murdered Philip Arrhidaeus, Philip II's bastard son, ten years before, and Roxane and her son by Alexander had been killed by Cassander in 311 BC.

118
14, 49, 5

Antigonus decided to strike at Ptolemy before he could recover from the defeat at Cyprus, and later in 306 BC he appeared before Gaza in Palestine with a huge army; the figures given are 80,000 foot, 8000 horse and 83 elephants, and there were 250 warships and transports commanded by Demetrius. But it was the wrong time of year; there were storms and several of Demetrius' ships were lost, while his attempts at landing were frustrated. Antigonus' army reached Pelusium to find that fortress city strongly held, the Nile crossings were well guarded and the river in flood.

Demetrius tried again for a landing but further west, and again his fleet was scattered by storm. During the delay many of Antigonus' men deserted to Ptolemy, who was popular with the army and ready with bribes. At last, mindful of the fate of Perdiccas fifteen years before, Antigonus abandoned the campaign, leaving Ptolemy even more secure in his fortress of Egypt.

THE SIEGE OF RHODES

The Antigonids could not rest and in 305 BC they commenced the famous siege of Rhodes, Ptolemy's ally, to which Demetrius brought 40,000 fighting men and 30,000 workmen in two hundred warships and one hundred and seventy transports. His siege engines included a great armoured tower full of stone throwers and catapults called 'Taker of Cities' (*Helepolis*). The Rhodians armed their slaves and manned the walls, beating Demetrius off. After a precious year and much waste and loss Antigonus ordered Demetrius to make terms with them; terms he could have had without the siege, that Rhodes should be free and Antigonus' ally *except* against Ptolemy. The triumphant Rhodians sold off the siege equipment left behind by Demetrius and with the proceeds erected a great bronze statue, sculptured by Chares, of the sun-god Helios, whose head is the obverse of their coinage.

The wars of the Diadochi ground on. Having completed the liberation of Greece from Cassander, in 302 BC Demetrius landed in Thessaly with an army of 60,000 men, determined to crush him. Cassander then came south against him with an army half as large, but took a strongly positioned defensive stand. At the same time he and Lysimachus sent urgent messages to Ptolemy and Seleucus, united action was imperative; if Demetrius prevailed over Cassander, before long they too would be destroyed. The allies agreed on joint action. The first essential was to relieve Demetrius' pressure on Cassander, and for that Lysimachus would cross over into Asia Minor and make for Phrygia, Antigonus' base satrapy. Cassander would give him ten thousand of his own men, whom he could ill spare (in the event their transports were intercepted by Demetrius' fleet). Second, Ptolemy would attack Antigonus' southern flank with an invasion of Syria and Phoenicia; and third, Seleucus would bring his entire strength north to meet Lysimachus, so that together they would be nearly equal to the Antigonids. But the difficulty was timing. Seleucus' army and transports could not be organized and make the long march across desert and mountains in time to join up with Lysimachus for that year's campaigning season so that, meanwhile, Lysimachus must avoid battle while still threatening the enemy.

Lysimachus got his army across the Dardanelles without opposition; there was treachery, apart from disaffection because of Antigonus' harshness. Like most rulers of his time and many other, Lysimachus would bribe freely; the cities of Lampsacus and Parium declared for him, and Phoenix, Antigonus' general in Lydia, handed over the fortress city of Sardis. Lysimachus sent one column south to Ionia where most of the cities, including Ephesus, came over to his cause. As planned he himself marched east to Phrygia where Docimus, who had been satrap of Babylon (p. 182) and his lieutenant Philetaerus, who later was to be governor of Pergamum for Lysimachus, came over to him with a considerable force and treasure.

Antigonus was celebrating in his new capital of Antigonea in Syria when the news of Lysimachus' invasion reached him.

THE BATTLE
OF IPSUS

147

He abandoned the festivities and hurried north to meet the attack, at the same time recalling Demetrius from his confrontation with Cassander in Thessaly. The first part of the allied plan had worked. As for Lysimachus, he was a capable tactician, and in a series of delaying actions he held off the Antigonids until the end of the year's campaigning season, going into winter quarters near Heraclea on the Black Sea coast. Early in the following year Ptolemy attacked the Antigonid garrisons in Palestine and Syria, and despite the enemy's attempts at interception, Seleucus and Lysimachus joined forces in western Phrygia.

And so toward the end of the eighth decade of his life, strong and vigorous still after more than twenty years of service to Philip and Alexander and over thirty years of the wars of the Diadochi, Antigonus, together with his son Demetrius, met the combined forces of Lysimachus and Seleucus on the field of Ipsus, in west central Asia Minor. Antigonus had 70,000 foot, 10,000 horse and 75 elephants. Their enemies had 64,000 foot, 10,500 horse, 120 chariots and 480 of the 500 elephants (reduced by some estimates to 150) Seleucus had gotten from Chandragupta of India three years before when a treaty of friendship had been signed (p. 186).

Like most battles, Ipsus was more lost than won. Demetrius opened with a cavalry charge against the allied horse under Antiochus son of Seleucus, breaking through and overwhelming them. But instead of then regaining his position in the battle line flanking Antigonus and the phalanx (the main body of infantry) Demetrius continued in hot pursuit of the fleeing enemy. When at last he did return to the field it was to find the mass of Seleucus' war elephants interposed between him and the main army, the phalanx being steadily ground down and Antigonus dead. It was a crushing and total defeat. Demetrius got away with but ten thousand of his eighty thousand men, after which most of the surviving mercenaries were incorporated in the armies of Seleucus and Lysimachus.

The winners carved up the Antigonid empire. Most of Asia Minor went to Lysimachus, and Seleucus got Syria, his doorway to the Mediterranean. Ptolemy held on to lower Syria and Palestine to which he was not entitled for earlier he had cut and run on false news of an Antigonid victory. Seleucus protested, but Ptolemy had been a friend in time of need and he was allowed to keep his gains, long to be a bone of contention between Seleucids and Ptolemies.

'The victors gave Antigonus a royal funeral. But later, under Lysimachus' harsher rule, a Phrygian peasant paid him a finer tribute. He was found digging a pit on his farm and when asked what he did, he replied sadly, "I seek Antigonus".'

Ptolemy had now been ruler of Egypt for more than twenty years and his kingdom had prospered. The Nile valley was rich, needing only water and cultivation to produce two or three abundant crops a year. New varieties of cereals, fruits, vines and olives were brought in, and high quality bulls, rams and boars as breeding stock. The oppressive tax system was over-hauled and its burdens lightened. Agriculture and commerce revived.

Immigration was encouraged, especially of Greeks and Jews. In Egypt there was opportunity, fortunes were to be made in this rich and ancient land. Greek civil servants were every-where, though the traditional forms of government were retained.

Especially compared with the problems of the Seleucids in their widespread empire, the governing of Egypt was easy, rendered so by its homogeneous population and its geography. For all its six or seven millions of population, except for the Nile delta Egypt was a long narrow strip of land rarely more than ten miles wide on either side of the river. The whole was en-closed, imprisoned, by desert. The Nile was thus a great high-way down the centre of the country, patrolled by the king's fleets, which could quickly reach and suppress any unrest, deal with any difficulty.

Administratively the country was divided into three governorships, the Thebaid, Lower Egypt and Central Egypt, each of which was again divided into nomes or counties. There were forty-two nomes, each in the charge of a civil servant who was both judge and tax collector. The whole responded to the *dioiketes*, the king's treasurer at Alexandria.

THE GOD SARAPIS

Unlike the camel, the god Sarapis may well have owed part of his design to a committee. Ptolemy realized the need for some unifying force or agent between his own people and the Egyptians. Alexander's plan for intermarriage and a common culture between Greeks and Iranians was certainly not applicable in Egypt, for in that densely populated country Ptolemy's Macedonians and Greeks would have quickly disappeared in any such intermingling of the races. The unifying force or agent might well be a new religion, and so there appeared the god Sarapis.

There are several accounts of the origin of Sarapis. One is that Ptolemy set up a consultative committee of philosophers and priests, which came up with the proposal for a combination of Zeus and Pluto of the Greeks and the Egyptian gods Apis and Osiris. Another story is that Sarapis originated in Babylonia, under a different name and with other attributes. A third, that his statue by the Greek sculptor Bryaxis, richly wrought of silver and gold and with jewelled eyes, was presented to Ptolemy by the people of Sinope on the Black Sea in gratitude for shipments of corn in time of famine.

At Alexandria a great temple was built within which sat the god, resembling a benign bearded Zeus crowned by the modius, the corn measure of Egypt, with Pluto's three-headed dog Cerberus at his feet. Sarapis worship became a state religion and there was a temple of the god in each of the forty-two nomes of Egypt; it was particularly strong in Alexandria and soon became widely spread in the Hellenistic world, with temples even at Delos and Ephesus. In his aspect of Pluto, god of the underworld, Sarapis offered assurance of life in the hereafter, a needed consolation for the tribulations of the present.

Ptolemy was a man of simple tastes and frugal habits; it was said that for a state banquet, gold plate for the royal table had to be borrowed from members of the court. He was intolerant of dishonesty and a just judge. There is a story of his having issued a proclamation that should he order anything that was contrary to the law of the land, he should be disobeyed.

He was a profound admirer of Hellenic culture, a friend of philosophers if not a philosopher king. Demetrius of Phaleron had built at Athens a home of the Muses, adjacent to the Lyceum. He came to Ptolemy's court, who decided now to build a second and greater Museum in his beautiful Alexandria. It was a university, with halls and lecture rooms and gardens, and Demetrius of Phaleron directed it. Scholars, poets, philosophers, scientists and artists were invited, famous and unknown alike, as teachers and as students. They were free of taxation and provided with their keep.

At the Museum they studied philosophy, dialectic, grammar, medicine, science and mathematics. Here Euclid wrote his *Elements of Geometry* and Archimedes for a time was his pupil. Working on condemned criminals, Herophilus of Chalcedon found, centuries before Harvey, that it was the constant pulsing of the heart that kept the blood circulating. Adjacent to the Museum was the building housing Ptolemy's collection of books, which was the nucleus of the great library of Alexandria. Here too, for the benefit of the Alexandrian Jews, who had largely forgotten their ancient tongue, the Bible was later translated into Greek.

It is one of those chances of history that we owe to Ptolemy most of what is known of the wars of Alexander the Great. In later life Ptolemy wrote an account of them, based on the daily 'Journal' kept by Eumenes, chief of Alexander's secretariat. Eumenes' 'Journal' and Ptolemy's history are lost but the Roman historian Arrian declares that Ptolemy's history was the prime source for his own *History of Alexander* and *Indica*, and thus of the numberless 'Alexander books' since written.

Ptolemy's first queen had been a daughter of Nectanebo, the last native Pharaoh of Egypt, but she had been set aside in 320 BC for Eurydice, daughter of Antipater, Regent of Macedon. One of Eurydice's ladies-in-waiting was Berenice, a widow with three children of whom one was a boy named Magas, later to become king of Cyrenaica under the overlordship of Egypt.

Some years later and after Eurydice had borne him four children, Ptolemy also married Berenice. Polygamy was no novelty in Macedon, and for Eurydice it was better to be half a queen than not at all. It was Berenice's son by Ptolemy who succeeded to the throne of Egypt as Ptolemy II Philadelphus.

16, 19

In 285 BC, having ruled as satrap and king of Egypt for thirty-eight years, Ptolemy made his elder son by Berenice co-ruler with himself. The rightful heir was Ptolemy called Keraunos, son of Eurydice. But Keraunos – the word means thunderbolt – was of unstable and violent character, disliked by Ptolemy and the court, while Berenice's son was a mild young man, popular with all and his father's favourite. There was celebration in Alexandria, while Keraunos went off to the court of Lysimachus in Thrace where his half-sister was queen.

Two years later, having seen his successor securely established on the throne and without bloodshed, Ptolemy's long career ended. If he was not the earth-shaker Alexander had been, in his own way Ptolemy too was a great man.

PTOLEMY II PHILADELPHUS 285–246 BC
Ptolemy II Philadelphus came to the throne as co-ruler of Egypt two years before his father's death. He was then about twenty-

15, 18

five years of age, born on the island of Cos during one of Ptolemy's campaigns. His early childhood was spent away from his plain-living father and without doubt he was thoroughly spoiled, but as he grew older Ptolemy found him suitable tutors among the scholars at the Museum.

The young king was interested in philosophy and zoology but not especially in matters of state, at least not at the time. To the delight of his subjects and unlike his thrifty father, he loved public entertainment, and quite early in his reign he decided to celebrate his accession with a pageant. It would be most splendid, intended to display to the world the strength and wealth of his kingdom. This pageant was to be the first of many such displays:

'Led by Lucifer, star of the morning and closed by Hesperus, star of the evening, there passed in file the gods of Egypt and Greece, the temple images of Osiris, of Ptah, of Dionysus and of Zeus. Keeping the roadway clear walked the Sileni, robed in purple and scarlet, behind the images walked a company of Satyrs, followed by a man of gigantic stature bearing the golden horn of Amalthea, and by a woman of surpassing loveliness waving in one hand a single palm branch, in the other a sprig of peace-blossom. Next there appeared a life-sized image of Dionysus seated on a golden throne drawn by 180 slaves, escorted by an army of priests, priestesses and initiates, and at their heels a representation of the bed-chamber of Semele, the mother of the god. Wine flowed freely, music rose and fell incessantly. It was generally agreed that never had there been, and there never would be again, so magnificent a pageant.

'The most absorbing spectacle was still to come, a long train of wild beasts and birds unknown to Egypt. First a hundred ponderous elephants harnessed to chariots, four to a team, next herds of buffalos, antelopes, gemsboks, ostriches, gnus, zebras and goats, ridden by boys attired as charioteers, and finally caged lions, panthers, tigers, a rhinocerus and a white bear. Following the wild beasts walked attendants carrying parrots, peacocks and pheasants from Ethiopia, cowmen leading bulls from India, Arabia and the Caucasus, and shepherds driving sheep from Greece and Ethiopia. There was a brief pause. The cheering ceased, the gossip died down, the royal party was approaching.

'Preceded by a life-sized image of the great Alexander, Ptolemy with Berenice and Philadelphus appeared. A roar of welcome broke out; the cheers grew louder when word passed that on the throne lay a crown made of ten thousand gold coins, when the eye caught sight of other golden crowns and chaplets borne by pages and ladies of the court, of wagons loaded with gold and silver plate that lumbered along in the rear.

'The procession made the round of the city, returned to the Stadium and there halted for the last scene of the pageant. Escorted by the bodyguard Ptolemy advanced to the centre of the arena and accepted from the delegates of states and cities Alexander had freed from the Persian yoke fresh gifts of golden crowns in memory of the services that great commander had rendered to the world.'

ALEXANDRIA

Both Philadelphus and his father Ptolemy Soter lavished wealth and effort on the building and enrichment of Alexandria. The Greeks might question Macedonian claims to be true Hellenes, but the Ptolemies' admiration for Greek culture was sincere. They determined to make their capital a worthy rival of Athens, and its grandeur and beauty brought them the fame and glory in the Greek world they so ardently desired.

The city of Alexandria was laid out in a rectangle four miles long from east to west and three-quarters of a mile from north to south. On the north it fronted on the sea, where a mile long mole ran out to the island of Pharos, whose beacon guided mariners from forty miles away. An inscription on the Pharos read:

Sostratus, son of Dexiphanes, the Cnidian
to the divine Soters,
in aid of mariners.

On either side of the mole were harbours, the westerly one for commerce, the easterly for war. On the south the city was bounded by the fresh-water lake Mareotis. This was connected to the Nile by canal, and its traffic handled by a conveniently placed third harbour.

The two main streets of Alexandria, lined with shops and bazaars, were over a hundred feet wide and colonnaded. One ran from the Canopus Gate on the east to the Moon Gate on the west, the other north and south. They crossed at the centre of the city where there was a great square. In this area were grouped the building housing the civic administration, the Halls of Justice, the Gymnasium, the central stores for corn, oil and other produce; and within its own walled enclosure the Sema, the tomb where Alexander the Great lay in his coffin of gold.

Beyond the east gate was the Stadium and the Hippodrome; to the west near the native quarter stood the great temple of Sarapis. Nile water was provided by a canal which fed conveniently spaced cisterns from which the populace could draw at will.

On the north of the city was the quarter Brucheum. Here stood the Palace with its north side to the sea, and a broad flight of steps led down to Philadelphus' pleasure fleet. Nearby were the barracks for the Royal Guard, the Museum, the famous Library and many temples to the gods, all set among spacious gardens and all of course walled off from the populace.

Alexandria at this time was the largest city in the known world, with a population of about half a million, including slaves. There were more than 100,000 in the Jewish quarter alone, for after the conquest of Palestine, Ptolemy brought large numbers of its inhabitants to Egypt. The general population was continually augmented from all parts of the Greek world, artisans and merchants and simple immigrants seeking a better livelihood than they could find at home, all eager to see this new, rich and beautiful metropolis.

Ptolemy Soter had been a great book collector and probably had commenced the building of the Library of Alexandria. Philadelphus certainly completed it and throughout his long reign continually added to it. The collection was said to have numbered several hundreds of thousands of volumes or papyrus rolls, each equal to thirty or forty pages of modern print. They were first catalogued, in 120 volumes, by Callimachus of Cyrene. The chief librarians continued to be eminent scholars and, conjointly with the Museum, the Library became the greatest centre of literary production and criticism of the Hellenistic world.

The Ptolemies' prime concern was of course security, internal and external. For a strong army and navy the native Egyptians were not good enough; only Macedonian and Greek mercenaries, trained in the best military techniques of the time, could be adequate. For this much money was needed and since this was to be had only in exchange for goods exported, Egypt was turned into a money making machine; its administration and economy were not so much revolutionized as tightened up. Greeks were brought in as managers of the tax system, to set up and expand manufactures, and as merchants and bankers. Egypt was primarily an agricultural country, wheat her most valuable crop. Improved irrigation and the development of new land

MEDITERRANEAN SEA

Prehistoric Harbour
Ras el Tin
ISLAND OF PHAROS
Pharos · Lighthouse
Fort Kait Bey
Temple of Poseidon
Catacombs of Anfouchy
Temple of Isis on Pharos
Timonium
EUNOSTOS HARBOUR
Present Coastline
GREAT HARBOUR
Present Coastline
Royal Harbour
Cape Lochias
Silsileh
Temple of Isis
Heptastadion Dyke
Place Mohammed Ali
Island Palace
St Antirrhodos
Gate of the Moon
Docks
Convent of St. Catherine
Cleopatra's Needles
Caesareum
Theatre
Area of Palace
Ch. of St. Mark
Ch. of St. Theonas
Canopic Street
now Rue
Race Course
Chatby
Gabbari
Ch. of St. Athanasius
Area of Mouseion
Library
el Horreya
Arab Walls
JEWISH QUARTER
Gate of the Sun
Porte Rosette
Shrine of Pompey
WESTERN CEMETERY
Arab Walls of A.D. 811
SOMA
Park of Pan
to Canopus
Canal
Temple of Serapis
Pompey's Pillar
Library
RHAKOTIS
Street of the Soma
now Rue Nebi Daniel
EASTERN CEMETERIES
Catacombs
Kom el Chogafa
Race Course
Canal following Course of
Probable Course of Walls
Lake Harbour
Mahmoudieh
BC 331
Canal
to Canopus & Nile
LAKE MAREOTIS
LAKE MARIOUT

3 *Alexandria*

by drainage in the Fayum produced a substantial surplus which was exported to the hungry lands of the Mediterranean and as far as Rome.

Mines and quarries belonged to the king and textiles and oils were a royal monopoly. The king decided how much and what kinds of oil-producing seeds, linseed, safflower, gourd and the like were to be planted, taking the entire yield at a fixed price and processing it in the royal factories. For every other kind of production the tax was assessed first, usually payable in kind, and any shortfall was the producer's loss, not the king's! There were taxes on rents and on sales, on cattle and on slaves, and a poll tax.

Thus managed Egypt produced more than enough to pay for the mercenaries and ships needed for protection from foreign enemies or domestic unrest. There was much private wealth, as shown especially by the opulence of Alexandria, but it was little beside that of the king.

ARSINOE I AND ARSINOE II

In about 285 BC Ptolemy Philadelphus married Arsinoe, daughter of Lysimachus of Thrace, a dynastic union of importance. She bore him three children, Ptolemy later called Euergetes, Lysimachus and a daughter Berenice who became a Seleucid queen (p. 191). But some six years later and despite her three children Queen Arsinoe came to disaster. She was accused of treason and there was none to defend her, for her father and the old Ptolemy were dead. She was dethroned and banished to Coptos in the Thebaid of Egypt, hundreds of miles from Alexandria and her children, there to end her days.

The cause of her tragedy and the successor to her throne was the full sister of her husband, also named Arsinoe, who had had two previous husbands. As her portrait coins show, she was a beautiful woman. She had many of the qualities of her father Ptolemy Soter except that where his inclinations were to kindness and honesty she was without scruple. As Arsinoe II Queen of Egypt she was practical, shrewd, hardworking and of balanced judgment, a far stronger character than her husband-brother. She had no children by him.

15, 18
20, 21

As a girl of seventeen she had been married to Lysimachus of Thrace, who then was about sixty years old. He came to be greatly influenced by his new young wife and as her special domain gave her the important towns of Tius, Heraclea, Amastris and Cassandrea. She bore him three sons and deciding that one of them should succeed to the throne she proceeded to intrigue against Agathocles, son of Lysimachus by his first wife and his legal heir. She was successful and Agathocles, a loyal son and a favourite with the army and the people, was put to death for alleged treason.

Then came the battle of Corupedion in 281 (p. 188) where Lysimachus was killed fighting against Seleucus Nicator. Six months later Ptolemy Keraunos assassinated Seleucus, himself becoming king of Macedon and Thrace (p. 189).

Ptolemy Keraunos, who was a half brother of Arsinoe, now persuaded her to marry him, thus again giving her a throne and helping to legitimitize his rule. But he soon decided that this strong-willed woman was a threat to him, and turned to do away with her and her children. The two younger boys were killed but the eldest, Ptolemaeus, escaped to Illyria, and Arsinoe was permitted to take sanctuary at Samothrace. Within a year Keraunos himself came to a bad end, killed by invading Galatians (p. 224).

Arsinoe was about forty years of age, a masterful woman of the world, when she returned to Alexandria in about 276 BC. Once settled there she decided to take the place of her brother's wife, Arsinoe I. This was quickly accomplished and Philadelphus, amiable and soft-tempered as he was, found in his sister-wife a worthy partner. He was wholly devoted to her and heart-broken when she died. He deified her and at least commenced the building of temples to her honour. He did not remarry.

During the seven years of her reign Arsinoe appears to have taken control of Egypt's foreign affairs and they prospered. Phoenicia and most of the coastal cities of Asia Minor from Miletus around into Cilicia, which had been lost to Antiochus I of Syria a few years before, were reconquered. In domestic matters, herself a usurper, she followed the practice of the time in removing any possible rival to the throne. Philadelphus' half-brother Argaeus was put to death on charges of conspiracy, and also another half-brother whose name is not known. Unlike many of her line Arsinoe was not wantonly cruel, for she adopted the three small children of the woman she had displaced, caring for their health and education. When she died in 270 BC they were the poorer for her going.

Philadelphus ruled Egypt for thirty-eight years, a long reign of which comparatively little is known. Because his interests were primarily in government, diplomacy and Greek culture, he has been pictured as an indolent dilettante of the arts. He was in fact a capable ruler, an intelligent man who understood his world and his country's place in it better than most monarchs of his time. (Rostovtzeff, in his *Social and Economic History of the Hellenistic World*, p. 262, says 'it is manifest from the evidence that Philadelphus displayed a feverish activity in dealing with the problems he inherited from his predecessor'.)

It must be remembered that Egypt's military and political problems differed from those of Philadelphus' contemporaries, especially from those of the Seleucids. Philadelphus had no need, as had Antiochus I, for long campaigns against rebellious satraps in countries far distant from his capital. Apart from the route along the Palestine coast, none of his boundaries needed protection against invasion by land. At sea he maintained a strong navy. Except for his possessions along the Asia Minor coast and in the Aegean, Philadelphus had to deal only with Egypt and Cyrenaica. Egypt's habitable area was no larger than modern Belgium even though it was strung out for several hundred miles along the banks of the Nile. Its six or seven million native Egyptians were a homogeneous people with a long history and an ancient culture, deeply religious and obedient to the priesthood, and through it to the government as personified by the king.

With the army and fleet made available by her wealth, Egypt under Philadelphus steadily increased her possessions. At one time or another during the third century BC these ranged from Abdera in Thrace along the coast to the Hellespont and, included the islands of Samothrace, Lesbos and Samos. She also held much of Phoenicia, southern Syria and Palestine.

In diplomacy Philadelphus exchanged credentials with Rome in 270 BC, but maintained a careful neutrality during her struggle with Carthage. To cement his alliance with the Seleucids he married his daughter Berenice to Antiochus II, a match that came to a bad end (p. 191), and a revolt by his half-brother Magas, sub-king or governor of Cyrenaica, was settled by the betrothal of Magas' daughter Berenice to Philadelphus' heir. This while both were children.

Of Philadelphus himself, it was said that by disposition he was kindly, expressing regret at being compelled by reasons of policy to order the death of men who otherwise were quite estimable. He died in 246 BC, aged about sixty, and by and large his reign was a successful one.

PTOLEMY III EUERGETES, 246–221 BC

Ptolemy Euergetes – meaning Benefactor – was thirty years old when he succeeded to the throne of the richest country in the known world. His father Philadelphus had added to the empire of Ptolemy Soter ('Saviour'), and Egypt was strong and secure. The Seleucid empire was in the hands of the weak Antiochus II whose queen, Berenice, was Euergetes' own sister, and Rome was preoccupied with her wars with Carthage.

The Egyptian army was large, well equipped and well officered, and comprised mainly of Greek and Macedonian mercenaries; the fleet of three hundred men of war, supported by hundreds of supply and transport ships, completely dominated the Aegean. The treasury is recorded as holding seventy thousand talents, and the revenue from the rich soil of the Nile valley and from commerce and manufacture was steadily increasing.

23, 27

His portrait coins show Euergetes as a burly, thick-necked man. He was no lover of the arts as his father had been, but rather of the chase. His early life had been difficult, for his mother, Arsinoe I, had been sent away into exile, leaving him and his brother and sister in the care of his father's second wife, Arsinoe II (p. 156). Despite her hard and dominating character Arsinoe II had cared well for her predecessor's children, but she had died while Euergetes was yet a boy.

20

The children's upbringing was then left to court functionaries, although tutors were found from the Museum for their schooling. Euergetes grew to be a rather spoiled and wilful young man, for who was not to indulge the handsome and likeable heir to the throne? But his youthful impatience led him to voice his contempt for his father's apparently indolent life. Philadelphus hearing of this decided to forestall any attempt at rebellion by getting this elder son of his out of Egypt, and the opportunity soon came to hand.

Trouble arose in Cyrenaica, where for over half a century Philadelphus' half-brother Magas had ruled as king under the suzerainty of Egypt. Years before it had been agreed that Magas' only child, his daughter Berenice, should marry Euergetes and there had been a formal betrothal. But after the death of Magas his widow Apama had decided instead on an alliance with the Antigonids, and Demetrius the Fair, son of Demetrius Poliorcetes and half-brother of Antigonus Gonatas King of Macedon, had come to Cyrene and married Berenice. (Whether Demetrius actually married Berenice, who was about fourteen years of age at the time, is disputed. He does appear to have ruled as king for a while.) They had ruled jointly until the young queen had found that her husband and her mother were lovers. She was not one to sit and grieve; her soldiers killed Demetrius in her mother's chamber. Much unrest followed and now Euergetes was sent to restore order; this he did quickly and firmly.

Euergetes stayed in Cyrenaica for some five years, but Cyrene was remote from Alexandria and he was an impatient man; when news came that his father was failing and that he should prepare to accede to the throne he gladly hurried home. Philadelphus died soon after and the new king was acclaimed with rejoicing – Alexandria had become a dull place during the old king's long illness. Euergetes, young, happy and proud, would bring back the sparkle of his father's early years.

Within a year of his accession word came to Alexandria that Euergetes' sister Berenice was in danger of her life, besieged in her palace near Antioch in Syria by partisans of her rival Laodice (p. 191). With that warmth and loyalty which the

Ptolemies sometimes gave to their sisters, though rarely to their brothers, Euergetes hurried to the rescue.

Four years before Berenice had been given in marriage to Antiochus II of Syria, part of a peace settlement with Egypt whereby she brought as dowry the revenues of lower Syria and Palestine. Antiochus' first queen, Laodice, went off with her two sons to Ephesus and Berenice took her place beside Antiochus at Antioch. It was a condition of the marriage settlement that should Berenice bear a son to Antiochus, that son should succeed to the Seleucid throne. Antiochus lived with his new wife long enough for her to produce a son and then, always a weak man, he left her to follow his first wife Laodice to Ephesus. He died shortly thereafter, poisoned it was said by Laodice, who then put her friends in Syria to work to destroy Berenice, whose young arrogance was resented by the court and populace alike. By the time Euergetes and his army had marched the more than seven hundred miles to Antioch Berenice and her child were dead, killed by Laodice's adherents. The city was put to siege and when at last it yielded with a plea for clemency, in revenge for his sister's death Euergetes turned it over to his troops to loot and burn.

Euergetes next turned to the conquest of the Seleucid empire's eastern territories, marching to Babylon and Seleucia-on-the Tigris. Their garrisons offered no resistance; they could not fight against this imposing invader. Campaigning of this kind was an affair of years, with progress governed by the speed of the wagon train and the necessity of living off the land. How much further Euergetes went is not known for he was no Alexander to take historians with him. Probably he turned into Media, and it was said that his embassies were welcomed at the Parthian and Bactrian courts.

25, 28   The governing of Egypt had been left in the able hands of Queen Berenice with, of course, a hierarchy of advisers and officials, for in that tradition-bound country little change was to be expected from year to year. Euergetes had been on campaign for nearly five years when word came of trouble in the land. A series of low Niles had brought famine, peasant uprisings and brigandage with which Berenice was quite unable to cope. The king was needed at home. Where he was at the time is not known, but perforce he abandoned his eastern conquests and turned back for Egypt, making an easy peace with Seleucus II, son and successor to Antiochus II, who during these years had established himself in Asia Minor and Syria.

Euergetes brought back to Egypt quantities of grain which were distributed to the people, while his soldiers put down the rebels and brigands. He also brought many sacred objects which Cambyses the Persian king had taken from the temples of Egypt centuries before, and forty thousand talents of silver to replenish the treasury. The veterans of his campaign were rewarded with grants of good land in the Fayum, and the Greek, Macedonian and Jewish prisoners of war and deserters from the Seleucid army were put to garrison duty. Before long government and people were again prospering.

There is little knowledge of the next twenty years of Euergetes' reign. He appears to have been energetic in restoring Egypt's position in the Aegean, regaining control of the Cycladic League. He also took Seleucia in Syria, Lysimachea, Ainos and Maronea in Thrace and the islands of Thasos and Samothrace in the northern Aegean.

Egypt was an agricultural, manufacturing and trading state and her prosperity depended on peace. She continued to maintain a strong army to keep order at home and to hold down the subject cities, and a large navy to protect her sea lanes but, inevitably, there was a slackening of interest in expansion abroad as Euergetes turned to home affairs.

Although his predilections differed from his father's Euergetes was yet a well-educated man, familiar with the best of Hellenic culture. It is notable that during his reign the Museum and the Library of Alexandria continued to flourish, magnets for scholars from all parts of the Greek world. He interested himself also in matters of religion, including temple building and the reform of the calendar.

Of the last decade of Euergetes' reign there is little record. The enthusiasms of his youth had been long forgotten when he died in 221 BC aged about sixty.

PTOLEMY IV PHILOPATOR 221–203 BC
Euergetes' elder son, Ptolemy IV Philopator ('son of a beloved father'), was twenty-four years old when he came to the throne. His younger brother Magas, his mother Berenice, his sister Arsinoe and his father's brother Lysimachus were still living. A second sister, Berenice, had died in childhood.

Egypt had prospered during the first hundred years of Ptolemaic rule and Philopator inherited a country still strong, secure and at peace. He was to leave it the worse for his reign. It has

29, 33

been said that the follies and weaknesses of the later Ptolemies arose from their having been spoiled in childhood in the quasi-oriental luxury of the Alexandrian court. But their mothers and sisters also grew up there, and many of them possessed the very qualities of character and good sense that their sons and brothers lacked. Be that as it may, too many of them were idle, self-indulgent and often silly. Such a man was Ptolemy IV Philopator.

During Ptolemy III's declining years his principal officer of state was an Alexandrian Greek named Sosibius. He was a man of high ambitions and few scruples. To ingratiate himself with the crown prince he encouraged his youthful dissipations, providing both the means and the companions for them. Now that the Prince was King, Sosibius saw to it that he was always surrounded with boon companions, loose women and the like. Philopator completely neglected his duties as king, and the conduct of affairs remained in the greedy hands of Sosibius. Soon the scandal of the King's manner of life, his wild self-indulgences and drunken orgies aroused such uneasiness that there were mutterings in Alexandria that the Queen Mother Berenice should move to replace the young sot with his manly and popular brother Magas. This came to the ear of Sosibius who, alarmed at the threat to himself, so worked on the king's fears that he agreed that his mother and brother should be disposed of. Berenice was poisoned, Magas was scalded to death in his bath and, for good measure, Philopator's uncle Lysimachus was also killed. This was the first year of Philopator's reign. His manner of life continued as before.

Philopator had one experience of war, a surprisingly successful one. Antiochus III of Syria, young, confident and aggressive, well informed of the dissolute life of the new Egyptian king and that under his rule the Egyptian army had been greatly weakened, decided to take lower Syria and Palestine. In the spring of 219 BC he marched over the hills down on Phoenicia and with the aid of bribes and the often tenuous loyalty of Graeco-Macedonian governors was soon in possession of Tyre and Acre. As things then were, Egypt was virtually defenceless and would have fallen with hardly a blow had he continued on to Pelusium. But he got a false report that Egypt was holding that fortress city in strength and agreed to a four months' truce during which a treaty of peace could be negotiated.

Sosibius now proved himself to be far more than another palace functionary. In his youth he had been a famous athlete, and in middle age was yet a man of courage and resolution. Because of his own and Philopator's neglect, for all practical purposes Egypt had no army. Sosibius sent emissaries with ample funds to recruit mercenaries in Macedon and Greece. Men and officers came in numbers, and as secretly as possible a camp was set up not far from Alexandria where with all possible speed an army was trained and equipped. But not enough mercenaries were available and twenty thousand Egyptians, hitherto despised as soldiers, were recruited or impressed. They were trained in the use of the sarissa, the long Macedonian pike, and the battle order of the phalanx. Antiochus of Syria meanwhile had returned to Seleucia and sent his troops to winter quarters. Sosibius sent representatives to the Syrian court to discuss peace terms.

By the spring of 218 BC Antiochus realized that these discussions were intended more to delay the making of a peace treaty than to make one and he proceeded with the second stage of his earlier plan, the reduction of southern Syria and Palestine. He continued as far as Samaria and again went into winter quarters, not realizing that time and Sosibius were robbing him of his opportunity. All the while the new Egyptian army drilled and trained at the camp near Alexandria.

Early in 217 BC Antiochus and his army, sixty-two thousand strong, reached Raphia on the Egyptian border. He had over 100 war elephants, 6000 cavalry and a phalanx of 20,000 men. The Egyptian army, with Philopator nominally in command, was 50,000, including a phalanx of 5000 Greeks and 20,000 Egyptians, 5000 cavalry and about 70 elephants. Sosibius was commander of the phalanx. Philopator was accompanied by his sister Arsinoe, whom he later was to marry, and as the armies approached each other she rode along the front of the Egyptian line, exhorting the men to strike in the name of Egypt and freedom.

At first, mostly on the wings, the fighting see-sawed but it was the Graeco-Macedonian phalanx of Antiochus' army that broke, the Egyptian-Greek phalanx that held. By the end of the day the Syrian king and his army were in flight and Philopator had proved himself a fighting king, at least worthy of his great-grandfather Ptolemy Soter.

The victory at Raphia enormously enhanced Ptolemaic self-esteem, but it left a long legacy of trouble. The 20,000 Egyptian soldiers who had fought there had shown themselves as good men as their masters, and they now decided that the time had

THE BATTLE
OF RAPHIA

163

come to throw off the foreign yoke. Revolts broke out, at first centred in the swamps of the Nile delta, in later years also in Upper Egypt. These rebellions continued intermittently during the life of the dynasty; they were put down with every resource of force and cruelty at the Ptolemies' command, but continued to reassert themselves.

After Raphia, sunning himself in the warmth of that unexpected victory, Philopator spent several months in Coele Syria and Phoenicia, re-establishing Ptolemaic rule there. The third Book of Maccabees gives an account of his welcome at Jerusalem, of his visit to the Temple, and of his indignation at being refused entry to the Holy of Holies – he who as Pharaoh was worshipped as a god in every temple of Egypt.

In that same year, probably at the urging of his prime minister Sosibius, Ptolemy married his sister Arsinoe and they were deified as the Gods Philopatores. But Philopator continued his dissipations 'spending his nights in debauchery and his days in gluttony'. Not until seven years after the marriage did Arsinoe give birth to a child, the son who was to be Ptolemy V Epiphanes. Then, having provided an heir to the throne, she was for all practical purposes set aside for Agathoclea, another creature of Sosibius. She and her brother Agathocles were the king's companions night and day. There are glimpses of Philopator during the later years of his reign, some temple building and restoring, the erection in Alexandria of a temple to Homer and the building of a great, luxuriously furnished Nile pleasure ship. There are records of gifts to Rhodes and various cities of Greece and also of shipments of corn to Rome during the time when Hannibal's invasion had laid waste much of Italy's agriculture. But Philopator and his follies did not change.

Natural or not, the immediate cause of Philopator's death at the age of forty-one is unknown. The victim of his own excesses, he had become ill and for some time had been in seclusion. With the king dead, his sister-queen Arsinoe was now regent for the five- or six-year-old heir to the throne, and thus a menace to Sosibius and Agathocles. She was poisoned in 203 BC.

The two royal deaths were kept secret until later in that year. Then, in a palace ceremony and amid lamentations, Sosibius and Agathocles announced the death of the king and queen, displaying to the assembled army chiefs and court notables two silver urns purported to contain their ashes. The will of the late king was read, appointing Sosibius and Agathocles as guardians for the child-king during his minority.

31, 34

There is a marble portrait bust of Arsinoe III of Egypt, Philopator's queen, in the Boston Museum of Fine Arts. It is the work of a sensitive artist, perhaps executed from life. The face is handsome, but the eyes, and especially the quite beautiful mouth, are sad.

PTOLEMY V THEOS EPIPHANES 203–181 BC

So it was that a boy of five, in the hands of a pair of scoundrels, sat on the throne of Egypt. But the circumstances under which Sosibius and Agathocles had assumed control aroused suspicion and hostility. To quiet the army a bonus of two months' pay was issued, a façade of orderly government was presented to the people and a capable Greek mercenary general named Tlepolemus was put in command of the frontier fortress city of Pelusium. For a time the unrest died down.

Agathocles, however, soon abandoned any concern for matters of state and according to Polybius 'he devoted the chief parts of the day and night to drunkenness and all the excesses which accompany drunkenness, sparing neither matron, nor bride, nor virgin, and doing all this with the most offensive ostentation'. It is presumed that Sosibius was now dead. Tlepolemus, the general at Pelusium, was proposed by some as the man to deliver Egypt from Agathocles, and when he marched on Alexandria he was enthusiastically welcomed by army and populace alike. Having a champion, the people of Alexandria demanded that Agathocles deliver up the person of the boy king, which was done. As soon as the king was safe the mob broke into the palace, seized Agathocles and his sister Agathoclea and tore them to pieces. Tlepolemus was now the darling of the army and the people, but he was no more than a good general of mercenaries. He wholly neglected his duties as prime minister, spending most of his time gaming and drinking with the soldiery.

Meanwhile the Egyptian overseas empire was rapidly dwindling. Philip V of Macedon took advantage of the power vacuum at Alexandria to drive the Egyptian garrisons from the island of Thasos off the coast of Thrace and from Abydos on the Hellespont, and began raiding Egyptian possessions on the Asia Minor coast. Then, in the year 200, at a place called Panion where the road through Lebanon enters Palestine, Antiochus the Great defeated the Egyptian forces under the mercenary general Scopas and took possession of the whole of Coele Syria down to Gaza, which he held under siege. At last Tlepolemus

THE BATTLE
OF PANION

was replaced by an officer of the Royal Bodyguard named Aristomenes, who is described as an admirable and virtuous administrator. He took control of the civil government and of foreign affairs. The command of the army was given to a general of mercenaries named Polycrates of Argos, who had been an outstandingly good viceroy of Cyprus.

There was much native unrest and in the hope of engaging the loyalty of the people to the monarchy it was decided to hold a coronation ceremony for the young king, although he was but twelve years old. The priesthood was the essential link between the king and his subjects, and the ceremony was held at Memphis and in accordance with Egyptian rites, instead of at Alexandria with Macedonian rites. Substantial grants were made to the temples and there were large remissions of taxation.

The Rosetta Stone, so named for its finding in 1799 by Napoleon's soldiers at Rosetta on the western branch of the Nile, deals with this coronation; it is now in the British Museum. In three scripts, Egyptian hieroglyphics, Egyptian demotic or cursive, and Greek, it records a decree passed by a synod of the Egyptian priesthood assembled at Memphis in 196 BC the year after the coronation. The decree commences with a list of the king's titles and genealogy, celebrates his accession to the throne and records his benevolences to the temples of the gods of Egypt and his gifts for their support. It was the Rosetta Stone which enabled the Frenchman Champollion to commence the decipherment of Egyptian hieroglyphics, and it is thus the foundation of much of modern Egyptology.

Peace was made between the Ptolemies and the Seleucids in 192 BC when the fifteen-year-old Ptolemy was married to Cleopatra, daughter of Antiochus the Great. As dowry the Seleucid princess brought the revenues of Coele Syria, or so the Ptolemies claimed though the later Seleucids denied it.

35, 39

The young king was neither aesthete nor statesman; his preoccupation, his passion almost, was the hunt, while the army was left to the command of Polycrates. Aristomenes remained as prime minister and chief advisor, but Ptolemy became increasingly impatient of his tutelage. One day Aristomenes had the effrontery to nudge the king awake when he dozed off during a diplomatic reception. Ptolemy took advantage of the unintended affront to compel this devoted servant to commit suicide; he was replaced by the more supple Polycrates.

Little is known of the next years of Ptolemy's reign. There was some meddling here and there in Syria and in Greece, some overtures to Rome, but nothing of importance. He died at about the age of twenty-eight, and there is no record of the cause of his death.

PTOLEMY VI PHILOMETOR, 181–145 BC

Ptolemy V left two sons and a daughter but the elder boy, the new king to be known as Ptolemy VI Philometor, was an infant, five or six years of age. However, the queen mother Cleopatra was a worthy daughter of Antiochus the Great and she promptly took power as Regent. She kept Egypt quiet and maintained good relations with her brother Seleucus IV of Syria and so far as possible with Rome. But within five years she too died, and then there arose something like the same tragi-comic situation as had occurred twenty-one years before after the death of Ptolemy IV, a boy king in the hands of a pair of scoundrels. Two palace functionaries, Eulaeus and Lenaeus, the first a eunuch and the second a Syrian, both probably ex-slaves, seized power as joint regents, and in silly opposition to the policy of the late queen they began a war against Antiochus Epiphanes of Syria. They were resoundingly defeated and disappeared. (For the subsequent history of this folly, the invasion of Egypt by Antiochus and its aftermath, see pp. 206–9 below.)

The early years of Philometor's reign were much troubled by his jealous younger brother Euergetes. For five years they ruled jointly, and then Philometor was forced to flee the country. He went to Rome to plead his cause and was awarded Egypt and Cyprus, while Ptolemy the Younger, as Euergetes came to be known, was given Cyrenaica. Ptolemy Philometor enjoyed a long reign and, exceptionally among the later kings of Egypt, he was a capable and kindly man. Polybius says of him 'none of his friends did he ever make away with on any pretext whatever'. He died in 145 BC of injuries received fighting in Syria on behalf of his daughter Cleopatra Thea (p. 215).

PTOLEMY VIII EUERGETES, 145–116 BC

After the death of Ptolemy VI the greater part of his army of mercenaries went over to the Syrian king, Demetrius II, so that his widow, Cleopatra II, now regent for her young son Ptolemy VII Neos Philopator, was quite unable to make a stand against Ptolemy Euergetes 'the brother' when he arrived at Alexandria in force, determined to take the throne. With her children and the treasury Cleopatra fled to Memphis, and for a time Egypt was again split between rival monarchies.

Then Euergetes offered to marry his sister – and ex-sister-in-law – Cleopatra II, now about forty years of age. Cleopatra, determined to stay in power, agreed provided that she and Euergetes should rule jointly as regents for her son, Ptolemy VII. But as soon as she had become pregnant by him, Euergetes had the boy king killed off, thus securing the succession to his own child by Cleopatra.

The child was duly born, a boy who was named Memphites, and then Euergetes became infatuated with his wife's daughter, also named Cleopatra, who agreed to marry him on condition that she too became queen. This he agreed, and now there was a Cleopatra II and Cleopatra III, both wives of this repulsively corpulent man who was nicknamed 'Physcon' – pot belly – by the people. In inscriptions the one is called Cleopatra the Sister, the other Cleopatra the Wife; and without doubt they hated each other.

So for some fifteen years Euergetes with his two queens reigned in Egypt, while revulsion against him grew, fed by his cruelties and extortions. Support mounted for Cleopatra the Sister, for her own sake and for Ptolemy Philometor's, the memory of whose virtues shone all the brighter for his brother's villainies. Realizing at last that both the army and the people were ripe for revolt and that his life was in immediate danger, Euergetes secretly took ship for Cyprus. With him went Cleopatra the Wife, her two children by him and the boy Memphites, his child by Cleopatra the Sister. A day later the Alexandrian mob broke into the palace, determined to kill him.

Established in Cyprus, Euergetes began to assemble an army of mercenaries with which to return to Egypt and overthrow his sister, who now reigned alone as Cleopatra Philometor Soteira. In Alexandria the hatred against Euergetes continued and one day in a public demonstration against him his statues were pulled down and broken. This the exiled king blamed on Cleopatra, and in revenge he killed his son by her, the boy Memphites, and sent the dismembered body neatly packed in a box to the child's mother as a birthday present.

In 129 BC Euergetes again landed in Egypt and although Cleopatra's supporters resisted they could not prevail, and a year later she went off to the court of her daughter Cleopatra Thea in Syria. After a time she returned to Alexandria to take her place again as Cleopatra the Sister. Euergetes died in 116 BC;

for him the wages of sin were a long life and success in his under-takings. Whether Cleopatra the Sister outlived him is not known.

PTOLEMY IX SOTER II, 116–80 BC AND PTOLEMY X ALEXANDER I, 106–88 BC

Ptolemy VIII Euergetes was survived by his wife-niece Cleo-patra III, two sons and a daughter. His will left the throne to his wife, she to decide which of her two sons should reign jointly with her. Her favourite was the younger son Alexander, but public opinion would not tolerate her passing over the rightful heir who, as Ptolemy IX (nicknamed Lathyrus, or chick-pea), became his mother's consort.

During her husband's lifetime Cleopatra had of necessity remained in the background but she now moved into control, a strong and able woman. Like most of the Ptolemies her passion for dominance left little room for scruple, and she was as murderous as any of her line. The Roman historian Justin describes her as a woman 'who had driven her mother from the bed of her husband, had made her two daughters widows by alternate marriage with a brother, had made war on one of her sons after driving him into exile and plotted against the other'. For the next sixteen years Egypt was in the hands of this formidable queen. She died in 101 BC aged about sixty; some said that she was murdered by her younger son Alexander, then her consort. Five years earlier the elder son, Lathyrus, had fled from Alexandria to Cyprus to escape charges of attempting to do away with the lady. Cleopatra had wanted to replace him with Alexander and trumped up the charge.

This last episode was in 106 BC since when Alexander had occupied the throne of Egypt. He maintained himself there for another eighteen years, a rather horrible man. He was so grossly fat that he had a man on either side to help him to walk, he was pimply and disgusting to look at, idle, drunken and extravagant in his way of life. In 88 BC his subjects at last rebelled and chased him out of the country, and in the same year he was killed at sea while shipping from Lycia to Cyprus.

Ptolemy Lathyrus was now free to return to his throne, which he held peacefully until his death at the age of 62 in 80 BC.

PTOLEMY XII NEOS DIONYSUS (AULETES), 80–58 BC; AND SECOND REIGN 55–51 BC

Ptolemy Neos Dionysus (father of the Cleopatra who was to

37, 40

169

be the last Ptolemaic ruler of Egypt) was a bastard, one of four children of Ptolemy Lathyrus by an Alexandrian Greek concubine whose name is unknown. When Lathyrus died the family left Egypt, for it was the prudent practice of Hellenistic monarchs to kill off promptly all possible rivals to the throne. On the other hand, in these circumstances hospitality was good policy, and all five were welcomed and given shelter at Sinope, the capital of Mithradates VI of Pontus.

Having no legitimate sons, Lathyrus bequeathed his throne to his daughter Berenice. But Egypt had to have both a king and a queen, and soon there arrived at Alexandria a nephew of Auletes named Alexander; he had gone to all-powerful Rome seeking support for his claim to the Egyptian throne and secured Sulla's blessing. He now found that he was expected, in fact required, to marry Berenice, though she was many years older than he and not at all to his liking. He did so and then, within three weeks of the wedding, he murdered her, intending to rule alone. His reign lasted nineteen days; when the Alexandrians learnt that he had done away with their popular queen he was torn to pieces by the mob.

In order to prevent Roman intervention the throne of Egypt must be filled, and now the only direct descendants of the first Ptolemy were the illegitimate children of Ptolemy Lathyrus, living at the court of Mithradates VI at Sinope. There were Seleucid cousins, but they were the poorest of alternatives. So the family was recalled and the elder son named Ptolemy King of Egypt. He later married his sister Tryphaena and once again Egypt had a pair of Ptolemy's on the throne. This Ptolemy took the title of Neos ('the young') Dionysus. Quite early in his career his dismal character and addiction to music had earned him his derisory title of Auletes (the flute player).

Without Rome's approval Auletes could not be crowned king of Egypt. It was asked for, debated in the Senate, and withheld. Meanwhile the Alexandrians clamoured for a coronation and to placate them a ceremony took place within the palace, conducted by the high priest of Memphis in accordance with Egyptian rites. Henceforth the prime aim of Auletes' policy, if it could be said that this dissolute and arrogant man had a policy, was to get Roman approval of his kingship.

After twenty-two years on the throne Auletes' follies, his oppressive taxation, his pro-Roman policy and the seizure of Cyprus by Rome at last aroused the Alexandrians to such resentment that he was driven out of the country. He fled to

Rome seeking support there for his reinstatement, leaving his wife and children in Alexandria.

Again the throne of Egypt could not be left vacant, and although Auletes' elder daughter Berenice was a capable young woman she could not rule alone. A husband was found for her named Seleucus, who claimed to be a cousin of the Ptolemies, and a marriage ceremony was performed. Within a week of the wedding Berenice decided that he was not to her liking and with the same forthrightness shown by that earlier Berenice (p. 159) she had him strangled by her soldiers. A new candidate appeared, an excellent young man named Archelaus from the court of Mithradates VI of Pontus who had befriended Auletes' family twenty-two years before. They were married, this was less than a year after Auletes' departure, and they ruled Egypt well though all too briefly.

In Rome, meanwhile, Auletes intrigued and plotted, seeking a lever with which to pry his daughter from the throne. At last, in 59 BC, a massive bribe to Julius Caesar, to be paid from the revenues of Egypt, secured him the Senate's recognition as 'a friend and ally of the Roman people'. He now needed military help, which was bought with another irresistible bribe to Gabinius, the Roman pro-consul of Syria. And so after some four years of exile Auletes appeared at the gates of Alexandria with three Roman legions under Gabinius' command. Archelaus was killed in the field, the city taken without opposition and Berenice thrown into prison to be killed later. Auletes once again ruled Egypt though only by virtue of Gabinius' legions, two of which were left behind under Lucius Licinius.

Auletes died four years later, aged about forty-five. His will stipulated that his daughter Cleopatra, now about seventeen, should marry the elder of her two younger brothers and reign jointly with him. This was in the year 51 BC.

CLEOPATRA VII, 51–30 BC

Cleopatra (the name means 'of a noble father'), daughter of Ptolemy Neos Dionysus, was the fourteenth and last of the Ptolemies to rule in Egypt. Our knowledge of her is mostly that which appears in the distorting mirror of Roman fear and hatred. But despite Plutarch's history and even Shakespeare's romance, Cleopatra was the only one of her line whom the Egyptians loved, and except for those in the army of Ptolemy IV (p. 163) the only one for whom they were willing to fight. They mourned her death and revered her memory.

45, 47

On most of her portrait coins Cleopatra is shown with a big nose and her father's heavy chin, quite unprepossessing; but tall or short, dark or fair, undoubtedly she was a graceful and accomplished woman. She was brave, loyal, and when policy or hatred decided, murderous, and she was dominated by an enormous drive for power. She was most intelligent, the only one of the Ptolemies to speak the Egyptian tongue; she was the wealthiest woman, perhaps the wealthiest person, of her time.

Like that other Macedonian, Alexander the Great, Cleopatra became a legend during her own lifetime, one of the few mortals who have moved the world. 'For Rome, who had never condescended to fear any nation or people, did in her time fear two human beings. One was Hannibal, the other was a woman'.

Proud and high-spirited, Cleopatra must have despised her father, his dissolute manner of life, his neglect of his kingdom and his fawning subservience to Rome, and have waited impatiently for the day when she would come to the throne. She was the second of his three daughters (the eldest, Berenice, had been killed four years before), and Auletes' will provided that Cleopatra was to marry the elder of her two young brothers and reign jointly with him. But during his later years Auletes had left the conduct of Egypt's affairs almost wholly to two favourites, a eunuch named Pothinus and an Alexandrian Greek mercenary named Achillas, who commanded the household troops. These men were determined to retain power, and Cleopatra was permitted only the nominal conduct of foreign affairs, little more than the reception of foreign emissaries.

Cleopatra was a strong-willed young woman, and as she became increasingly self-assured and demanding her two 'counsellors' decided that one Ptolemy on the throne was enough, and they prepared to do away with her. A palace faction opposed to Pothinus and Achillas warned Cleopatra of her danger and she fled to Syria. There friends rallied to her support, and in the tradition of these indomitable Macedonian women she was soon on her way back to Egypt with a substantial army, determined to oust her enemies and regain her throne.

Meanwhile Alexandria had learned of Cleopatra's preparations and movements; she and her army reached the frontier fortress of Pelusium to find it held by a force as strong as her own, nominally under command of her fifteen-year-old brother but actually under Achillas. Neither side was eager for battle so that for the time being both armies sat there, each waiting for the other to withdraw or offer terms.

JULIUS CAESAR

It was at this juncture that Rome entered directly into Egyptian affairs. At the battle of Pharsalus in Thessaly on 9 August 48 BC Julius Caesar had overwhelmingly defeated his rival Pompey, who fled to Macedonia. There his officers urged him to rally what was left of his army and continue the fight, but his nerve was gone. He took ship for Asia Minor, seeking a refuge and perhaps support for his cause. But he was unwelcome there and continued on to Cyprus, which gave him a small contingent of soldiery and some money. He sailed for Egypt, where a year earlier his son Cn. Pompeius had secured 50 ships, a supply of corn and 500 men; and ten years before in Rome he had given Ptolemy Auletes hospitality and political help (with financial profit to himself), and he could reasonably expect a welcome from Auletes' children.

At Alexandria Pompey was refused a landing 'without Ptolemy's permission', and Ptolemy was at Pelusium. He proceeded there and was brought to shore in a small boat which held Achillas and two Roman officers who belonged to the legions left behind in Egypt by Gabinius one of whom, Septimius, Pompey recognized as having served under him. Pothinus had received the news of Pharsalus, and realizing that Julius Caesar was now master of the world he and Achillas decided to bid for his favour. As Pompey prepared to step from the boat Septimius stabbed him in the back, and he fell forward and died. It was the 28 September 48 BC.

In hot pursuit of his defeated enemy, Caesar reached Alexandria a few days later to be presented on landing with Pompey's severed head and signet ring. He was relieved that Pompey was dead, but for these Egyptians to take it on themsevles to be his executioners was another matter. Pothinus was later executed and Achillas was killed by order of Cleopatra's younger sister Arsinoe on another count.

With due ceremonial Caesar marched his men through Alexandria to the Palace, where he was told of the confrontation of Cleopatra and Ptolemy before Pelusium. He summoned them to Alexandria. This was an opportunity to put Egyptian affairs in order and to collect some part of the debt contracted to him years before by Auletes, for Caesar always needed money. The story that Cleopatra smuggled herself into Caesar's presence inside a roll of carpets has inspired historians, dramatists and novelists – it may even be true; certainly she dared not travel openly in what was for her enemy territory. The

43

young Ptolemy also presented himself, but soon realized that Cleopatra was to be the favourite, and ran from the audience mouthing threats to destroy both Caesar and his sister.

In Alexandria, Caesar and his three thousand or so legionaries were soon under heavy siege, the Alexandrian populace vigorously joining Achillas and his soldiery in the attack. Ptolemy was drowned during the fighting for the mole that ran out to the island of Pharos, but his sister Arsinoe took his place. It was during this time that a store of books belonging to the Library of Alexandria was accidentally burned. Caesar had need of all his military skill merely to survive, for it was months before reinforcements came. Then he quickly put down the rebels and made Cleopatra and her surviving brother, to whom she was now married, joint rulers of Egypt.

41, 46

Caesar stayed with Cleopatra four months longer, luxuriating in her youth and ardour. He left her knowing that she was carrying his child (some say the child was born in Rome), and she followed him to Rome in 46 BC where he installed her in a handsome villa across the Tiber. But despite her lavish hospitality 'the Egyptian', as they derisively called her, was hated by the Romans. They feared the prospect of Caesar as emperor and Cleopatra as his consort, a possibility to which she was not shy of alluding.

Two years later Caesar was assassinated. Seneca remarks ironically that among his murderers were to be found more of his friends than of his enemies. About two weeks later Cleopatra slipped quietly out of Rome, taking ship for Egypt.

MARK ANTONY

For Rome, Caesar's death was followed by a civil war that ended at Philippi in September of 42 BC when the senatorial party of Brutus and Cassius was crushingly defeated by Antony and Octavian. Brutus committed suicide and Cassius was killed later.

The victors agreed that Octavian should have Italy and the west and Antony the governance of Rome's eastern empire. Antony proceeded to Asia Minor to be welcomed with all ceremony and flattery by the Greek cities of the coast; Ephesus hailed him as the new Dionysus. He revelled in pomp and adulation but he needed money, and he levied taxes – or tribute – with a heavy hand. Recalling the wealth of Egypt he sent word to Cleopatra to present herself to him at Tarsus.

She delayed until Antony's emissary broadly hinted at the wisdom of compliance.

When at last Cleopatra reached Tarsus she came not as a suppliant but in full panoply, queen of a rich and ancient country, sailing up the Cydnus river in her magnificent pleasure barge, a delight to the eyes of gods and men. She banqueted Antony on board with a lavishness unknown to him; Cleopatra remembered the young cavalry captain who had come to Egypt fourteen years before with Gabinius. Then she had been a girl – now she was a woman of the world, confident that the charms which had captivated Caesar would conquer Antony also.

This was the summer of 41 BC. Antony was infatuated with Cleopatra; there was a special charm, he wrote Octavian, in bedding a queen. He followed her to Egypt and for months they feasted and pleasured together. But their 'love affair' held little of the unselfishness of the genuine emotion: each knew that the other was bent on wholly personal ambitions. Cleopatra wanted Antony to marry her and thus to secure Egypt's safety and her throne. Antony needed Cleopatra's wealth to help him to dominance in the Roman world.

Early in the following year Antony left for Greece. His wife Fulvia together with his brother Lucius had raised a revolt against Octavian. This failing, they had come to Athens, where Fulvia died. Continuing to Italy, Antony made peace with Octavian and married his sister Octavia. The alliance was to be a guarantee of peace and goodwill between the two men who now ruled the Roman empire.

Antony lived with Octavia for three years and then returned to Syria to launch the great campaign against the Parthians for which Caesar had been preparing at the time of his death. This was to be his great triumph, to set the capstone on his military career. But he was short of money and sent for Cleopatra and her help. She came to meet him but now her price was marriage, nothing less.

It was folly, but Antony paid it. True, the ceremony was according to Egyptian rites, not recognized in Rome as legal, and Antony was careful not to call himself king of Egypt. But he was already married to the sister of Octavian, and this unworthy alliance was with the woman who had seduced Julius Caesar and who was hated and feared in Rome. His second blunder was to give Cleopatra as dowry what was not his to give, Cilicia, Coele Syria, Transjordan and the Jericho valley.

44, 45

These territories together with Palestine had belonged to Egypt, being taken by Ptolemy I Soter after the defeat of Antigonus the One-eyed in 301 BC, and won from his successors by the Seleucid king Antiochus the Great a century later. But in 64 BC the remnants of the Seleucids and their kingdom had been swept aside by Pompey the Great, and Syria had become a Roman province; it certainly was not at Antony's disposal, and the news of his gift to 'the Egyptian' aroused yet more resentment in Rome. Cleopatra wanted Judaea also, but despite his infatuation for her Antony would not agree. It was Roman policy to maintain Judaea as an independent kingdom, a frontier fortress state against the Parthians. Besides, King Herod was a personal friend whom he, and Caesar also, had helped to place on the throne in Jerusalem, and he knew that Cleopatra hated him and would destroy him.

In the spring of 36 BC Antony marched against Parthia. His campaign was a disaster. He was a first rate general, proven on many battlefields, but here his strategy and his tactics were wrong. The Parthians were no wild Gauls or plodding mercenaries; they were masters of hit and run warfare, fierce and indomitable. Within a few months Antony's huge and sluggish army was worn down and in desperate retreat. Scarcely a hungry and mutinous half of his men got back to Phoenicia, to the shiploads of food and clothing sent from Alexandria.

Antony returned to Egypt and before long was again buoyant. In 34 BC he mounted a second campaign, this time against Armenia. It was a success, and he returned with the Armenian king as captive and much treasure. To celebrate his victory Antony staged a Roman triumph, but it was at Alexandria, not Rome, and the Romans sneered at the news of it.

Then came word that Rome had repudiated Antony, disowned his conquests and denounced him as an enemy of the Republic. It was a shock, but not wholly unexpected. If Octavian wanted war, Antony was confident of victory.

In preparation, Antony commenced in 33 BC to assemble men and munitions at Ephesus on the Asia Minor coast. To his nineteen Roman legions were added contingents from many parts of Rome's Asiatic empire, and Cleopatra joined him with seventy ships and a considerable war chest. Also to Ephesus came many of Antony's Roman friends and others who were rather against Octavian than for Antony. He was the better general, had a stronger force than Octavian and was far more popular with the people and the army.

Antony's weakness was his infatuation with Cleopatra, which made him yield to her where his own judgement and the advice of his friends should have prevailed. Cleopatra was a strong and clever woman but not a wise one; she could not comprehend that a war between Antony and Octavian must now be a war to the death. She strove for a continuance of the *status quo*, with Octavian ruling in the west and Antony as her consort on the throne of Egypt, ruling Rome's eastern conquests. So far as she could prevail there would be no great battles, no final victories, for should Antony oust Octavian from Rome he would return there to live again with Octavia, and this Cleopatra was determined to prevent.

She now demanded that Antony divorce Octavia. He yielded to her despite his own doubts and the urgings of his advisers, making enemies of many who had been friendly or undecided, and sending waverers over to Octavian's camp. The letters of divorcement were sent to Octavia from Athens in May 32 BC after Antony and a considerable part of his army had crossed over from Asia Minor. Octavian retaliated by seizing and publishing Antony's will which, as was customary, had been deposited in the care of the Vestal Virgins in Rome. The will directed that on his death Antony's body should be sent to Cleopatra for burial, and provided large legacies for her children by him. On the strength of this scandal Octavian prevailed on what was left in Rome of the Senate to put him at the head of the army and to swear fidelity to him. Then, in the name of Rome, he declared war on *the Queen of Egypt*.

By the autumn of 32 BC most of Antony's army was in Greece and his fleet stationed in the Gulf of Ambracia to repel any landing by Octavian. But by a ruse Octavian's admiral Agrippa succeeded in getting a substantial force ashore on the Epirus coast to the north. To protect his fleet Antony promptly moved his army into camp at Actium.

For almost a year the confrontation – it was hardly a war – continued with skirmishes, Octavian slowly strengthening, and his warships interrupting Antony's corn supplies from Egypt. Negotiations were started, faltered, revived and died. Ferrero puts it 'Octavian did not attack Antony because he did not dare, Antony did not attack Octavian because Cleopatra would not let him'. At last Antony was compelled to action; his friends, even his generals, demanded that he either fight or make peace. Despite his inexperience in sea warfare he decided to battle it out on the water and on the morning of 2 September 31 BC the

THE BATTLE
OF ACTIUM

rival fleets, about evenly matched, faced each other off Actium.

The fighting see-sawed for several hours until Antony's line was seen to falter and some of his ships turned off from the battle. At the same time, and on the heels of a fresh northerly wind, Cleopatra's seventy ships came sailing between the opposing fleets, heading south for Egypt. Then Antony's own ship broke away from the line to join Cleopatra in flight.

Soon the whole enormous fiasco became apparent, Antony's massive betrayal of his friends and himself. He had never intended a fight to the finish. Earlier he had embarked 20,000 of his best troops with orders to make for Egypt when he broke off from the battle, and he had given instructions for the remainder of the army and fleet to follow as soon as they could. In Egypt, with even half the force with which he had faced Octavian at Actium he would be secure against any strength his rival could bring against him, and there he would continue to rule as master of the Roman empire in the east. Of that he was sure.

Antony was a capable general, likeable, generous, possessed of an iron constitution, a natural leader of men. He had campaigned with Caesar in Gaul, had been his second-in-command against Pompey at Pharsalus and in senior command at Philippi against Brutus and Cassius. For more than a decade he had ruled the Roman east. He was fifty-two years of age and at the height of his powers when his career ended at the 'no' battle of Actium.

To a Roman soldier the prime virtue was steadfastness, no matter how dark the face of fortune. For Antony to run away, to abandon the men who were fighting and dying at his command was a total betrayal, an incredibility. He had not thought it that when Cleopatra had persuaded him – perhaps she had called it a strategic retreat. But betrayal it was, and by the time Antony reached Egypt he realized it, and that now he was better dead.

Arriving at Alexandria he and Cleopatra made a brag of victory, but the truth soon came through. Antony still had eleven legions in Egypt and made some preparations for defence, but after a time he isolated himself in a small house on the shore, brooding on his disaster, while Cleopatra busied herself with fruitless plans, repressions, intrigues: both awaited the inevitable.

Octavian was in no hurry; after Actium he did not pursue Antony as Caesar had Pompey after Pharsalus. Ever cautious, he waited for a time and then sent back to Italy the men who had come over from Antony's army and disbanded them there, also a large part of his own forces. He turned to the many problems that come with peace.

By the following spring Italy was simmering with unrest, the people clamouring for revenge against Antony and 'the Egyptian', the veterans demanding their promised pay and land allotments. To placate the masses Octavian must make an end of these two in Egypt who were still so feared and hated; to pay off the soldiers and to buy land for them – and also to pay off his friends – he had to have money, a great deal of money. This only the treasure of Egypt could provide.

Octavian's forces advanced on Egypt from two sides, Africa and Syria. They encountered little resistance and at the end of July his army stood before Alexandria. Antony roused himself to lead a last sortie and then his men went over to Octavian. Word came that Cleopatra had committed suicide – it was false – and Antony stabbed himself, to die later in Cleopatra's arms. On the same day, 1 August 30 BC, Octavian and his army marched unopposed into Alexandria.

There are romantic tales of Cleopatra's death but little knowledge. Near the tomb of Alexander the Great she had built an imposing mausoleum, where in due time she and Antony would rest in grandeur as the founders of the great new Empire of the East. In the lower part of this building was now stored the vast treasure of Egypt, precious stones, gem-encrusted vessels, silks and rare spices and a great quantity of gold. Cleopatra and her women occupied the upper floor of this barred and bolted edifice. She sent word to Octavian that she wished to talk with him, but that if she were attacked she would set fire to the building and all that was burnable in it, and herself die in the flames.

Octavian came, or she went to him at the Palace – there are conflicting accounts. Cleopatra offered her crown and her life if he would assure her that one of her children would succeed to the throne of Egypt and that the Ptolemaic dynasty would continue. There is no record of this remarkable conversation but Octavian appears to have made no promises. For the present all that he wanted was the treasure, intact.

So matters rested for a day or two, until one of Octavian's men climbed unseen through a window into Cleopatra's chamber and seized her, thus giving Octavian access to the treasure below. For Cleopatra this was the end. Octavian was implacable, death was her only alternative to 'gracing' his triumph in Rome as her sister Arsinoe had Caesar's almost twenty years before. Probably the story of the asp hidden in a basket of figs was an invention; as a Hellenistic queen Cleopatra would have been familiar enough with poisons. With her maids and in full regal array, she was found dead in her chamber.

Octavian honoured Cleopatra's last wish, that she be buried with Antony, but her eighteen-year-old son by Julius Caesar he put to death. Antony's former wife Octavia, Octavian's sister, took Cleopatra's three children by Antony to Rome, and adopted them. The girl, also named Cleopatra, later married a Numidian prince named Juba, whom the Romans made king of Mauretania. Their son Ptolemy succeeded to the throne but was killed by Caligula. The two boys disappeared from history, and thus ended the line of Ptolemy Soter, son of Lagus.

Octavian took Egypt as his personal property. He ordered that henceforth no member of the senatorial order might even enter the country without his express permission.

CHAPTER THREE

The Seleucids of Syria

SELEUCUS I NICATOR, 321–280 BC

Seleucus son of Antiochus, founder of the Seleucid dynasty of Syria, who at his death was ruler of an empire reaching from Macedonia and Thrace across Asia to the confines of India, was born into the Macedonian aristocracy. His father was a general in the army of Philip II and Seleucus was one of the boys chosen to share Alexander's classes with Aristotle. Boyhood friends, Seleucus was with Alexander when he embarked on the expedition to Asia, the conquest of the Persian Empire.

As the Macedonian army fought its way eastward against Darius and on into India, Seleucus became one of Alexander's trusted generals, commander of the Hypaspists, a body of light armed infantry. He comes into special notice in the fighting on the approaches to India and in the battle against King Porus on the Jhelum river in the Punjab (p. 29). He joined with Alexander in the mass marriage at Susa, when his bride was Apama, the Iranian princess who was to become the mother of his son and successor, Antiochus I, and for whom he named several cities of his empire. And he was with Alexander at Babylon when the great conqueror died there in 323 BC.

At the age of thirty-five Seleucus was a first-rate field commander, pleasant natured, determined and ambitious. He had stood aside when, following Alexander's death, the Council of State at Babylon re-allocated many of Alexander's satrapies, although he was certainly high enough in the army hierarchy for one had he so desired. Perhaps he foresaw the conflicts that inevitably must arise among these strong-willed men with whom for years he had lived and fought. Or it may have been that Babylonia, the one satrapy he wanted, had been pre-empted by Perdiccas as his own power base. For the meantime he elected to remain with the army as first lieutenant to Perdiccas, his own command being the élite 'Companion Cavalry' corps. In this capacity in 321 BC he was with Perdiccas in his attempt to bring Ptolemy to heel, and if not the leader he was one of the three senior officers who murdered Perdiccas in his tent (p. 143).

Following the killing of Perdiccas the army offered the command to Ptolemy, who was popular with both officers and men, but he declined, all he wanted was to be secure in Egypt. Pending the arrival of the regent Antipater from Macedon, he suggested an interim leadership, and the army moved from Egypt to Syria. Antipater, together with Antigonus the One-eyed, the ex-satrap of Phrygia, arrived some weeks later and a second meeting of the Council of State was convened at Triparadisus in Syria. There a second allocation or re-allocation of satrapies was made, especially of those held by appointees of Perdiccas. Seleucus now asked for the satrapy of Babylonia. After his part in the killing of Perdiccas he would not have wanted to remain with the army and Antigonus, for he certainly was not one of the new commander-in-chief's men. Babylonia also had the advantage of distance from Antigonus' base satrapy of Phrygia.

Seleucus had earned the right to his request and it was granted. Together with a group of officers and men who elected to follow his fortunes he set off without delay for his satrapy, arriving at Babylon several weeks later where he found Perdiccas' satrap Docimus still in possession. There was some fighting but before long Docimus was gone and Seleucus the master of the ancient city.

FIRST SATRAPY OF BABYLONIA, 321–316 BC
Babylon – The Gate of God – sitting astride the Euphrates river, was no longer the great metropolis of old. Darius the Great had razed its walls and Xerxes had despoiled its temples, but it was still the prosperous and populous capital of a rich and fertile country. Seleucus was careful. Whatever fancies or hopes he may have had as he looked across the three-thousand-year-old city he proceeded prosaically with the business of government, dispensing even-handed justice and respecting the customs and traditions of the people. The reputation, the affection even, which he earned during this period of his rule in Babylon was later to stand him in good stead.

In those years Antigonus the One-eyed was the strongest power in Asia. He was commander-in-chief of the sixty thousand strong Grand Army, he had possession of Alexander's treasure chest of over twenty-five thousand talents of gold and silver and his revenues from the satrapies were more than ten thousand talents a year. He maintained the fiction that he was no more than a general, ruling in the name of the heirs of Alexander the Great; in fact he was king of all.

With his army and an immense baggage train Antigonus proceeded to make a round of the empire's eastern territories, replacing – killing off those who did not escape in time – those satraps whose total loyalty to himself might be suspect. He reached Babylon in 316 BC and Seleucus received him with all due formality. When the preliminary courtesies were over Antigonus demanded from Seleucus an accounting of the revenues of his five years of office, brushing aside his protests that he was not accountable to anyone. This continued for a few days and then, realizing that his own head was next for the block, Seleucus fled in the night with a handful of followers for Egypt and Ptolemy, hoping to find there 'but a corner in the shade of his friend's good fortune'. Ptolemy cordially received his old companion in arms. Seleucus was a competent general, and against the threat of Antigonus, Ptolemy needed all the fighting men he could get.

During the next three years Seleucus is seen commanding an Egyptian fleet in the Aegean and fighting on Cyprus. Meanwhile an alliance of necessity was made between the men Antigonus was seeking to devour, Cassander of Macedon, Lysimachus of Thrace and Ptolemy of Egypt. It came into action in 312 BC when Antigonus was about to invade Thrace. To guard his rear against Ptolemy he sent his son Demetrius to Syria with a strong army. A diversion was essential, and the army which Ptolemy had been building and training for ten years now marched against Demetrius, who came south to meet it. At Gaza in Palestine the army of Ptolemy, in part led by Seleucus, gave battle to Demetrius and wholly defeated him. Lysimachus and Cassander were safe from Antigonus and the alliance was secure.

As a return for his part in the victory Seleucus asked Ptolemy for a force, however small, with which to attempt the recovery of his lost satrapy of Babylonia. He got a thousand men, foot and horse, little enough. With them Seleucus crossed over into Mesopotamia and at Carrhae on the road to Babylon his reputation brought him eager recruits from among the Macedonians who had settled there in Alexander's time. More came as he entered Babylonia, and at Babylon itself most of the garrison troops came over to him, they and the populace alike rejoicing that Antigonus' harsh satrap had been killed in the fighting at Gaza. Such resistance as remained was quickly overcome and once again Seleucus was ruler in Babylon. This year, 312 BC, the Seleucids took as the foundation date of their dynasty.

Seleucus realized that he would not be left for long to enjoy his regained glory, and he set to work to build an army. But Babylon was remote and there were few men to hand; most of the Antigonid garrison troops had been sent to join Demetrius at Gaza, to be lost on the field or to go over to Ptolemy. The thousand or so men left behind had of course joined Seleucus. Beside these he had a couple of thousand of his own men and about as many more came to hand. Then word came that Peithon son of Crateuas, Antigonus' satrap of Media, was on the march against him with 20,000 men. Seleucus could not wait to stand siege against such odds. Leaving a small force in Babylon under the command of an officer named Patrocles, he crossed the Tigris with 3000 foot and 400 horse and fell on Peithon in a surprise attack which was followed by a complete rout. Peithon barely got away and the bulk of his army went over to Seleucus. Most of these men were Greek mercenaries to whom soldiering was a trade; do or die was not for them, and Seleucus had a fine reputation and was a coming man.

Seleucus now had an army worthy of the name and he followed Peithon into Media, again fighting and then killing him. After which, with Peithon's end as a persuader, the satraps of Persis and Susiana came over to Seleucus without demur.

Meanwhile, Ptolemy's victory over Demetrius at Gaza could not be left unchallenged, and Antigonus himself moved south and re-occupied Syria and Palestine in preparation for an attack on Egypt. Then came the news of Seleucus' success against Peithon in Media and the threat to all Antigonus' eastern satrapies. To create a diversion to Seleucus' rear, Demetrius was sent on a raid against Babylon with 15,000 foot soldiers and 4000 cavalry, but he was given a strict time limit. He arrived at Babylon to find it virtually undefended, with his tiny force Patrocles dared not challenge Demetrius' army, and he sent his men off into the desert to hide. Demetrius could only loot, and when his time ran out he returned to Syria from his fruitless errand. Seleucus continued with his campaign, then or later possessing himself of all the eastern satrapies, including Parthia and Bactria.

48, 52   With these conquests Seleucus became ruler of an empire, and after his return to Babylon in 312 BC, proceeded to build

himself a new capital city away from the malarial swamps
around Babylon. (Malaria is thought by some to have been the
cause of Alexander's death.) Named Seleucia-on-the-Tigris and
situated near where a canal joined the Tigris and Euphrates
rivers, it was to be a Greek city, although Jews and Syrians were
admitted to its citizenship. Before long Seleucia overshadowed
Babylon, from which it took much of its commerce, and for
centuries to come was the most important city of the East. In
the early first century AD Pliny gave its population as 600,000,
enormous by the standards of the time.

Seleucus was a statesman; whatever he may have thought of
Alexander's ideas for a Graeco-Persian state they were not for
him. He realized that the peoples of the diverse countries he
held would never give him more than the consent of subjection.
He was a king *in*, not *of*, the countries he ruled and he followed
Alexander in building cities at strategic points within his empire, garrisoned and largely peopled with Macedonians and
Greeks. They were a minority, but a master race among the
native peoples. He and his son Antiochus I devoted much
wealth and energy to the creation and support of these new cities,
which almost within a generation were secure with a strong
Graeco-Macedonian population which provided a trained military force in time of need. Besides Alexander's foundations, by
the end of the reign of Antiochus I there were more than ninety
of these Seleucid garrison towns.

Appian tells us (*Syriaca* 57), that

'Seleucus founded cities throughout the whole length of his
empire – sixteen Antiochs in honour of his father; five Lao-
diceas in honour of his mother; nine in his own name: and
four in the name of his wives, three Apameas and one
Stratonicea. The most celebrated of them today are the
Seleucia on the sea-coast and the one on the river Tigris, the
Laodicia in Phoenicia, the Antioch under Mount Lebanon
and the Syrian Apamea. The rest he called after Greek or
Macedonian cities or after achievements of his own or in
honour of Alexander the King. Hence it comes that there are
many Greek or Macedonian city names in Syria and in the
barbarian lands beyond it: Berrhoea, Edessa, Perinthus,
Maronea, Kallipolis, Achaea, Pella, Oropus (Europus)
Amphipolis, Arethusa, Astacus, Tegea, Chalcis, Larissa,
Heraea, Apollonia, and among the Scythians Alexandres-
chata; and in honour of Seleucus's own victories there are

Nicephorion in Mesopotamia and Nicopolis in the part of Armenia nearest Cappadocia.'

Not until 304 BC does Seleucus again appear in recorded history, marching from Bactria into India, claiming the right to the conquests of Alexander the Great with whom he had fought against King Porus more than twenty years before. But now he was faced with a far stronger power than Porus; in the Punjab the emperor Chandragupta stood to meet him with an enormous army, said to have included three thousand war elephants.

Instead of battle a treaty of friendship was signed whereby Seleucus exchanged his dreams of Indian empire for 500 war elephants (perhaps fewer), and with these four-legged tanks he turned back to Babylon. Meanwhile a mutual liking and respect had arisen between the two monarchs and for years Seleucus maintained an ambassador named Megasthenes at Chandragupta's court at Pataliputra (modern Patna) and letters and gifts were exchanged.

In 302 BC Lysimachus sent word of Cassander's confrontation with Demetrius in Thessaly, urging that only united action could save Cassander and in the long run all of them. Lysimachus proposed that he would relieve the pressure on Cassander by an immediate invasion of Asia Minor and then hold the Antigonids in delaying action until Seleucus could join forces with him in the following year. At the same time Ptolemy would mount an attack on the Antigonid southern flank in Palestine and Syria.

THE BATTLE
OF IPSUS

Lysimachus' plan was agreed and, as expected, Demetrius was ordered back into Asia Minor as soon as word reached Antigonus of Lysimachus' having crossed the Hellespont. Seleucus and his precious elephants marched north, wintering in Cappadocia. He joined up with Lysimachus in the following year, and the final battle was fought at Ipsus in western Phrygia. It was the elephants that tipped the scale; Antigonus was defeated and killed and Seleucus took his place as the strongest force in Asia.

49

In the division of Antigonus' territory after Ipsus, Seleucus got control of northern Syria, a prize of the greatest importance because it gave him access to the Mediterranean. In about 300 BC he proceeded to build a western capital there, which he named Antioch for his father. It was situated on the left bank of the Orontes river about fifteen miles from the sea and for a quarry he used the building stones of the nearby city of Antigonea, founded seven years before by Antigonus as his Mediterranean capital. The Graeco-Macedonian population of Antigonea, numbering about five thousand, was also moved to Antioch and successive Seleucid kings added to its size and population; Antioch continued as an important city into Byzantine times. At the sacred grove of Daphne four miles away Seleucus built a magnificent temple to Apollo, who became the patron deity of the dynasty and he also founded the city of Seleucia-in-Pieria at the mouth of the Orontes as a port for Antioch.

55, 57, 59

Although he was now stronger by far than either Ptolemy or Lysimachus in Thrace, together they would be a threat and Seleucus looked about for allies. Despite the crushing defeat at Ipsus, Demetrius the Besieger, son of Antigonus, still had strength. He held the Phoenician cities of Tyre and Sidon, the island of Cyprus and some of the Greek cities of the Aegean coast. Also, and most importantly, he possessed a powerful fleet while Seleucus had none. In 298 BC Seleucus offered Demetrius an alliance, proposing that he take Demetrius' daughter Stratonice as his queen. The offer was gladly accepted and after a magnificent wedding ceremony Seleucus took his young bride to Antioch.

Then comes an odd tale. About five years later Seleucus' physician told him that the sickness from which his son Antiochus was suffering was love for his stepmother Stratonice. Seleucus was over sixty years of age. Wives could be replaced but not sons. An assembly of the army was called before which Seleucus proclaimed Antiochus and Stratonice man and wife, declaring that 'what the king willed was law'. Antiochus was to be joint-king and to rule the eastern satrapies from Seleucia-on-the-Tigris.

Off went Antiochus with his queen, but what she thought or felt of all this is not recorded. Stratonice had already borne one child to Seleucus, a girl, and was to provide two sons and a daughter to Antiochus. As shown by the number of her dedications, especially at Delos, she was a religious woman. On none of these dedications does she describe herself as the wife of Antiochus.

At Antioch and at Seleucia alike the day-to-day work of government proceeded. Order had to be maintained, revenue gathered, armies trained and equipped. Embassies came and went to and from the cities and states of the Mediterranean and

the Aegean and the east as far as India. The empire was now a
sea power and there were fleets to build, while the building and
manning of military posts and cities demanded much time and
money.

LYSIMACHUS OF THRACE

In Europe and Asia Minor Lysimachus too was tireless. In 285
BC he ousted Pyrrhus from Macedon and now his territories
reached from the Pass of Thermopylae through Thessaly to
Macedon and Thrace and across the Dardanelles. He controlled
most of the Greek cities of the Aegean coast and the tableland
down to the Cilician Gates. He was strong and secure.

Then came tragedy. After the battle of Ipsus in 301 BC when
Seleucus had become the strongest power in Asia, Lysimachus
in middle age had allied himself with Egypt by taking to wife
Arsinoe, the beautiful daughter of Ptolemy Soter. He got more
than he bargained for; Arsinoe matured into a strong-willed,
ambitious and unscrupulous woman. She bore Lysimachus
three sons and made up her mind that one of them rather than
Agathocles, Lysimachus' able and popular son by his first wife,
should succeed to the throne.

To this end she so worked on the ageing Lysimachus that she
convinced him that Agathocles was plotting treason. On
spurious evidence Agathocles was accused and put to death;
his friends who offered protest were held to be proven accom-
plices. Agathocles' widow and children, along with those
friends who escaped execution and a number of army officers
who had turned against Lysimachus at his crime, fled to Seleucus
in Syria.

Several of the Greek cities of Asia Minor now sent word
urging Seleucus to come north against Lysimachus, offering aid
should he do so, and at last the old lion was persuaded. He was
a Macedonian, and being the man he was may well have long
held the dream that one day he too might sit on the throne of
his native land. In 281 BC he crossed the Taurus mountains
with a strong army. The cities of the coast gave him joyful welcome, for with advancing years Lysimachus had become an
increasingly harsh master. At Pergamum, Philetaerus surrendered the city and the 9000 talents in his keeping (p. 251). Sardis
yielded without siege and Zipoetes of Bithnyia with his army
came down to join the invader.

At Corupedion in the Hermus valley north of Smyrna
Seleucus and his reinforced army defeated and killed the

50, 53

eighty-year-old Lysimachus. It was said that his body was found amid the heaps of slain only by the fidelity of his dog, which had stood guard over it. Thus ended the Wars of the Diadochi.

PTOLEMY KERAUNOS

After more than forty years of struggle Seleucus could now say that except for Egypt and India he was master of the empire of Alexander the Great. He was in his seventy-eighth year. What he planned is unknown; he may well have decided that to end his days as king of Macedon was enough, his son Antiochus could have the rest.

For the next six months he busied himself with the aftermath of his victory and then turned to the land of his birth. One day he paused at a place called Argos near Lysimachia in Thrace to look at a pile of stones which legend claimed had been an altar of the Argonauts. With his small party was Ptolemy Keraunos, eldest son of Ptolemy Soter of Egypt. Keraunos had been denied the succession to his father's throne and had gone first to Lysimachus, whose queen Arsinoe was his half-sister, and then after the death of Agathocles to Seleucus. Keraunos was capable of any crime; in an unguarded moment he came up behind Seleucus and struck him down.

The murder of Seleucus had been planned. Keraunos, waiting for the opportunity, had already suborned a number of Seleucus' officers. He immediately galloped off to the camp near Lysimachia, where the news brought confusion and dismay. Who was now to lead the army, who was to replace the dead king? Seleucus' son Antiochus was far away in Babylonia. Into the turmoil stepped the friends of Keraunos with a proclamation that he should be the new king. To Lysimachus' men he was the avenger of their king and as for the others, Keraunos was a son of the royal house of Egypt, a king and leader by natural right. Mistrusting and hesitant, the soldiery at last accepted him, and thus suddenly Keraunos was king of Macedon and Thrace and, did he wish it, a power in Asia Minor to boot.

Within his limits Keraunos was able and vigorous. Given his own military training and the quality of the Macedonian army he probably could have held his own, and he was quick to placate Egypt by renouncing any claim there. As for Antiochus, for the present at any rate he was far away, trying to establish his rule in Syria. But Keraunos' victory was short lived. Early in the following year, when the Macedonian levies were scattered to their homes for the winter, the Galatians, as the Greeks called the eastern Celts, came down from the north in strength. Keraunos, fighting with what small forces he could hastily assemble, was defeated and killed. The invaders, plundering and ravaging as they went, swept across Macedonia into Greece with Keraunos' head stuck on a spear carried in triumph before them.

ANTIOCHUS I SOTER, 280–261 BC

54, 60

Antiochus I Soter was forty-four years old when he succeeded to the throne of his father Seleucus Nicator. He had ruled the eastern satrapies from Seleucia-on-the-Tigris for thirteen years and his earlier coins show him full fleshed and strong-jawed, a determined man. On later issues his mouth is somewhat pursed, perhaps because of the loss of his teeth. Coin die-cutters were realists.

He arrived in Syria to find the country in a revolt of which practically nothing is known, and only after much fighting was his rule there secure. Meanwhile urgent appeals came from the Greek cities of the Aegean coast for help against the Galatians. During the political chaos that had followed the deaths of Lysimachus and Seleucus these barbarians from the north had been brought over as mercenaries by Nicomedes of Bithynia. But they had run out of control and were now ravaging the countryside and demanding heavy tribute from the cities as the alternative to siege and destruction. Not until four years later and with the help of a troop of Bactrian armoured elephants was Antiochus able to deal effectively with the Galatians. In battle, the very appearance of these huge fearsome creatures drove them into headlong flight and Antiochus was hailed as Soter – 'Saviour'. There is an inscription of the city of Ilium to this effect.

Little is known of Antiochus' reign. In 262 BC he suffered a defeat by Eumenes I of Pergamum and before that had his personal tragedy in similar fashion to Lysimachus. His elder son Seleucus, whom earlier he had made joint-king ruling at Seleucia-on-the-Tigris, was accused of intent or attempt to revolt. He was put to death and the second son, also named Antiochus, succeeded him. Antiochus I died in 261 BC – how or where, in battle or in bed, there is no record.

ANTIOCHUS II THEOS, 261–246 BC

56, 61

Antiochus II was only twenty-four years old when he came to
the throne. A heavy drinker, he was surrounded by paltry
favourites, including a buffoon and a dancer. With the throne
he inherited a dreary and indecisive war with Egypt. Ptolemy
II Philadelphus had command of the sea and he pulled and
pried at the Seleucid cities of the Aegean coast. During this time
Antiochus adventured north of the Taurus and was once in
Thrace. He regained some of the territories that had slipped
away during his father's last years but this was offset by the
secession of Parthia and Bactria (pp. 197, 234).

A few years before the end of his reign the war with Egypt
died down and a peace was made. To reinforce it Ptolemy
offered Antiochus his daughter Berenice, to bring as dowry the
revenues of lower Syria and Palestine. The marriage would
require Antiochus to set aside his queen Laodice, the mother of
his two sons. Laodice was half-sister or cousin to her husband,
wealthy in her own right and a woman of strong character, but
Antiochus wanted a solid settlement with Egypt and he was
greedy. The marriage with Berenice was made in 252 BC and
a boy was born of it; meanwhile Laodice went off to Ephesus
with her two sons, where she had a strong following. Then,
after five years of marriage, Antiochus left his second wife and
her child at Antioch and went off to rejoin Laodice at Ephesus.
The actual reason is not known, perhaps it was a matter of the
old shoe being more comfortable than the new.

It was folly for Antiochus to have taken Ptolemy's bait, setting aside Laodice for Berenice of Egypt. Little foresight was
needed to see the trouble that must ensue should Berenice provide a rival heir to the throne. It was folly compounded to
leave her after she had provided a son, to go and live with Laodice who, whatever she thought of Antiochus, would be
determined that her son should inherit the throne.

Antiochus died after a short time in Laodice's company,
probably poisoned by his 'prudent' wife. He was forty-one
years of age.

SELEUCUS II CALLINICUS, 246–226 BC, AND
ANTIOCHUS HIERAX, 246–227 BC

58, 62

Soon after the death of Antiochus II at Ephesus his elder son by
Laodice was proclaimed ruler of the Seleucid empire as Seleucus

II Callinicus – 'gloriously victorious'. Promptly a similar announcement was made at Antioch for the child of Berenice; it was a declaration of war between the two queens, but Laodice was by far the stronger. She had friends at Antioch who kidnapped Berenice's child and soon Berenice herself was besieged in her palace at Daphne and the baby was killed.

When the news of Antiochus' death and Berenice's danger reached her brother, Ptolemy III Euergetes of Egypt, he assembled an army and marched to her support. But he arrived at Antioch to find that Berenice was dead and Syria in turmoil. Euergetes besieged the city and, when it surrendered with a plea for mercy, in revenge for his sister's death he turned his troops loose on it. Then, after installing garrisons in the larger Syrian cities he marched on Mesopotamia and Babylonia. Of his further plans there is no record. He was at Babylon when word came of famine and unrest in Egypt, and leaving garrisons at Babylon and Seleucia he hurried home (p. 160).

With Euergetes gone, Seleucus took the field with some success, but he needed money for mercenaries and turned to his rich mother for help. She gave it, but her price was that her younger son, Antiochus named Hierax (the Hawk), was to be king of Asia Minor; not joint-king, but sole and independent. Of necessity Seleucus agreed; with the money and support from his own people he drove the Egyptian garrisons out of Syria and re-established Seleucid rule in Babylonia and Mesopotamia. Meanwhile at Sardis in Lydia, Laodice held firm in the name of his brother, Antiochus Hierax.

63, 69

There was a stalemate between Syria and Egypt until an agreement was made – or was being discussed – between Seleucus and Antiochus Hierax for a joint attack on Egypt. The brothers did not actually meet, but the threat was enough for Ptolemy to offer a ten years' peace, which ended that war. This was soon followed by the Laodicean War, the first to be named after a woman. From Sardis, Laodice issued a proclamation that her younger son Antiochus – named Hierax – was the rightful heir to the Seleucid empire, not his elder brother Seleucus who had reigned now at Antioch for five years. This was a declaration of war and Seleucus marched his army over the Taurus. He won a battle but could not take Sardis, and then his brother-in-law, Mithradates II of Pontus, intervened on the side of Antiochus, bringing with him the Galatians. There was a battle near Ancyra – modern Ankara – and Seleucus was heavily defeated, barely escaping with his life to Syria, while the bar-

barians were again loose in Asia Minor, ravaging the countryside and levying tribute on the cities as in the days of
Antiochus I.

In 228 BC Antiochus Hierax made another try at his brother
by way of an invasion of Mesopotamia. Defeated there, and
again in several battles against Attalus I of Pergamum he finally
escaped to Egyptian-held Thrace. There he was put under
guard, escaping only to fall in with a band of marauding Gauls
who killed him. The victim of his mother's arrogance and his
own folly, he died a total failure, aged thirty.

His brother Seleucus was killed a year later by a fall from a
horse.

SELEUCUS III 226–223 BC

Seleucus II had left two sons and the elder, Alexander, assumed
the throne with the dynastic name of Seleucus. His sixteen-year-
old younger brother, later to be Antiochus the Great, was sent
to Seleucia-on-the-Tigris in Babylonia as titular head of the
Seleucid empire in the east. Meanwhile the king's uncle Andromachus, with what should have been a sufficient force, marched
over the Taurus to recover those areas of Seleucid Asia Minor
which had been taken by Attalus I of Pergamum. In the event
Attalus proved the better general; Andromachus was beaten
in several engagements and finally captured.

Seleucus III was then about twenty years of age, and addicted
to violent rages which earned him the derisive title of Keraunos
('thunderbolt'). Though he had little knowledge of war he
decided to inaugurate his reign with a military campaign, and
after Andromachus' failure against Attalus of Pergamum, now
the dominant power in Asia Minor, Seleucus assembled a
second army and marched against him.

Attalus, however, was a capable strategist and tactician and
Pergamum a stronghold, and after several indecisive battles
Seleucus abandoned the attack and turned eastward to Phrygia,
the country which according to legend had been invaded by the
Amazons before the Trojan War. There was more fighting and
again no victories and Seleucus' officers, of whom Nicanor and
Apaturius were the leaders, decided at last that this king was
unlikely to bring them glory or loot. He was put to death, by
poison it was said. There followed much confusion in the camp,
which was ended with the arrival of Achaeus, another uncle of
Seleucus and governor of Sardis in Lydia, a capable man. He
restored order, executed Nicanor and Apaturius and, under the

65, 70

67, 71

orders of a veteran general named Epigenes, the army marched safely back to Antioch.

ANTIOCHUS III THE GREAT 223–187 B C

At first glance an account of the early years of the reign of Antiochus III has all the flavour of Viennese opera. There is a youthful and hesitant king, a wicked vizier, a loyal general, a young queen and babe and a wise old physician. There are rebellious governors whose armies melt away when the rightful king appears on the battlefield and friends who dispose of the wicked vizier. And there is a cousin of the king, a would-be usurper, whose army refuses to advance when it suspects the purpose of its commander. But here is no make-believe.

70

When he had gone off on campaign against Pergamum three years before, Antiochus' elder brother, Seleucus III, had left the government at Antioch in the hands of his prime minister or vizier Hermias and an advisory council, but by now Hermias was in full control, an oriental despot, unscrupulous and greedy for power and money. With Seleucus dead, he would have preferred to leave his younger brother and successor where he was, at Seleucia-on-the-Tigris, but the Syrian populace wanted their new king at Antioch, and in due course he arrived. He was then about eighteen years of age, uncertain and untried; in fact if not in name the government continued in the hands of Hermias.

All was quiet for a couple of years, but then came trouble in the eastern satrapies. About thirty years before, during the weak reign of Antiochus II, the satrapies of Bactria and Parthia had broken away from Seleucid rule (p. 234) and now Molon, the Seleucid satrap of Media, decided to follow this earlier example and declared himself an independent king. His brother Alexander, satrap of Persis, followed suit.

During the discussions at Antioch as to the measures to be taken against the rebels, Epigenes, the loyal general who had brought the army safely back from Phrygia after the murder of Seleucus III, proposed that Antiochus in person should lead the army against Molon, urging that his appearance on the battlefield would bring Molon's Macedonians over to him. But Hermias wanted to keep the young king under his own eye at Antioch, so instead the punitive force was commanded by two generals, Xenon and Theodotus (nicknamed One-and-a-half). Molon, meanwhile, had greatly strengthened his forces and instead of offering battle the generals dug in behind fortifications and sent for reinforcements. So a new Syrian army marched eastward under an Achaean named Xenoetas, who was given supreme command. He got as far as Molon's main camp at Ctesiphon but found it a trap, for in a surprise attack Molon completely overwhelmed the Syrian army. Now the advice of Epigenes prevailed. A new army was assembled and Antiochus marched at its head. As predicted, the very presence of the Seleucid king aroused the basic loyalties of the Macedonians in Molon's army and they came over to Antiochus almost in a body. Molon and his brother committed suicide to escape being tortured to death.

Antiochus had come to the throne an untried young man under the tutelage of the vizier Hermias, but after this victory he began to think for himself, a portent to Hermias of the loss of his power. A year before Antiochus had married a daughter of Mithradates II of Pontus and she had given birth to a son, so that if Antiochus was removed Hermias, as regent for the child, would be assured another term of authority. Poison was an ever present hazard at Hellenistic courts and the king's friends feared for his life. Antiochus' physician Apollophanes warned him of the danger, and on a pretext Hermias was separated from his guards and killed.

Now firmly on the throne, Antiochus turned to settle the ancient grudge of Syria against Egypt, the possession of Coele Syria, the territories to the south of Syria proper, including Palestine. But after two years of campaigning and some early victories he was resoundingly beaten by Ptolemy IV at Raphia (p. 163). His next move fared better. His uncle Achaeus, governor at Sardis for Seleucid Asia Minor, was an able and ambitious man whose scruples prevented him from seizing power at the time of the death of Seleucus II. This he had later repented and had marched south to take Antioch and the throne, but as with Molon's men in Media, when his Macedonians learned his purpose they would not continue against the true Seleucid king. Nonetheless he posed a threat to Antiochus' rear. In the summer of 216 BC Antiochus marched over the Taurus mountains against him. Little is known of the fighting, but two years later Sardis had fallen and Achaeus was penned up in the citadel with a handful of faithful followers. He attempted to escape but was betrayed to Antiochus, who had him beheaded.

The career of Antiochus III emerges from conjecture into history with Polybius, though there are periods of several years of which little or nothing is known. In 212 BC Antiochus was

72, 76

67, 71

in rebellious Armenia, besieging its young king Xerxes in his capital city of Arsamosata. When at last Xerxes asked for terms he was generously treated; no more was demanded than partial payment of the arrears of tribute owed by his father and himself and a promise of future good conduct. Antiochus was a statesman, he wanted allegiance, not mere conquest, for he could not hold these outer provinces by force alone. To assure Xerxes' continuing loyalty he was given Antiochus' sister Antiochis as queen. It is to be noted that later, when Xerxes failed to live up to his promises, his wife dutifully – to her brother – had him done away with. The Seleucid women were not sentimental.

The next few years are a blank, presumably devoted to the ordering of affairs in Syria and Asia Minor. Then Antiochus set out to re-establish Seleucid rule over the outer eastern provinces of Bactria and Parthia. He reached Ecbatana in Media in 209 BC, where eleven years before his satrap Diogenes had been set in the place of the rebel Molon. Here was the vast summer palace of the Persian and now the Parthian kings. Its walls and columns once had been sheeted in gold and silver, but this had been taken away by Alexander and his Diadochi. They had not dared to commit the sacrilege of looting the great temple of Anaitis, but Antiochus had no scruples. Antiochus needed money and he seized all the gold and silver the priests could not hide, taking a considerable treasure to the value of over four thousand talents. But this temple robbing was a blunder, for Seleucid strength stood on two legs; one, a spread of Greek and Macedonian military settlements, strategically placed along the main trade routes and frontiers; and second, the acquiescence of their native subjects. The peoples of the diverse countries of the Empire, peasants and townsfolk alike, were largely unconcerned with the battles, marchings and countermarchings of their masters. In the main fighting was between armies of mercenaries and went on over the heads of the masses, so to speak, though the effect on those unfortunates who chanced to be close to the actual fighting could be cruel and ruinous. Although there was little if any sense of nationhood among these people, religion was deeply rooted in their lives and, following Alexander's example, the Seleucids had been careful not to interfere with their religious or social life and customs so long as taxes were paid and order maintained. It was here that the influence of religion, through the priesthood, was most important, but when Antiochus took to temple robbery he changed the tolerance of his subjects to bitter enmity. This he perhaps realized but his need for money grew and he continued the practice. It was temple robbing that caused his death; twenty-two years later he was killed by an enraged mob when he attempted to seize the treasure of the temple of Anaitis in Elymais.

From Media the army moved east to Parthia, the mountainous country south of the Caspian Sea. The first Macedonian satrap, Andragoras, was one of Alexander's generals. Seleucus Nicator and his son Antiochus had planted military townships here, Soteria, Charis, Achaea, Calliope, and others of which we have no names. Parthia was important and must be strongly held. Some sixty years later the Seleucid satrap of Parthia, also named Andragoras, revolted or seceded from his overlord Antiochus II. As a declaration of independence he struck coins with his portrait and name, though he did not call himself king or wear the diadem. But his rule was brief. His eastern neighbour, Diodotus of Bactria, expelled a tribe of Scythian nomads from the western part of his territory. They were thus pushed into Parthia and, led by an able chieftain named Arsaces, they attacked Andragoras, killed him and became masters of the country. Arsaces was the first of a strong line of Parthian kings.

The Parthians formed a military establishment in the countries they conquered. Their principal striking force was a body of heavily armoured cavalry – even the horses were clad in iron mail – called the Cataphracti. They were armed with a heavy lance or spear and a bow, but there was the basic disadvantage for the mounted spearmen that the stirrup had not yet been invented. To offset this in some measure their horses were especially bred as big and heavy as possible. Supporting the Cataphracti were the light cavalry, archers who would gallop within bowshot of the enemy, let loose a cloud of arrows and, almost in the very act of firing, wheel off out of range – the Parthian shot. In all else, administration, official language, literature, art, royal titles, the Parthians adopted Greek practice.

Antiochus reached Parthia in 210–209 BC. Arsaces II was on the throne, and his capital city was Hecatompylos – the Hundred Gates. He had been watching Antiochus in Media and knew that he was no match for him in open battle. He abandoned Hecatompylos and fell back on the mountain country below Hyrcania, fighting rearguard actions and attacking in the passes as Antiochus followed. One by one his citadels were taken, and Syrinx, the capital of Hyrcania, was stormed; there was nothing for it but to sue for terms. We have no details, but probably they were similar to those imposed on Xerxes in Armenia, tribute to be paid and a promise of future loyalty, as well as provisions for the conquering overlord and his army. Antiochus wanted formal submission, he could not continue in possession by force of arms.

A campaign such as this was an affair of months and years. The days when kings went to war when the harvest was in, much more of blitzkriegs, were long in the future. This was slow marching with baggage train and siege engines, the sick and wounded in wagons, mountains and deserts to be crossed. Living as they must off the country, forage for the animals and victuals for the men could be a first prize of battle. So that it was not until the following year, rested and recouped, that the army of Antiochus appeared on the west bank of the Arius river, the boundary of Bactria. The satrap of this breakaway Seleucid state at the time of Antiochus II had been a Greek general named Diodotus. He had not so much rebelled as withdrawn from Antioch, and indeed, to keep a tie he had been given a sister of Antiochus as queen. But his son and successor, Diodotus II, had been overthrown and killed by another Greek general, Euthydemus, who came from Magnesia in Asia Minor. An account of the two-year siege of Euthydemus in his capital

74, 77

city of Bactra, and of the settlement with Antiochus, is given below (p. 235). The settlement included the acknowledgement of Antiochus' suzerainty and the gift of a number of war ele-

75

phants together with provisions for the army. From Bactria Antiochus continued over the passes of the Hindu Kush into India where Seleucus Nicator had gone almost a hundred years before, claiming to be the heir of Alexander the Great and entitled to *his* conquests.

Since then Chandragupta's empire, although later strengthened and enlarged by his grandson Asoka, had been torn apart. A mere local king now faced Antiochus, with little strength to measure against this third Macedonian invader. His name was Sophagasenus and he offered Antiochus submission, provisions for his army, more war elephants and a promise of tribute in silver and gold. With this Antiochus was content, for the time had come for his return to Antioch, and the road home was long. He had been on campaign for almost four years, two of them taken up by the siege of Euthydemus in Bactra. He went south-west by way of Arachosia and wintered in Carmania. In 205 he was at Seleucia-on-the-Tigris and a year later at Antioch in Syria. The circuit of the empire in the east had been completed and Antiochus, now called 'The Great King' after the fashion of the Persians, could proclaim that he had restored Seleucid power over the territories in Asia that had been won by his great ancestor, Seleucus Nicator.

Now in his late thirties and at the height of his powers, Antiochus was indeed the 'Great King' by virtue of his achievements, but these were restorations of empire, not gains. His ambitions turned again to the task at which he had failed at the battle of Raphia twelve years before, the conquest of Coele Syria. This territory between Syria and Egypt had been seized by Ptolemy I immediately after the defeat of Antigonus the One-eyed in 301 BC by Seleucus Nicator and Lysimachus of Thrace. Ptolemy had been their ally, but he had not fought and Seleucus claimed that he had unfairly seized the fruits of his and Lysimachus' victory. Ever since Coele Syria had been a bone of contention between Syria and Egypt.

Now Egypt was weak. Ptolemy Philopater had died in 203 BC and his throne was now occupied by a child, Ptolemy V Epiphanes, and the country was disunited. Antiochus made an alliance with Philip V of Macedon for a joint attack on Egypt's possessions. Philip was to get Cyrene in North Africa, and Egyptian possessions in the Aegean and Thrace; Antiochus would take Cyprus and Coele Syria. In 202 BC both moved to the attack. After some three years of fighting, for the Phoenician cities resisted bitterly and most were taken only after long siege, Antiochus was in possession of all the territory between Syria and Egypt down to and including Gaza. In Judaea the people of Jerusalem welcomed him with rejoicing. By 198 BC Antiochus was back in Antioch, the permanent conquest of Coele Syria achieved. As to Egypt, Antiochus betrothed his daughter Cleopatra to the young Ptolemy, and his immediate ambitions in that quarter were satisfied.

Antiochus was now at the height of his career, the strongest man in the known world. Except for Pergamum, the independent Greek cities of the Aegean coast and a handful of small states bordering on the Black Sea and the Sea of Marmora, all Asia west of India was subject to him, and in India itself one king did him homage. He dominated Egypt. Of the conquests of Seleucus Nicator only Thrace and Macedon were not in his grasp but like most conquerors he was insatiable, and in 197 BC he set out to impose his authority on the Greek cities of the Aegean coast. By the end of that year most of them had submitted, and troops were sent by sea to the Hellespont and the occupation of Thrace planned for the following year. It had been agreed that Philip V of Macedon should have Thrace, but after his defeat by the Romans at Cynoscephalae (p. 227) he had been forced to abandon that project.

Antiochus reached Lysimachia, old Lysimachus' capital, to find the city in ruins, destroyed by the native Thracians. He rebuilt and fortified it, restoring all those he could find of the former population and bringing in new settlers.

To expect Antiochus now to be content with his achievements is to forget that he was still the man who had achieved all this. Strong and ambitious, his flatterers doubtless comparing him with Alexander the Great, there were still worlds to conquer.

From the days of Alexander I of Macedon, who had given warning to the Greeks on the eve of Plataea, the Macedonian and then the Hellenistic kings had wished to be well thought of in Athens. It was Greek culture as well as Greek and Macedonian mercenaries that they had planted throughout Asia. But beyond Greece was Rome. She carried no romantic mystery as did Carthage but was a fact, hard and solid as a mountain. Antiochus maintained an embassy in Rome and was informed and respectful of her. Caution urged restraint but pride and ambition pushed him forward, and he looked towards Greece. He was still at Lysimachia when Roman ambassadors arrived. They presented a formal protest against Antiochus' incursion into Europe and his subjection of the Greek cities of Asia Minor, declaring that the freedom of the Greeks was a prime aim of Roman policy. Antiochus courteously but firmly rejected Rome's right to intervene. In any event, he asserted, his policies were not directed against Roman interests and were pacific.

During the following years Antiochus continued to strengthen himself in Thrace and on the Asia Minor coast. The expansion aroused fears of encirclement in Pergamum, which encouraged the Greek cities to appeal for support directly to Rome. Rome was watchful and mistrustful of Antiochus, especially now that Hannibal, the greatest soldier of the age and the hated foe of Rome, was at his court. But she was not ready for war. Then, in 192 BC, the always simmering Greek pot again boiled over, and in defiance of Rome the Aetolian League called on Antiochus to 'liberate' Greece.

Following her victory over Philip V of Macedon at Cynoscephalae in 197 BC Rome had withdrawn her troops, declaring, as had other earlier 'liberators', that she wanted no more than 'to secure the freedom of the Greeks'. But Antiochus knew that any intervention there by him must arouse Roman resistance. At his headquarters at Ephesus there was division among his advisers, some urging an early massive landing in Greece, others counselling delay and Hannibal proposing an attack by Antiochus on Italy, while he himself would bring Carthage over to his cause. Only after much hesitation and delay did Antiochus commit his great blunder, the direct challenge to Rome. Late in the same year he landed at Pteleum in Greece with an army of 10,000 men, 5000 horse and six elephants. Of course this could be no more than an advance guard, and Antiochus promised massive reinforcements which, through mismanagement or whatever, never arrived. Because of this the Greeks, at whose invitation Antiochus had come, refused to join him; the Achaeans formally declared war on him. 'Better the devil you know than the devil you don't.'

Rome declared war, and in 191 BC an army of 20,000 foot and 2000 horse under command of Acilius Glabrio left for Greece, and was joined by Philip V in Thessaly. Antiochus was brought to battle at Thermopylae, which he had fortified, but a Roman contingent under command of Cato made its way over the Callidromus Pass as had the Persians under Hydarnes in 480 BC. The Syrian army was overwhelmed, and Antiochus with a handful of his men escaped, wounded, to Chalcis, whence he took ship to Ephesus.

What emerges is that somewhere, somehow, there was a 'failure of nerve'. Perhaps it was the strangeness of the enemy. For twenty-five years Antiochus had been fighting against men like himself, whose soldiers were in the main Greek and Macedonian mercenaries like his own, and whose thinking and tactics were like his own. The Romans were different. They had little élan of battle, only a grim purposefulness that was unaccustomed and disconcerting. The Roman legion, tougher and more resilient than the Macedonian phalanx, was organized in thirty *maniples* of 120 to 200 men, ten to each line of the three lines of its battle formation, each maniple drilled to deploy within the line as reinforcement was needed. The legionary was armed with two short throwing spears and a considerable sword, and trained in open fighting, gladiator style. In contrast, the three lines of the Macedonian phalanx were tight packed, shoulder to shoulder, and because of the great length of the sarissa (the Macedonian pike) could manoeuvre only slowly.

It was vulnerable on the flanks and especially in the rear, and in battle could only advance frontally, stand, or break. But over all there now appeared a hesitancy, a lack of determination and of preparation, an inadequacy of force at the right time and place that was wholly out of keeping in a field commander of Antiochus' experience and proven quality. He appeared to be yielding while attacking, almost expecting defeat.

At Ephesus, Antiochus took stock. To get at him a Roman army must come by sea or make the long march across Macedonia and then across Thrace where he held several fortified cities. In any case a Roman army in Asia Minor must be supplied by sea and Antiochus was strong in the Aegean and held the Hellespont. Rome had a small fleet in the Aegean and was supported by Rhodes, which had decided to back her as the likely winner. In the first sea battle with the Syrian fleet under command of the Rhodian Polyxenidas the Romans won, using the grappling tactics which had been so effective against the Carthaginians. Antiochus set Ephesus to shipbuilding and Hannibal was charged with the task of getting another fleet built in Phoenicia. A few months later he sailed these new ships to join Polyxenidas, but they were caught en route and destroyed by the Rhodians. Then the Romans under Caius Livius, aided by a number of Pergamene ships, inflicted a decisive defeat on Antiochus' main fleet. Many of his ships were lost and the remainder bottled up in the harbour at Ephesus. Rome now held command of the Aegean.

Antiochus had been assembling his army at Magnesia, about thirty-five miles up the Hermus river and as many west of Sardis. It totalled 75,000 men and included contingents from all parts of the Empire. They were good fighting men but as Antiochus well realized, far inferior in weapons and organization to the Roman legionaries. Meanwhile, having lost command of the sea Antiochus had been compelled to evacuate Thrace, across which a Roman army of 30,000 men under the command of Scipio now marched unopposed against him. It crossed the Hellespont also without interference. Antiochus now offered to treat with the Romans, withdrawing all claims to Thrace and proposing to pay half the cost of the war. The offer was refused. The Romans demanded that Antiochus evacuate all of Asia Minor north of the Taurus mountains and pay the *entire* cost of the war. Antiochus had no choice between an impossibly humiliating surrender, a denial of his very kingship, and battle.

In 190 BC at Magnesia, a field of his own choosing, Antiochus was overwhelmingly defeated. His army was destroyed and he fled to Syria, leaving his generals to rally the fugitives. A few days later he sent emissaries to the Romans asking for terms, terms which he must now accept whatever they might be. They were stiff, but little more than had already been put forward. Henceforth Antiochus was excluded from Asia Minor west of the Taurus mountains. An indemnity of 15,000 talents of silver was levied, 3000 to be paid within one year, the remainder in ten annual instalments. He was to hand over all but five of his decked warships and twenty named hostages, among whom was the son who later reigned as Antiochus IV Epiphanes. Eumenes II of Pergamum had helped in the Roman victory and he too was to get an indemnity, 400 talents of silver. Hannibal and other named enemies of Rome were to be extradited, and corn was to be provided for the Roman army during its stay in Asia Minor.

Antiochus accepted without demur, and the peace treaty was signed at Apamea in the following year: meanwhile the hostages were delivered up but of those to be extradited, Hannibal had escaped.

For Antiochus the defeat was shattering. Like Perdiccas, Antigonus the One-eyed and Seleucus Nicator, he too had hoped to master the empire of Alexander the Great. Now with his dreams of glory gone he was shut out of Asia Minor and Europe, although he could offset this in some measure with his gains of Phoenicia and Palestine. His army was lost. The Romans had no regard for the Hellenistic practice of sparing the defeated, and with the help of Eumenes of Pergamum they had slaughtered most of Antiochus' men, including his precious and irreplacable Macedonians. Also he had now to find the heavy annual indemnity payments to Rome, and there was news from the eastern satrapies of revolt, consequent on his defeat at Magnesia. But it was in the east that his triumphs had been won, and leaving his elder son Seleucus as joint-king (Seleucus IV Philopator) at Antioch, he turned his back on Syria and with a small force marched eastward. There was no word of his plans or of his route until news came that he was dead, killed by a mob of his rebellious subjects while attempting to despoil the temple of Anaitis in Elymais.

THE BATTLE
OF MAGNESIA

SELEUCUS IV PHILOPATOR 187–175 BC
ANTIOCHUS IV EPIPHANES 175–164 BC

One of the terms of the Treaty of Apamea was the delivery to Rome of twenty named hostages, and foremost of these was the twenty-three-year-old younger son of Antiochus the Great, also named Antiochus. It was Roman practice to treat such political prisoners with courteous generosity, and Antiochus was provided with a suitable residence and with the means to maintain himself fittingly in his 'honourable captivity'. He was a personable young man and was well received into Roman society.

Antiochus' mother tongue and education were Greek, and throughout his life he demonstrated his admiration for Greek culture with gifts to Greek temples and cities, notably to Athens. But at Rome where he was to stay for twelve years he learned also to know and to admire Roman institutions.

Meanwhile in the year of his arrival at Rome, Antiochus' father, Antiochus the Great, had been killed in Persia by a mob of his rebellious subjects, to be succeeded by his eldest surviving son as Seleucus IV. In his thirties at the time, Seleucus was an able man, and his reign was a period of quiet recovery from the great defeat at Magnesia. He was much hampered by the drain of the 1200 talents a year payable to Rome under the terms of the Treaty of Apamea.

Antiochus continued to live quietly and enjoyably at Rome until 176 BC when the Senate demanded changes among the Syrian hostages. Foremost again among these was the replacement of Antiochus by the eleven-year-old son of Seleucus IV, named Demetrius. As heir to the Syrian throne, Demetrius was a far better guarantee of his father's good conduct than Antiochus, for brothers were readily expendable among Hellenistic monarchies. Seleucus had little option and Demetrius arrived in Rome, leaving Antiochus free to return to Syria.

During his twelve years in Rome, Antiochus had made influential friends who were interested in his political as well as his personal well-being. He made a round of farewell calls, received the customary assurances of continuing good will, and took ship for Athens, intending to make a lengthy stay. He was in no hurry to reach Antioch for he had been away for a long time and was unsure of his welcome there. At Athens he was warmly received as an ardent philhellene and a cultivated prince of a reigning house. He had been in Athens only a short time when his placidities were shattered by news from home.

Seleucus IV was dead, murdered by his prime minister Heliodorus, who had seized power as regent for Seleucus' five-year-old son, also named Antiochus.

Suddenly, what had been a dream of Antiochus' youth that some day he might sit on his father's throne had become possible, perhaps probable. There were three candidates: the youth Demetrius who was hostage in Rome, the infant at Antioch and himself. His self-confidence was boundless, he was shrewd, and he had friends in Rome. Perhaps it was these friends at Rome who suggested to Eumenes II of Pergamum that here was an opportunity to change Seleucid hostility into the friendship he so much desired. There were letters and messengers and Antiochus sailed for Pergamum. There he was provided with men and money and escorted to the Syrian border.

What followed is a clouded tale. Heliodorus disappears as the regent and before long Antiochus was co-regent with the queen-mother Laodice for the child-king. Five years later the boy-king was gone and his uncle reigned at Antioch as sole ruler of the Seleucid empire; the dream had become a reality.

History has little good to say of Antiochus IV Epiphanes. He was the vain and foolish king who called himself 'Theos Epiphanes' (god made manifest). He was the practical joker who affected a most unkingly familiarity with his subjects, who used the public baths at Antioch and who gave the rich cities of Mallus and Tarsus to his mistress Antiochis. He was the king who so loved pomp and display that he tried to outdo the Romans with his 'triumph' at Daphne a scant year after his outrageous humiliation by them in Egypt. And he was the king responsible for the desecration of the Temple in Jerusalem.

This is one aspect of the man, but a recent study proposes that 'Antiochus IV, in spite of some miscalculations, was actually a shrewd politician who may even deserve to be called a statesman. His campaigns in Egypt and Armenia show him to be an able general'.

Antiochus seized power in 175, four years before Rome's *80, 85* second war with Macedonia. In 173, he sent an embassy to Rome asking for a renewal of the treaty of friendship which had been made with his father Antiochus the Great. The request was accompanied by a substantial payment of indemnity due under the terms of the Treaty of Apamea. In effect he was assuring Rome of his neutrality in her coming war with Perseus of Macedon. The embassy was warmly received and the Senate voted a renewal of the treaty.

Meanwhile Antiochus had concerns nearer home. His father Antiochus III had at last resolved the old dispute between Egypt and Syria over the possession of Coele Syria when, after the battle of Panion in 200 BC, he had annexed this rich territory, which included Palestine. Ptolemy V of Egypt was preparing for the reconquest of Coele Syria when he died in 181, but his widow, who for some years ruled as regent for her son Ptolemy VI, was a Seleucid, a sister of Antiochus Epiphanes, and while she lived there was peace. After her death in 176 BC power fell into the hands of two court officials, a eunuch named Eulaeus and an ex-Syrian slave named Lenaeus. These two, bedazzled by dreams of glory and loot, persuaded the army chiefs and the Alexandrians that Antiochus' hold on Syria was weak and that Coele Syria was ripe for reconquest. They commenced the build-up of an invasion army.

Antiochus of course was kept fully informed of events in Egypt, and while sending a delegation to Rome to protest against Egypt's threatening conduct he made his own preparations. In his youth he had naturally received military training and he took to war with the ardour common to all the Seleucid kings. So that when in November 170 BC, the Egyptian army, led by Eulaeus and Lenaeus, set out to march against Syria, Antiochus with a stronger force stood ready near the Egyptian frontier. At a place a few miles to the east of Pelusium the two armies met and in the ensuing battle the Egyptians were defeated and put to flight.

The victor was moderate, almost mild, forbidding the killing of captives and fugitives and granting an amnesty. Then by some sort of subterfuge he gained possession of the fortress of Pelusium, the key to Egypt from the east.

Next, the young ruler of Egypt, Ptolemy VI Philometor, fell captive to Antiochus. There is an unlikely story that, in panic after the defeat at Pelusium, Eulaeus and Lenaeus had sent him off for sanctuary to the island of Samothrace and that his ship was captured by a Syrian man-of-war. At any rate he was with Antiochus as the Syrian army moved across Egypt by way of Memphis to the Greek city of Naucratis on the western arm of the Nile. Alexandria then sent a delegation to Rome pleading for help, and since the king was captive to his uncle Antiochus his younger brother, also named Ptolemy, and his sister Cleopatra were enthroned in his stead. Antiochus also sent a delegate to Rome protesting that he was in Egypt only to assure the rights of his nephew Ptolemy Philometor. Meanwhile he put

Alexandria to siege, but the city held and after a time he with-drew.

Antiochus returned to Syria in 169 BC leaving Egypt divided, with Ptolemy Philometor ruling at Memphis and his younger brother Ptolemy Euergetes enthroned at Alexandria, jointly with his sister Cleopatra. Thus, by an adroit combination of force and diplomacy, and without any open challenge to Rome, Antiochus had become the dominant power in Egypt. Ptolemy Philometor was man enough to realize that his position at Memphis as Antiochus' protégé was an unworthy one and as soon as his uncle was gone he opened negotiations with his brother and sister in Alexandria. Soon the three were united there, ruling Egypt jointly. They then sent another delegation to Rome to ask for help against Antiochus. The year before Rome had been too deep in her war with Macedonia to consider intervening in the Syrio-Egyptian conflict in support of her policy of preventing any of the Hellenistic kings from becoming over-strong, as would be the case with a Seleucid king in control of Egypt. The war against Perseus (p. 228) was now going better and a three-man delegation, headed by Caius Popilius Laenas, was sent to settle the dispute, but to go no further than the island of Delos until the Macedonian war was over.

Of course Antiochus was not the man to sit idle while his hold on Egypt slipped away. Early in 168 BC his fleet sailed for Egyptian-held Cyprus, where after a victory at sea its governor surrendered and went over to the Syrian side. At about the same time Antiochus again appeared before Pelusium, there to be met by an embassy come to plead that he halt his invasion and to ask for his terms of peace. He granted an armistice for negotiations, but now there was no pretence that he was in Egypt to protect his nephew's rights to the throne. He demanded the formal cession to Syria of both Cyprus and Pelusium, and waited while the embassy went to Alexandria and returned. The terms were impossible. Cyprus perhaps, but to cede the fortress city of Pelusium would be to give Syria an ever-open door to Egypt. To that Alexandria could never agree.

Antiochus advanced to Memphis where he was warmly received. From Memphis at a leisurely pace he moved on to Alexandria, arriving in July and there to meet disaster – the 'day at Eleusis'. At the battle of Pydna on 22 June the Romans under Aemilius Paullus had finally beaten the army of Perseus of

Macedonia, and on receiving the news the mission which had been waiting at Delos sailed for Alexandria. It arrived to find the Syrian army encamped at a place near the city, called Eleusis.

When Antiochus was told of the arrival of the Roman mission he came forward courteously to greet it. But instead of responding in like manner the leader, Caius Popilius Laenas, silent and stony-faced, handed him a brass tablet. On it was a harshly worded ultimatum, a formal resolution of the Senate requiring that Antiochus and his army should immediately evacuate Egypt.

As a matter of course Antiochus asked for a little time to consult with his 'friends' and then came the famous episode of the 'Circle in the Sand'. As he stood there waiting a response to his request, Popilius with his walking stick traced a line on the ground around Antiochus' feet, and stepping back demanded, 'yes or no before you cross that line'. Standing there within the circle, Antiochus realized that there could be no refusal to the Senate's demand; that Syria, like the other surviving Hellenistic monarchies, was now no more than a client state of Rome. Hiding his rage at this open humiliation he told Popilius that he would obey and turned to give instructions for the march back.

The Roman mission waited in Egypt until Antiochus and his army were gone and then sailed to Cyprus, remaining there until the last Syrian soldier had left the island.

Antiochus' attempt to seize control of Egypt had failed, but he was left with a measure of gain. He had defeated the Egyptian army and also had secured a considerable booty, part of it the war chest of Eulaeus and Lenaeus, the remainder mostly loot from temple treasuries. Most important, Syria's right to possession of Coele Syria had been accepted by Rome, tacitly if not explicitly.

He now decided to present the Egyptian affair to his subjects and to the Greek world as a great victory, and to celebrate it with a 'triumph', which was to outdo the 'games' which Aemilius Paullus had held at Amphipolis to celebrate the Roman victory over Perseus of Macedon. Representatives from the Greek states were invited to the festivities, which were to take place in September of the following year.

The festivities opened with a procession which showed the world the wealth and range of the Syrian empire, in much the same way as that with which Ptolemy Philadelphus had celebrated his accession to the throne of Egypt a hundred and twenty years before. It was headed by a march past of 46,000 infantry, 5000 of them armed Roman style, and 10,000 cavalry, and it ended with troops of war elephants, altogether an impressive display of military strength by the standards of the time.

In his *The Greeks in Bactria and India*, W. W. Tarn proposes that this 'triumph' was in part at least a celebration of the reconquest of Bactria by Antiochus' cousin and general, Eucratides (p. 238), but other historians and a number of numismatists have challenged this.

The festivities lasted a full month and they included games of every kind, gladiatorial contests and theatrical performances. There were lavish banquets for visitors and the populace, while wine instead of water flowed from the fountains of Antioch. The Romans might sneer at Antiochus for his humiliation at Eleusis, but his visitors left Syria convinced that he was still strong, rich, and generous.

Antiochus had been expelled from Egypt and Cyprus but he remained ruler of a considerable empire, and he turned now to deal with its problems. The growing strength of Parthia was an external threat, while internally Seleucid rule was being steadily and increasingly weakened by the shrinkage of the empire's Macedonian and Greek population. Seleucus Nicator had known that to endure, his empire must have a strong Graeco-Macedonian population, settled in cities strategically placed along the main trade routes and boundaries. He and his son Antiochus I had devoted much energy and wealth to the building and peopling of these cities, but since their time there had been much intermarriage with the native peoples, while the Seleucid expulsion from Asia Minor west of the Taurus had greatly reduced the flow of new settlers.

Realizing this and himself an ardent philhellene, Antiochus proceeded to strengthen the Greek element in those cities and to refound many which had lapsed to local customs and Asiatic gods. There was much building and rebuilding of temples, gymnasia, theatres and the like, while taxation and citizenship privileges were freely granted. As a unifying force between his Greeks and Macedonians and the native peoples he instituted a cult of himself as Theos Epiphanes, 'the god manifest'. A century and a half before Ptolemy Soter of Egypt had attempted something of this sort with his cult of the god Sarapis (p. 149) and in 196 BC Ptolemy V had also received the title of Theos Epiphanes.

Only in one place was there difficulty over the acceptance of a cult of Antiochus for, as with the Greeks, a plurality of gods was common to the religions of Asia as was the deification of kings. The exception was the tiny monotheistic state of Judaea.

Within the Seleucid empire the state of Judaea was a subsection of a province, a bare fifty miles from north to south and sixty from west to east. But the fortress city of Jerusalem was important, a strongpoint above the road from Syria into Egypt.

Antiochus first visited Jerusalem in about 173 BC when he was welcomed by a cheering crowd carrying torches. The Seleucids had a good record there. He returned in 169, on his way to Syria after his first Egyptian campaign, but this time he robbed the Temple of its treasury, taking also even the sacred vessels used in its service. Begun by Antiochus the Great, temple robbing had by now become a Seleucid practice.

He came again a year later, after his ignominious eviction from Egypt. A false report of his death while in Egypt had aroused a revolt in Judaea against Menelaus, the High Priest appointed by Antiochus. The rebels held the city and Menelaus had taken refuge with the Syrian garrison in the citadel. Smarting as he was from the affront at Eleusis, Antiochus mistook what was really a civil war for a revolt against his own rule, and he punished Jerusalem. He recaptured the city and then turned his soldiers loose to plunder, rape and kill.

To ensure against further revolts a Syrian regiment under the command of a general Apollonius arrived in Jerusalem in 167 BC and attacked the populace, many of whom were sold into slavery. The city walls were torn down and a new fortress, known as the Acra, was built on the site of the ancient city of David. Within this area were housed those Jerusalemites who were for Antiochus and hellenization together with Menelaus the High Priest, and it was garrisoned with Apollonius' troops.

Three months later, on the 25th day of Kislev, in pursuit of Antiochus' policy of vigorous hellenization, a heathen altar, the 'Abomination of Desolation', was set up within the temple precincts and ten days after a pig was sacrificed on it. The Temple itself was dedicated to Zeus Olympius and an image of the god set up therein.

The First Book of Maccabees is the prime source of our knowledge of the Maccabean revolt which followed. It deals with the years 167 to 134 BC and appears to be an eye-witness account of the struggle between Judas Maccabaeus and his followers against the overwhelming strength of the Syrian forces sent against him. The story is vivid and immediate, especially when read against the Israeli-Arab conflict of our time.

In the spring of the year 165, Antiochus set forth from Antioch at the head of an army 40,000 strong, horse and foot, marching for the eastern provinces. He left the home government and the care of his young son in the hands of a 'kinsman' named Lysias.

The army marched north-east to Armenia, where, after the battle of Magnesia twenty-four years before, the military governor of this province of the Seleucid empire had set himself up as an independent ruler, King Artaxias. There is no record of the fighting but Antiochus put an end to Artaxias' pretensions to independence though allowing him to remain as a vassal king, subject to payment of annual tribute. Then, with the same purpose of strengthening and reasserting Seleucid rule in the outlying provinces, Antiochus marched on to Persis and Elymais.

Meanwhile the revolt in Judaea, that is to say in the countryside, continued. Lysias had been left with forces ample to deal with this or any other unrest in the western states, and he sent a considerable army under the generals Gorgias and Nicanor to deal with the Maccabean revolt. This army was soundly defeated and after another failure Lysias himself in the following year marched to put an end to the rebellion. The narrative is clouded, but near Beth Sur on the frontier between Idumaea and Judaea the Maccabees won another victory against the overwhelmingly superior Seleucid forces, and Lysias returned to Antioch. From there, in the name of Antiochus, he offered an amnesty to all the rebels who returned to their place of residence and took up their former occupations. The offer was accepted.

Of Antiochus' movements after leaving Armenia hardly anything is known. He died of illness somewhere in Persia, in the same year of 164 BC. The account of his death given here is taken from I Maccabees 6, 1–16:

'About that time king Antiochus travelling through the high countries heard say, that Elymais in the country of Persia was a city greatly renowned for riches, silver and gold; and that there was in it a very rich temple, wherein were coverings of gold, and breastplates, and shields, which Alexander, son of Philip, the Macedonian king, who reigned first among the Grecians, had left there. Wherefore he came and sought to take the city, and to spoil it; but he was not able, because they of the city, having had warning thereof, rose up against him in battle: so he fled, and departed thence with great heaviness, and returned to Babylon.

'Moreover there came one who brought him tidings into Persia, that the armies, which went against the land of Judaea, were put to flight; and that Lysias, who went forth first with a great power, was driven away by the Jews; and that they were made strong by the armour, and power, and store of spoils, which they had gotten of the armies, who they had destroyed: also that they had pulled down the abomination, which he had set up upon the altar in Jerusalem, and that they had compassed about the sanctuary with high walls, as before, and his city Bethsura. Now when the king heard these words, he was astonished and sore moved: whereupon he laid him down upon his bed and fell sick for grief, because it had not befallen him as he had looked for. And there he continued many days: for his grief was ever more and more, and he made account that he should die. Wherefore he called for all his friends, and said unto them, "The sleep is gone from mine eyes, and my heart faileth for very care. And I thought with myself, Into what tribulation am I come, and how great a flood of misery it is, wherein now I am! for I was bountiful and beloved in my power. But now I remember the evils that I did at Jerusalem, and that I took all the vessels of gold and silver that were therein, and sent to destroy the inhabitants of Judaea without a cause. I perceive therefore that for this cause these troubles are come upon me, and behold, I perish through great grief in a strange land". Then called he for Philip, one of his friends, whom he made ruler over all his realm, and gave him the crown, and his robe, and his signet, to the end that he should bring up his son Antiochus, and nourish him up for the kingdom. So King Antiochus died there in the hundred forty and ninth year'.

DEMETRIUS I SOTER 162–150 BC
In preparation for his last campaign Antiochus Epiphanes had appointed one of his 'kinsmen' (in the Macedonian tradition 'kinsman' was an honorary title for a close and trusted friend of the king) named Lysias as regent for his nine-year-old son, also named Antiochus. Distances were great, communications at best poor and slow, and there could be no absentee administration of the Seleucid empire.

82, 86

Meanwhile Demetrius, the elder son of Seleucus IV and rightful heir to the Seleucid throne, was still held hostage in Rome under the terms of the Treaty of Apamea (p. 203). He was a serious and cultivated young man who had profited greatly by the exchange of the pettiness and intrigues of the half-oriental court of Antioch for the company and friendship of men of affairs and intellect in Roman society. Important among these was Polybius, the Greek historian, soldier and diplomat, who like himself was a hostage in Rome.

Against the advice of Polybius, who better understood Roman temper and policy, Demetrius now addressed himself to the Senate, urging that he be permitted to return to Syria to take up his inheritance, and that he was a respectful friend and admirer of Rome. But those shrewd men were reluctant to release so forceful and capable a prince to a position of power, especially in the east, where they preferred weakness and dissention to strength and unity. Frustrated, Demetrius at last acted on Polybius' advice 'to be bold' and with a few friends slipped away by ship from Rome, where his absence was unnoticed until it was too late for pursuit. Landing at Tripolis in Phoenicia he was told that there was much unrest in Syria under the rule of the regent Lysias, and indeed, as soon as word of Demetrius' landing reached the troops at Antioch they rose in revolt, seizing Lysias and the boy-king Antiochus and sending word to Demetrius asking how they should be dealt with. He ordered that they should be disposed of; 'let me not see their faces'. A poor way to begin a reign, but in the context of the time no more than common prudence.

Thus, suddenly, Demetrius was master of the Seleucid empire in the west but the eastern provinces were in the hands of Timarchus the Milesian. Timarchus, a favourite of Antiochus Epiphanes and made governor by him, now declared himself king of Media and asked for Rome's approval. Rome was suspicious and resentful of Demetrius' escape and his easy taking of the Syrian throne and did not disapprove Timarchus' claims, who forthwith prepared an army to march on Syria. But Demetrius was no man to sit and wait, and he hurried to meet Timarchus in force, coming up with him at the Euphrates above Babylonia. As with the confrontation of Antiochus the Great and Molon (p. 195) there was no battle; in the presence of a true Seleucid king the army of Timarchus melted away and Demetrius was greeted at Seleucia as Soter – 'Saviour'. His father's empire was now his, entire.

87, 88, 91

There remained a matter of great importance, Rome's recognition of Demetrius as king. Following his flight the Senate had sent a commission to Syria to enquire as to its affairs, but they did not arrive until Demetrius was firmly in the saddle. Forewarned, he made sure the commissioners were handsomely met en route and at Antioch they were received and treated in such fashion as to secure, however reluctantly, the Senate's acknowledgement of his legality as king. Like his father, Demetrius too had friends in Rome.

Demetrius was to reign at Antioch until 150 BC, but not happily. He was the son of a sober and forthright Macedonian and his five years in Rome and his own native temperament led him openly to despise the luxuries and vices of the Levant. He was no man for circuses and display, and his people grew restive and resentful as over the years Demetrius shut himself up in the castle he built near Antioch, where he entertained philosophers and poets, and also indulged in the Seleucid vice of heavy drinking. Antiochus Epiphanes, luxury loving, colourful and supple, had been more to the Syrian liking. Nor did his foreign affairs prosper, hampered as he was by the constant enmity of Egypt, Cappadocia and of Pergamum especially. Then came word of a claimant to Demetrius' throne, a youth who purported to be a son of Antiochus Epiphanes, who had escaped when his elder brother had been killed at Demetrius' orders (p. 213). His name was Balas and he was at the court of Attalus II of Pergamum. Perhaps he was no more than a handsome youth who happened to resemble his putative father; certainly he later proved to have little of the Seleucid quality. But he was a useful tool for Attalus, who crowned him as the true Seleucid king, with the evocative name of Alexander.

After a time Attalus sent Alexander to one of his clients, a Cilician chieftain named Zenophanes, and with his help he took the city of Ptolemais, on the coast of Pamphylia about thirty miles to the east of Side. Here he set up court and was promised further help from Attalus and also from Ptolemy Philometor of Egypt. It came, but there is scant knowledge of the events. There was fighting in which at first Demetrius was successful but in the final battle he was cut off from the main body of his troops and almost alone fought his last fight and died. It was the year 150 BC and Demetrius was then thirty-five years of age.

ALEXANDER BALAS 150–146 BC

Alexander Balas, the pretender put forward by Attalus II of *89, 92*
Pergamum and supported also by Ptolemy Philometor of
Egypt, was a handsome young man, pleasure loving and
friendly, a welcome change from the gloomy and withdrawn
Demetrius Soter, and at first immensely popular with the
Syrians. To strengthen his influence in Syria, Philometor gave
the new king his daughter Cleopatra Thea in marriage.
Alexander, however, soon surrounded himself with dissipated
friends and mistresses; the government of the country was left
to favourites and to his prime minister Ammonius, who removed the important adherents of the late king by assassination, confiscating their estates. Within a few years the populace
that had hailed Alexander with delight had become disgusted
with him and his court.

Three years after he took the throne Alexander's pleasures
were interrupted. The elder son of Demetrius I, also named
Demetrius, landed on the Syrian coast with a force of mercenaries under command of a noted Cretan condottiere named
Lasthenes, and with the presence in the country of a genuine
Seleucid resentment against Alexander boiled into revolt. In
the confusion Ptolemy Philometor arrived with a strong army,
having taken and garrisoned the cities of Phoenicia on the
way, and determined that Alexander must go. Philometor prevailed on the Antiochenes to accept the young Demetrius as
king, and Cleopatra Thea, who after bearing a son to Alexander
had returned to Egypt, was brought back and married to
Demetrius. She was a dutiful daughter.

Now Alexander's own intimates turned against him and he
fled to Cilicia. There he raised a body of mercenaries and in
145 BC he came into northern Syria destroying and burning all
along his way. Ptolemy Philometor met him in force and
Alexander was routed, again fleeing for his life, although Philometor was mortally wounded in the fighting. A group of
Alexander's officers offered to kill him in exchange for a pardon
from Demetrius, now hailed as Demetrius II of Syria. The
bargain was made and Alexander's severed head was shown to
Philometor before he died. This vicarious success apparently
justified Demetrius in reviving the title Nicator, previously
borne with more justification by Seleucus I.

DEMETRIUS II NICATOR, FIRST REIGN, 146–140 BC

93, 97

For him and his kingdom the six-year-long first reign of Demetrius II was an unhappy one. The mercenaries, mainly Cretan, who had helped to put him in power ran out of control, looting and ravaging, while Demetrius, or rather his ministers for he was still a youth, made savage reprisal against Alexander's supporters and those who resisted the heavy imposts they levied. Within a few months of Demetrius' accession civil war again broke out. A general named Diodotus, in command of the fortress city of Apamea, brought forward the infant son of

99, 105

Alexander Balas and Cleopatra Thea as Antiochus VI Dionysus, rival heir to the Syrian throne, and Antioch and inland Syria declared for him. Soon all that was left of Syria to Demetrius were the cities of the coast, though Mesopotamia and Babylonia still acknowledged him as king.

The civil war dragged on and the people suffered. Three years later it was given out that the boy-king Antiochus VI Dionysus had died of illness, presumably put away by Diodotus,

101, 106

who now proclaimed himself king with the name Tryphon, the 'Magnificent'.

By 140 BC Demetrius, now some twenty years of age, made his own decision to break out into the eastern provinces in the hope of there rebuilding his strength. Leaving Cleopatra at Seleucia he marched with what forces he could muster; in Mesopotamia he was welcomed and reinforced, and continued on to Babylonia. He next engaged in a series of actions against Mithradates of Parthia, in which he appears to have been the victor, but somehow, by treachery or chance, was made captive. He was taken to Hyrcania, and there at the court of the Parthian kings he was to remain in 'honourable captivity' for the next ten years. So ended the first reign of Demetrius II Nicator.

ANTIOCHUS VII SIDETES 139–129 BC

The capture of Demetrius II by the Parthians left the field clear for his younger brother Antiochus. While yet a boy he had been sent for safety to Side in Pamphylia and from that connection

104

came to be known as Sidetes. Side was a vigorous seafaring town, where Antiochus had grown to manhood in a better atmosphere than the hothouse court at Antioch. In character and competence he was an exception among these later Seleucids, a worthy descendant of the founder of the line. Seleucus Nicator would have approved of him.

Antiochus was a personable and serious young man, and though Demetrius was still alive, Cleopatra Thea's counsellors urged her to marry him as her third husband and thus, hopefully, bring order to the state. She did so, and he took the throne as Antiochus VII. He was at least ten years younger than she, but he proceeded energetically with the immediate task of ridding Syria of Tryphon, who within a year was defeated and dead.

103, 107

With Syrian affairs in some sort of order Antiochus then moved against the rebellious Judaeans. He took Jerusalem after siege, but his treatment of the vanquished was generous, earning him the title of Eusebes – the Pious. He reconquered Babylonia from the Parthians in 130 BC and then, with his now considerable army, moved north into Media, where he went into winter quarters. His ostensible aim was to attempt in the following year to rescue his brother Demetrius from his Parthian captivity, but in the early spring of 129 BC the towns among which Antiochus' soldiers were scattered rose in simultaneous planned revolt. With what forces were immediately to hand Antiochus hurried to the rescue, to find himself faced with the main Parthian army under Phraates II. In the ensuing battle Antiochus was isolated and killed, and Cleopatra Thea, who had borne him five children, was again widowed.

Phraates dealt with the dead Antiochus with kingly courtesy, returning his body to Syria in a silver casket. Seleucus, the young son of Antiochus who had accompanied him on the campaign, was taken into the Parthian court and brought up there as befitting a prince.

DEMETRIUS II NICATOR, SECOND REIGN, 129–125 BC

For the past ten years Demetrius II Nicator, the elder brother of Sidetes and his predecessor on the Syrian throne, had been held captive at the Parthian court. Some day he might be a useful tool of politics or war, and so despite several attempts at escape he was maintained in luxury and even given a royal daughter in marriage.

Late in 129 BC with the Syrian army encamped in winter quarters in Media and a spring offensive against Parthia in prospect, Demetrius was at last put to use. Phraates II, the then king, sent him back to Syria under escort, there to create a diversion in Sidetes' rear by claiming, or reclaiming, his right to the Syrian throne. As it happened, Demetrius reached Syria at about the same time as the news of the defeat and death of Sidetes, thus unexpectedly to find himself again ruler of what was left of the Seleucid empire, with Cleopatra Thea once more his queen.

95, 98

The second reign of Demetrius lasted four years. During his long sojourn in Parthia he had adopted the Parthian style of a beard and robes, shown on the coins of this second reign. Cleopatra had borne him two sons, and one can but conjecture what she thought of this strangely un-Macedonian figure. But in folly and intemperance Demetrius had·not changed; he had as little regard for the needs of the state and its people as during his first reign. A great army had been lost in Media and much treasure, hardly a family but mourned a husband or son. A few years of rest and recovery were essential, but soon Demetrius was busy draining away what was left of men and money in order to mount an attack on Egypt.

In 127 BC Demetrius marched down the Phoenician coast to the Egyptian fortress city of Pelusium, to find facing him there a far stronger army than his own under the command of Ptolemy VIII Euergetes, while at the same time news came that northern Syria was in revolt. A new pretender to the Syrian throne had appeared, named Alexander as the earlier one but nicknamed Zebina – the Bought One, an imputation of servile origin. He had been put forward by Ptolemy Euergetes with the aid of a contingent of Egyptian troops and promptly accepted by Antioch and the inland cities, although Seleucia and the coastal towns had remained loyal to Demetrius. Demetrius forthwith abandoned any thought of attack on Egypt and hurried back to deal with the rebels.

Intermittent war between the two kings continued until some time in 126–5 BC when the final battle was joined near Damascus. Demetrius was heavily defeated and retired to Ptolemais, where he had left Cleopatra. But when he arrived the city gates were shut against him, and when he boarded ship at Tyre in an attempt to escape he was killed on Cleopatra's orders.

CLEOPATRA THEA AND ANTIOCHUS VIII GRYPUS 125–121 BC

Cleopatra Thea was the daughter of Ptolemy VI Philometor of Egypt and queen in Syria for twenty-nine years. She had borne eight children to three of its kings. In 125 BC she was in her early forties, a strong, determined and intelligent woman with no more scruples than were common to her time and place. On her coins she is quite handsome. She now decided to take control of affairs as sole ruler, though half the country was in the hands of the pretender Alexander Zebina, who three years later fell into the hands of Antiochus Grypus and committed suicide. Cleopatra must have had the support of the court and nobility as well as what was left of the army, who would have welcomed her in place of Demetrius II. Once enthroned she would brook no challenge to her authority, and is said to have killed her son Seleucus with her own hands when he presented himself as the rightful successor to his father Demetrius. But before long there was resentment among the people against the sole rule of a woman, and Cleopatra took her younger son Antiochus, then about seventeen years of age, to rule conjointly with her. Both their heads appear on the coins of this reign, but Cleopatra's predominates.

108, 114

110, 115

Antiochus, called Grypus, 'hooked-nosed', like most of the later Seleucids was little more than another hunting, drinking and fighting man, intent on his pleasures and with little thought for the welfare of his kingdom. As the years passed he became increasingly resentful of his mother's dominance and she, disliking him and his incompetence, decided to do away with him. The story goes that one day when Grypus returned from the hunt she offered him a cup of cool wine; the courtesy was unaccustomed and he, being suspicious, insisted that she drink it instead. She did so, and died.

ANTIOCHUS VIII GRYPUS 121–96 BC

The reign of Antiochus Grypus differed from that of his successors chiefly in its length, twenty-five years. He was murdered by his general Heracleon in 96 BC and after him Syria endured seven more Seleucids. Throughout this time, except during the rule of Tigranes of Armenia (83–69 BC) until the end of the dynasty there was almost continuous civil war. Syria was divided between the coastal cities and the area of the upper Orontes river centred on Antioch, and at one time there were three minor kings struggling for dominance. The great empire of Seleucus Nicator, reaching almost 2500 miles from the Hindu Kush to Macedonia·was now little more than a memory, and the once rich and populous centre of that empire, the land of Syria, was eaten up by extortion and war, its coasts the haunt of pirates.

112, 116

Rome saw all this, yet although Syria was to be had for the taking she was reluctant to add to the burden of empire until her war with Mithradates of Pontus had been won. That twenty-year struggle ended in 68 BC with Pompey's over-whelming victory at Nicopolis in Pontus (p. 269). Four years later the victor came south, bringing with him order and discipline, and Syria became a Roman province.

CHAPTER FOUR

The Antigonids of Macedon

When Alexander left Macedonia in 334 BC he put his country and his ultimate base in the charge of an elderly general named Antipater. This position was no sinecure, for he had both to organize a regular supply of recruits for Alexander's army and at the same time to maintain for himself a sufficient military establishment to control the Greek states. Although wholly loyal to his king, Antipater's remoteness from Alexander in Asia gave him a quasi-regal authority. On his death in 319 BC he was succeeded by his son Cassander, who later assumed the title of King, just as did the other *de facto* rulers of portions of Alexander's empire.

Though Cassander's ambitions were limited his ruthlessness in realizing them was unbounded, for he was largely responsible for exterminating the house of Alexander. Olympias, Alexander's mother, now a refugee in Epirus, had murdered in 317 BC Philip III, the half-witted and illegitimate son of Philip II, who had been chosen by the army as joint-heir to the empire. She then invaded Macedonia, but fell into the hands of Cassander who had her put to death. At the same time Cassander attempted to legitimize his royal position by marrying a half-sister of Alexander, and by holding as hostage Alexander IV, Alexander's posthumous son by Roxane and joint-heir to his empire. This Alexander, however, was a pawn who was killed as soon as his usefulness ended. When Cassander died in 297 BC his dynasty virtually ended with him, for three years later Demetrius Poliorcetes was proclaimed King of Macedon.

DEMETRIUS POLIORCETES 306–283 BC
Demetrius Poliorcetes (the 'Besieger'), son of Antigonus the One-eyed, was one of the most colourful and forceful men of his time, yet his tremendous energy seems to have been an end in itself, without constructive purpose. His reign in Macedonia

117, 121

221

was short, only five years, but it was important because it legalized Antigonid rule which was to last until the Roman conquest one hundred and thirty years later.

When scarcely twenty Demetrius was already in command of part of his father's army, and in 313 BC he was put in charge of Syria and Phoenicia, Antigonus' vulnerable southern flank. But the next year he was heavily defeated by Ptolemy at Gaza in Palestine and lost these territories until Ptolemy, ever cautious, abandoned his gains and fell back on Egypt.

For the next ten years Demetrius was mainly occupied in maintaining his father's rule in the Aegean against the en-croachments of Cassander and Ptolemy. In 307 BC he compelled Cassander to evacuate Athens, Megara and Chalcis. At the same time he was building up a powerful navy with which he won the strategically important island of Cyprus by heavily defeating Ptolemy off Salamis in 306 BC (p. 145). After his un-successful attempt to follow up this victory with an invasion of Egypt, Antigonus next directed Demetrius to capture Rhodes, a close ally of Ptolemy. The result was one of the famous sieges of antiquity lasting for a whole year, during which every known device of attack and defence was employed. In the end Rhodes remained untaken and the two sides were induced by Aetolian mediators to make peace. Demetrius nevertheless was held to have earned the title Poliorcetes, the 'Besieger'.

After Rhodes, Antigonus' enemies concentrated against him: Lysimachus and Seleucus joined hands in the north, Ptolemy threatened from the south. In the great battle of Ipsus in 301 BC Demetrius played a fatal part, for, like Prince Rupert, he and his cavalry defeated their immediate opponents and then pursued them beyond the field of battle, so exposing his infantry to the charge of Seleucus' elephants. Antigonus was killed and Demetrius escaped with only ten thousand of his men. Though after Ipsus the Antigonid provinces in Asia were divided among the conquerors, Demetrius' garrisons still occupied Corinth, Megara and Argos in Greece and his fleet secured the Cyclades, Cyprus and parts of the coasts of Asia Minor and Phoenicia, so that he remained a power to be reckoned with.

In 297 BC Cassander of Macedon died leaving no strong heir, presenting Demetrius with an opportunity for intervention which he was unable to use, for he was preoccupied with a siege of Athens. Ten years before he had been welcomed there as a liberator, ousting Cassander's garrison from the city and pro-claiming freedom for all. But because of his arrogant and dissolute conduct (he was accused of converting the house of the Virgin Goddess into a brothel), the earlier enthusiasm had cooled, and now Athens had shut her gates and manned her walls against him. The siege was long and bitter but at last in March 294 the city capitulated, and the 'Besieger' this time justified his name.

Soon after this victory Demetrius was invited by one of Cassander's sons to intervene in Macedonia on his behalf. He accepted the invitation but used the opportunity to get himself proclaimed king of the country, his former marriage to a sister of Cassander providing him with some show of legitimacy.

Demetrius' five-year-reign as king of Macedon was undistinguished, in fact he was held to have been her worst king. Far from being concerned for the welfare of his subjects, he regarded Macedonia and Greece only as bases from which to attempt the recovery of his father's Asiatic dominions. In the past Demetrius had been too dynamic and successful, and now his possession of Macedonia was a menace which united his enemies. Ptolemy of Egypt proceeded to avenge his defeat by undermining Demetrius' naval power in the Aegean and then in 288 BC Pyrrhus of Epirus and Lysimachus of Thrace invaded Macedonia from east and west. The Macedonian army went over to Pyrrhus, and he and Lysimachus partitioned the country between them. Demetrius fled to Asia Minor hoping to rally support, but was soon captured by Seleucus, and died in comfortable captivity five years later.

ANTIGONUS GONATAS 277–240/39 BC
The heir of Demetrius was his son Antigonus, surnamed Gonatas, but as long as Macedonia was occupied by Pyrrhus and Lysimachus all that Antigonus could do was to maintain his hold on Greece. But the division of Macedonia between Pyrrhus and Lysimachus was short-lived, for Lysimachus soon forced Pyrrhus to retire to Epirus, becoming sole ruler of Macedonia and Thrace and much of Asia Minor.

119, 122

Lysimachus was now eighty years of age and his family and court were rent with dissension. Also, co-existence was not a viable policy in the political climate of the time, perhaps because the protagonists, these last of the Diadochi, were still men who had lived under the spell of Alexander and his single, world-wide kingdom. Finally Seleucus and Lysimachus met in battle at Corupedion in Lydia in 281 BC. Lysimachus lost both his kingdom and his life and Seleucus, now also in extreme old age, was for a few months ruler of all Alexander's empire except for the Egypt of Ptolemy.

Seleucus, a Macedonian by birth, decided to return to his homeland and take over the inheritance of Alexander; but on the way, outside Lysimachia in Thrace he was assassinated by Ptolemy, a son of Ptolemy Soter, nicknamed Keraunos ('Thunderbolt'). The name was appropriate both in expressing the aimless violence of its possessor, and as the name of a son of Egypt's ruler, who had adopted the eagle and thunderbolt of Zeus as his personal device. Keraunos was no agent of his father, by whom he had been disinherited, but was trying to carve a realm for himself out of the chaos of the time, and for a brief while he succeeded in being recognized as *de facto* king of Macedonia. His reign was terminated not by an avenging Seleucid, but by a new menace from the north, with which other Hellenistic rulers had to cope.

In 279 BC a tribe in search of plunder and land on which to settle, known to the Greeks as Celts or Galatae (to the Romans as Gauls) broke into Macedonia. Rulers with experience of frontier warfare in semi-barbarous lands would no doubt have acted differently, but Keraunos lived up to his name; he flung himself upon the barbarians with a small force, and both he and it were cut to pieces. Macedonia was without an effective king and – more important – Greece lay exposed to the ravages of the invading Gauls. Their invasion of Greece, their abortive raid on Delphi, and their eventual repulse mainly by the Aetolian League lie outside the main theme of this chapter, but the story of the Gallic invasion shows the vital role of a strong Macedonian state as the northern bulwark of the Greek peninsula.

After the death of Ptolemy Keraunos the principal claimant to the Macedonian throne was Demetrius Poliorcetes' son, Antigonus Gonatas, who since the flight of his father ten years before had maintained himself in central Greece in a small realm based on the three fortress harbours of Corinth, Chalcis and Demetrias (in Thessaly).

His chances did not look good, but the fact that he had survived as an independent power for so long was significant. We do not know how he came to be accepted as king of Macedonia, but it is clear that the principal occasion was provided by the Gauls. Those who had invaded Greece were no longer a menace, but at the same time another horde had overrun Thrace, and by 277 were threatening the Greek cities of the Thracian Chersonese (the Gallipoli peninsula).

There, near Lysimachia, Antigonus by a stratagem trapped the Gallic host between his fleet drawn up on shore and his army inland; the Gauls were so mauled that they withdrew and gave no further trouble. Such was the terror they inspired, and such the relief at Antigonus' victory, that the prestige he gained thereby won him the throne of Macedon, which he held until his death thirty-eight years later.

By a treaty with Antiochus I of Syria, Antigonus secured his eastern frontiers, and Thessaly and the southern chain of fortresses were protected against attack by an understanding with Aetolia. Trouble on the northern frontier would have to be dealt with as it arose, but to the west, with the death of Pyrrhus in 272 BC, the power of Epirus declined, removing the last serious threat to Macedonia.

Antigonus was a very different character from either his father Demetrius or his grandson Philip V. Though all three had evident practical and military ability, Antigonus alone showed keen interest in poetry, philosophy and history. As a young man he had frequented the circle of Menedemus of Eretria, and members of that circle were later attracted to Antigonus' court at Pella. There Aratus became court poet and wrote, at the request of Antigonus, his long and still surviving astronomical poem, the *Phaenomena*. Another habitué of the court was the historian Hieronymus of Cardia, to whose history of his times we owe much of our knowledge of the period. Antigonus formed a close and lasting friendship with Zeno, the founder of Stoic philosophy, though Zeno himself refused Antigonus' invitation to leave Athens and settle at Pella. To Zeno he may have owed the plain common sense characteristic of sayings attributed to him, such as 'no man is a hero to his valet'.

The long reign of Antigonus ended with his death in 240 or 239 BC and in its broad outlines it must be accounted a success. The central object of his policy had been the protection of Macedonia from the ravages of war. The country had been drained of men by Alexander, had been fought over by his successors, had been ravaged by the Gauls; a period of repose and recuperation was necessary for national survival. Never does Antigonus appear to have indulged in gratuitous attacks on his neighbours; but in mainland Greece he was always ready to deploy his strength, for this area formed the outer defences of Macedonia. Only at the very end of his reign did this protective policy begin to crumble when a new Peloponnesian power, the Achaean League, captured Corinth and attempted to roll back the Macedonians from the south.

DEMETRIUS II 240/39–229 BC AND
ANTIGONUS DOSON 229–221 BC

The aged Antigonus was succeeded by his son Demetrius II, who had long been the principal lieutenant of his father. His reign of ten troubled years ended in 229 BC, when he was overwhelmed and perhaps killed in battle by the Dardanians, a mountain people who had invaded Macedonia. At the same time Thessaly revolted to join with the Aetolians. In this crisis the son and successor of Demetrius was a boy aged nine, the future King Philip V.

Fortunately for Macedonia and for Philip the choice for regent fell upon a man who was an able general and politician and also completely loyal to the royal house. Antigonus Doson was a grandson of Demetrius Poliorcetes and a cousin of the late king; his surname Doson perhaps means 'generous'. He checked the Dardanian invasion, a direct threat to Macedonia itself, and then turned to deal with the situation to the south. Thessaly, which had defected to the Aetolians, seems to have been quickly recovered, but this success was offset by the loss of Athens and the Piraeus.

By 223 BC Antigonus, now in alliance with the Achaean League, had defeated an anti-Macedonian coalition led by Cleomenes, King of Sparta, and supported by Ptolemy III of Egypt. But at the height of his success, when he had extended Macedonian power over the whole Peloponnese, he was recalled to deal with yet another barbarian invasion from the north. Already a sick man, the strain of this campaign proved too much, and he died during it in 221. His short reign had re-established the dominant position of Macedonia in Greece and had allowed Philip, now aged seventeen, to reach an age at which he could himself take over his kingdom.

PHILIP V 221–179 BC

123, 127

Philip V survived as king of Macedonia for over forty years until his death from natural causes in 179 BC; mere survival in such an age was no mean achievement. He was endowed with superabundant energy, but the final picture is an unattractive one. Like so many leaders of the Hellenistic age Philip seems to have waged war simply for the sake of action, without any long or even short-term aim in view. His restless and ruthless activity, sometimes marred by what even in those times were regarded as atrocities, stirred up more opposition than he could ever overcome and ended by precipitating the intervention of Rome in the affairs of mainland Greece. Thereafter he could maintain a precarious independence only by acceding to every Roman demand.

The involved conflicts between different groups of powers which had long plagued mainland Greece continued during the first period of his reign and there were clashes with the Romans, who in 229 BC had established a bridgehead in Illyria. Rome did not forget that Philip had signed a treaty with Hannibal of Carthage in 215 BC at the very moment when her fortunes were at their lowest ebb in the Second Punic War. Later, another treaty, between Philip and Antiochus III of Syria directed against Ptolemy IV of Egypt, persuaded the Roman Senate that the time to take action against Philip had arrived.

In October 200 BC two Roman legions (about 10,000 men), under command of Sulpicius, landed in Illyria. After two indecisive campaigns the Roman general T. Quinctius Flamininus at last brought Philip to battle at Cynoscephalae in Thessaly, where the Macedonian army was totally destroyed. In the ensuing negotiations, at which a certain mutual sympathy between Philip and Flamininus became apparent, Philip was allowed to retain his throne, but had to surrender territories outside Macedonia, in particular the three key fortresses of Demetrias, Chalcis and Corinth in Greece; he also had to give up most of his fleet, pay an enormous indemnity, and provide hostages.

Thereafter Philip had to collaborate with Rome when called upon to do so, sometimes against his former allies as, for example, Antiochus III, who was Rome's next victim at the Battle of Magnesia in 190 BC (p. 203). Now at last he devoted some attention to the needs of his kingdom by reorganizing finance and re-opening mines. His last years were, however, poisoned by one of those domestic tragedies so typical of the age. On the accusation of his elder son Perseus, Philip was persuaded to execute his younger son Demetrius, who had been a popular hostage at Rome; then in remorse he was about to disinherit Perseus when he died at Amphipolis in 179 BC.

PERSEUS 179–168 BC

125, 128

Perseus, the last king of Macedon, bore a name which had no precedent in the Macedonian royal house. In legend Perseus had been the slayer of the Gorgon and the saviour of Andromeda, but it was probably the hero's Argive origin, and the fact that Philip's wife was an Argive which induced Philip to adopt Perseus as his patron deity, place his head upon his coinage, and to name his eldest son after him.

The new king of Macedonia received a difficult inheritance, which required all his tact to consolidate. Rome was suspicious of him for having apparently caused the death of his popular and pro-Roman brother Demetrius, but he tried to disarm her suspicions by negotiating a renewal of his father's treaty, and by keeping the Senate informed of his intentions in Greece. At home he countered opposition by recalling exiles, freeing prisoners and cancelling debts.

In character Perseus differed greatly from his father, from whose failures he had certainly learned. Though, like him, a trained soldier, he was courteous in manner and diplomatic in his dealings with the Greek states; these he clearly recognized as his only allies in the inevitable conflict with Rome. Yet when that conflict came in the last years of his reign, his parsimony in buying support and his hesitation in action contributed much to his final ruin. But it was his foreign policy which aroused fears which no tact could allay. The elimination of Seleucid power in Asia Minor had made Eumenes II of Pergamum Macedon's most formidable neighbour, against whom Perseus must necessarily be on his guard. By marrying the daughter of Seleucus IV of Syria, and by giving his own half-sister as wife to Prusias II of Bithynia, Perseus secured useful allies against Eumenes. He also strengthened the Macedonian hold upon parts of Thrace, an area where Pergamene interests were in conflict with his own.

In the end it was the intrigues of Euemenes coupled with Roman fears and suspicions which precipitated the final Macedonian War (171 BC) – a desultory conflict which dragged on ineffectively for three years. Only in 168 BC was the consul, Aemilius Paullus, an experienced commander, able to co-ordinate the operations of the Roman fleet and army and bring Perseus to battle at Pydna in Macedonia. The issue was soon decided, for though afterwards Paullus often described the onset of the Macedonian heavy infantry as the most frightening sight he had ever seen, his tactics enabled the more flexible Roman

units to disorganize and eventually to slaughter the Macedonians. Perseus fled to Samothrace where he surrendered to
the Romans. He was taken to Rome to adorn Paullus' triumph,
and died two years later in Italy.

This was the end of Macedonia as a national state: the Antigonid dynasty was dethroned, and the country divided into four
republics between which no political or economic intercourse
was permitted.

CHAPTER FIVE

The Greek Kings of Bactria and India

Until comparatively recently the very notion of Greek kings of Bactria and especially of India would have been a fanciful one. There is a verse in Chaucer from 'The Knight's Tale':

> With Arcite, in stories as men find
> The grete Emetrius, the King of Inde,
> Upon a steede bay, trapped in steele,
> Covered with clothe of gold, diapered wele
> Came riding like the God of Armes, Mars.

There is an account of the siege of Bactra by Antiochus the Great (p. 235) and mention of the Eucratides who 'ruled the thousand cities of Bactria'; little more.

Yet we now know that commencing with Diodotus in about 250 BC and ending with Hermaeus some two centuries later, more than forty Greek monarchs, in kingdoms large and small, ruled and held court there. Their conquests reached from Bactria northward over the Oxus to the foothills of the Himalayas and south to the Indian Ocean. They went over the mountains of the Hindu Kush and across the Punjab, the Land of the Five Rivers, to Pataliputra on the Ganges (modern Patna), more than fifteen hundred miles further east.

The literary and epigraphic evidence for the rule of these Greek kings of Bactria and India is scant. Greek writers ignored or were largely ignorant of their distant kinsmen. There are fragmentary references, but nothing that can be called a history or even an attempt at one.

There is little trace in Bactria or India of Greek rule there. French archaeologists have recently uncovered the site of a Greek city in northern Bactria, the first discovery of its kind. In his recent book, *Flames over Persepolis*, Sir Mortimer Wheeler describes and illustrates this find. An outpost at the north-east gateway into Bactria, the as yet unnamed city is situated at the confluence of the river Oxus and a tributary stream called the Kikcha, near a village called Ai Khanum (Lady Moon). The oblong gridiron plan of the streets, with a broad avenue running down the centre, is similar to that of many Hellenistic cities, and the foundations of public buildings and columns, capitals, sculpture and inscriptions have been uncovered.

There is an inscription of King Menander (p. 245) at Bajur and another relating to King Antialcidas at Besnagar. In Indian literature there is the *Melinda-panha* (Tales of Melinda) which is an account of a discussion between King Menander and a Buddhist sage who converts him. There is a story in the *Yuga Purana*, part of a larger work on astrology, which describes the march of the Greeks on Pataliputra and of how they were compelled to abandon their conquest of this great city. There is the often quite beautiful sculpture of Gandhara which shows much Graeco-Roman influence; and there are the coins.

The discovery of these Greek kings of the East is in fact almost wholly a numismatic one, for most of our knowledge of Greek Bactria and India derives directly from the coins which they issued. Here are their portraits, often striking ones, their names, their titles and their emblems.

These coins first came to notice in 1733, when Theophilus Bayer published in St Petersberg a treatise in Latin describing and illustrating a coin of Eucratides of Bactria. He proposed that this was the Eucratides recorded in the history of the Seleucids, and he also showed a coin of Menander, though wrongly attributing it to Theodotus.

The interest of western scholars and numismatists during the decades following was maintained by a trickle of such coins coming from Russia and Persia, and from time to time papers were read before learned societies. In 1835 and 1836, about a hundred years after Bayer's publication, James Prinsep published a description of a number of Graeco-Bactrian and Indo-Greek coins. Three years later the American Charles Masson published part of his large collection of these coins, illustrated with five plates. By 1838 Prinsep had recognized sixteen of the thirty-three letters of the Kharoshti script on the reverses of most of these coins. The obverse legends were usually in Greek.

In 1835 Sir Alexander Cunningham, later Director of Archaeology in Bengal, published an article on Indo-Greek coins in the *Journal of the Asiatic Society of Bengal*; his *Coins of Alexander's Successors in the East* was published in 1884. His collection of these coins went to the British Museum, and comprised most of the coins in the Museum's catalogue of

The Greek and Scythic Kings of Bactria and India by Percy Gardner, dated 1886. In 1914 there appeared a catalogue of the Indo-Greek coins in the collection of the Punjab Museum, Lahore, by R. B. Whitehead. Then, in 1933, W. W. Tarn published *The Greeks in Bactria and India*, a full and detailed history which in substantial part rests on the evidence of the coins. Necessarily, Tarn theorizes much. Many of his conclusions have been challenged, notably by A. K. Narain in *The Indo-Greeks*, 1957.

But despite uncertainties and contradictions the account of the rise and fall, the triumphs and defeats, of the Greeks who were the heirs to Alexander's conquest of the farther east is a fascinating one, a most brave and romantic story.

There is much overlapping in time and place among the three dynasties of the Greek kings of Bactria and of India, so that in order to make a reasonably plain tale for the general reader this account is given in two parts, 'The Greek Kings of Bactria' and 'The Greek Kings of India', rather than as a continuous and intermingled narrative. Dating the Indo-Greek kings is a chancy business. Percy Gardner in 1886, W. W. Tarn in 1933, A. K. Narain in 1957, all differ, often widely. Illustrating these uncertainties, A. N. Lahiri's *Corpus of Indo-Greek Coins* published in 1964 gives no dates at all. The dates given here are largely those of A. K. Narain.

BACTRIA

The Kingdom of Bactria was that reach of the Iranian plateau (now part of Afghanistan) which is bounded to the south and east by the Hindu Kush mountains and on the north by the Oxus river. Its western frontier was the river Arius, beyond which lay Parthia. Called the 'Jewel of Iran', Bactria was a rich country of high valleys where, as in Babylonia, a network of irrigation canals watered a fertile soil. The Iranian nobility in their castles were the landowners, and it was they who supplied the cavalry for which Bactria was famous. The capital city, Bactra, was called 'The Paradise of the Earth', 'The Mother of Cities'. It was the traditional home of Zoroastrianism.

Greek rule in Bactria commenced with the arrival of Alexander the Great in 329 BC but Greeks were there more than two hundred years before. They had come in the service of the Persians as artisans, administrators and merchants, and especially as mercenaries. The Greeks were first-rate fighting men who hired themselves out to all who could pay. There were Greeks in the army of Xerxes when he invaded Greece in 480 BC and the *Anabasis* of Xenophon is the account of the homeward march of ten thousand of such mercenaries, recruited into the army of Cyrus the Younger for his unsuccessful rebellion against Artaxerxes II in 401 BC. Rather than make the long march home to an uncertain welcome and a chancy future, some of these time-expired soldiers elected to settle among the Persians, especially in Bactria and the countries around. They took native wives, but continued to cherish a strong sense of their Greek identity.

In the Swat valley north of Bactria, Alexander was welcomed by the people of a town called Nysa who claimed descent from the soldiers of the god Dionysus, the mythical conqueror of India. According to Arrian they entertained him with a ten-day Bacchanalia, and gave Alexander three hundred cavalrymen for his army. Probably their ancestors were such time-expired soldiers, settled there by the Persians. Grouped in small townships, these Greek fighting men were excellent frontier guards against the northern nomads.

Alexander took Bactria and its capital city against little opposition, and after much fighting against the hill tribes to the north in the summer of 327 BC, he marched his army over the passes of the Hindu Kush into India. To guard his rear he left in Bactria a garrison of 3000 cavalry and 10,000 foot, mostly Greek mercenaries. When Alexander died in Babylon four years later these Greek soldiers wanted to go home, and revolted against their Macedonian officers. The revolt was crushed and many of them were killed, but there remained in Bactria a large number of Greeks, soldiers and others, who became the foundation of the future Graeco-Bactrian kingdom.

When in 312 BC Seleucus Nicator came into control of the eastern satrapies (p. 184) he continued the practice of settling Greeks in Bactria, so that within a couple of generations that country was truly a Graeco-Bactrian state. So much so that Seleucus, himself a Macedonian, appointed a Greek general as his satrap there, as did his son and grandson, Antiochus I and Antiochus II.

DIODOTUS I AND DIODOTUS II 256–235 BC

The first Greek king of Bactria was an officer of mercenaries named Diodotus, who was appointed satrap of the country by Antiochus I and of whose origins nothing is known except that he was a Greek. Diodotus then set himself up as an inde-

129, 133

pendent monarch during the time when his then overlord, Antiochus II, was at war with Egypt.

Bactria had been a satrapy of the Seleucid empire since the days of Seleucus Nicator, but by this time there would have been little loyalty to the Seleucids in distant Antioch among the Greeks or the Iranian landowners, who probably regarded them as little more than receivers of tribute for which they got little or nothing in return. Bactria was a frontier state, under constant threat from the northern nomads against whom they and the Greeks were left to make their own defence.

Diodotus made no sudden revolt; there was no proclamation or waving of banners; only a gradual withdrawal from the Seleucid authority and first a reduction and then a cessation of tribute payments. Parthia also revolted about this time, and it is a measure of Antiochus' weakness that there is no record of action against either rebellion. Instead, a face-saving alliance was made when, in about 247 BC, Antiochus gave one of his sisters as wife to Diodotus, hoping perhaps to persuade where he could not command.

129
130

The coins show how gradual Diodotus' revolt was; first come those with his own portrait in place of Antiochus, but with Antiochus' name still on the reverse. Coins with 'of King Diodotus' on the reverse come next, and lastly those with the title of Soter (Saviour) added. Probably these last were issued by Diodotus II.

Diodotus died in about 235 BC after a long and successful career. His son and successor, Diodotus II, was not a child of the Seleucid princess – he would have been too young. Little is known of his reign except that he reversed his father's policy of hostility to his Parthian neighbours, a move which caused his downfall and death at the hands of the man who became King Euthydemus I.

EUTHYDEMUS I *c.* 235–200 BC

Euthydemus was a Greek from Magnesia in Asia Minor, an army officer commanding one of Bactria's northern satrapies;

131, 134

his coin portraits show an able and forceful face. It is noteworthy that in a time when few kings lasted long he appears to have reigned for some thirty-five years.

He came into power in the following circumstances. After the death of Diodotus I his son, Diodotus II, preferring peace, made a treaty of amity with the Parthians, Bactria's western neighbours and the traditional enemies of the Iranian people.

The army however became dissatisfied with a king who was content merely to hold his inheritance, while at Bactra the widow of Diodotus I had married her daughter by him to the promising young general Euthydemus.

After a time unrest in the army, the disaffection of the native Iranian chieftains and palace intrigue flared into open revolt. It was led by Euthydemus, who killed Diodotus II and seized the throne to become the founder of the second dynasty of the Greek kings of the Farther East.

Little is known of his reign, but the character and capacity of Euthydemus is illustrated in Polybius' account of the siege of Bactra by Antiochus the Great, who in about 210 BC had set out to emulate Alexander the Great and march to the conquest of India (p. 28).

After subduing Parthia in about 208 BC, Antiochus appeared in battle array at the river Arius, the western boundary of Bactria. Euthydemus stood to meet him on the river's eastern bank with an army which included a strong contingent of war elephants and 10,000 cavalry. It is a measure of Bactria's prosperity under Euthydemus that such a great force of armed horsemen should be available to him.

In a surprise move Antiochus and part of his army crossed the river during the night and Euthydemus retreated to Bactra, his capital city, which had been fortified and provisioned for a long siege. For two years Antiochus invested it in vain. By then Euthydemus' supplies were running low but he knew that Antiochus' soldiers were becoming intractable by reason of long idleness and he entered into negotiation through, among others, a certain Teleas, a fellow Magnesian in Antiochus' entourage. Polybius (XI, 34) gives us the details:

'For Euthydemus himself was a native of Magnesia, and he now, in defending himself to Teleas, said that Antiochus was not justified in attempting to deprive him of his kingdom, as he himself had never revolted against the king, but after others had revolted he had possessed himself of the throne of Bactria by destroying their descendants. After speaking at some length in the same sense he begged Teleas to mediate between them in a friendly manner and to bring about a reconciliation, entreating Antiochus not to grudge him the name and state of king, as if he did not yield to his request, neither of them would be safe; for considerable hordes of Nomads were approaching, and this was not only a grave danger to both of them, but if they consented to admit them, the country would certainly relapse into barbarism. After speaking thus he dispatched Teleas to Antiochus. The king, who had long been on the look-out for a solution of the question when he received Teleas' report, gladly consented to an accommodation owing to the reasons above stated. Teleas went backwards and forwards more than once to both kings, and finally Euthydemus sent off his son Demetrius to ratify the agreement. Antiochus, on receiving the young man and judging him from his appearance, conversation, and dignity of bearing to be worthy of royal rank, in the first place promised to give him one of his daughters in marriage and next gave permission to his father to style himself king. After making a written treaty concerning other points and entering into a sworn alliance, Antiochus took his departure, serving out generous rations of corn to his troops and adding to his own the elephants belonging to Euthydemus.'

It is uncertain whether Demetrius ever got his promised Seleucid princess.

DEMETRIUS I *c.* 200–185 BC

135, 141

152, 155

Just when Euthydemus died is unknown. When his son Demetrius succeeded to the throne he was secure in a strong Bactria, with a well-trained and large army ready-to-hand for conquest. His portrait coins show him strong and stern-faced, wearing the elephant-scalp head-dress of a conqueror of India, a worthy successor to Alexander the Great. Now that the Treaty of Apamea (p. 203) had so weakened the Seleucid power as to remove any threat from that quarter, Demetrius struck north and west. Before long he was in possession of the satrapies to the south-west and west of the Caspian sea, of Ferghana and Margiana, and also some of the Parthian satrapies.

But it was to the east that the great prizes lay. Bactria was on the main trade route to India, whence from the time of Darius I travellers and merchants had brought back tales of the great cities of the Punjab and of the Ganges, a mightier river yet than the Indus or the Nile. Meanwhile the empire of Chandragupta (p. 241) and Asoka had fallen apart into the hands of many smaller and weaker kings. Demetrius began probing over the passes of the Hindu Kush into Gandhara and the Punjab.

The Hindu Kush – Paropamisadae to the Greeks – is a five-hundred-mile-long south-westerly spur of the Himalaya mountains which divide India from Tibet. Its width varies from less than fifty to over a hundred miles, and several of its peaks rise over 24,000 feet above sea level. To the west the mountains level out to the high plateau which is Afghanistan, of which Bactria was the northern part. Today much of this area is desert but it was then a fertile land, watered by the rivers which rose amid the snow and ice of the mountains. In these mountains also was mined the silver which supplied the plentiful coinage of the Bactrian kings.

There are no dates for the initial phase of Demetrius' invasion of India. First would come the subduing of the hill tribes within the Hindu Kush and the establishment of forward bases. Then scouting raids, followed by heavier incursions into Gandhara and the taking of Pushklavati, its principal city, and at last the march into Taxila in the Punjab. All this would have been spread over several years. The early organization may well have been the work of Euthydemus, whose coins show him as a heavy and aging man; the field commander was Demetrius.

134

To govern Bactria during his absence, Demetrius had left his eldest son, Euthydemus II, to rule there as joint-king. His second son, Demetrius II, was set up as a subordinate king to govern the Paropamisadae and the country up to the Indus, which would include Gandhara. The story is now best continued under the Greek kings of India (pp. 240 ff.).

137, 142

ANTIMACHUS I *c.* 190–180 BC
The portrait coins of Antimachus rank with the best in the gallery of Hellenistic coin portraiture; they appear to be the work of the same considerable artist who was responsible for those of Euthydemus I and Demetrius I. Antimachus, with his odd flat hat – the Macedonian *kausia* – and his mouth in a wry half smile, on the reverse of his coins calls himself Theos – God. A little later Antiochus IV of Syria called himself Epiphanes – God made manifest. But unlike him, Antimachus appears to be a man of few illusions, one who would have little belief in the divinity of kings and certainly not of Bactrian ones. Rather he would realize how much chance had gone into setting him in his high and precarious state.

139, 143

Antimachus' origins are uncertain, he may have been a son of Euthydemus and younger brother of Demetrius I. He appears to have ruled for a decade or so north and east of Bactria, in Sogdiana across the Oxus river, and in Margiana. The Poseidon on the reverse of his coins perhaps refers to a naval victory against the Sacas, fought on the Oxus river, and after the death of Demetrius I he appears to have held part of the Paropamisadae. All this is based on the find-spots of his coins. His period of rule is given as five years or so on either side of 187 BC

EUCRATIDES I *c.* 171–155 BC

146, 149

Eucratides was the founder of the third dynasty of the Greek kings of Bactria and, unlike Diodotus and Euthydemus, something is known of his antecedents. Late in his career he struck commemorative portrait coins of his parents, Heliocles and Laodice. Laodice wears the royal diadem; she may have been a grand-daughter or daughter of Euthydemus; Heliocles was a commoner, probably a satrap of one of Bactria's provinces. Meanwhile, judging from Eucratides' own portrait coins, he does appear to have been a formidable person in his own right.

144, 147, 148

His bronze cavalry helmet is reminiscent of the Anglo-Indian solar topee.

Whether it was his own ambitions or those of Antiochus IV that set him off, some time about 176 BC Eucratides appeared in Bactria with a small force and, perhaps with the aid of an element still loyal to the Diodotids or even to the Seleucids, he raised a revolt against the Euthydemids. Demetrius at the time was campaigning in India. There were years of intermittent fighting and there is a reference to Eucratides escaping from a besieged fortress. Finally the revolt became a civil war in which Eucratides triumphed. It is assumed that Demetrius I was killed by Eucratides as he hurried back to fight this usurper, and his son Euthydemus II also disappears at this time. The life expectancy of a defeated monarch, and of his relatives for that matter, was short.

Having established himself as king of 'The Thousand Cities of Bactria' and with the same passion for conquest that was the *raison d'être* of most ancient monarchs, Eucratides set out to enlarge his kingdom. During the fifteen years of his reign he conquered across the Hindu Kush following in the steps of Demetrius I, and south into Arachosia. There is record of one heavy defeat at the hands of Mithradates I of Parthia, so that he would appear to have fought around Bactria north, east, south and west.

'Count no man happy until you know the manner of his death', and Eucratides' death was a horrifying one. He had two sons, Plato and Heliocles, and while returning from one of his campaigns he was set upon and killed by one of them. It was thought that the murderer was the elder, Heliocles, but opinion now names Plato as the parricide. Plato seized the throne and ruled for about five years. Then, probably with the support of an anti-Parthian party or group, Heliocles rebelled and avenged his father by killing Plato. On his coins Heliocles calls himself Dikaios (the 'Just'), asserting his right to the throne and justifying his fratricide.

HELIOCLES I *c.* 155–140 BC

Heliocles was the last Greek king of Bactria and, like his father Eucratides, very much of a fighting man. The Parthians had occupied much of western Bactria during the reign of his brother Plato and Heliocles now drove them out, making the river Arius once more the country's western boundary. He stood firm against the increasing pressure of the Saca nomads on southern Sogdiana and Ferghana, as well as holding the Paropamisadae and Arachosia, conquered by Eucratides. How far east into Gandhara his writ ran is not known. His coins have been widely found, moving in trade beyond the frontiers of his rule.

150, 154

The reign of Heliocles lasted some fifteen years; his dates are given as from 155 to 140 BC. Spending much of his time outside Bactria he set up his son or brother Eucratides II as sub-king there, with the right to strike his own coinage. But the end of Greek rule in Bactria was inevitable. Over the generations the fighting strength of the Bactrian Greeks had shrunk by reason of intermarriage and the constant attrition of war, while the flow of new blood from Greece and the Greek cities of Asia Minor had been cut off by the Parthians. In about 141 BC the Saca horsemen from the northern steppes broke through in overwhelming strength. They overran Ferghana and swept down over Bactria. The army of Heliocles was destroyed and he and his son killed. The Sacas, no longer nomads, settled down in the rich lands north of the Oxus. They did not occupy Bactria itself.

There is an account of the Sacas in their new home written some twenty years later in a report to the Han emperor Wu-Ti by a Chinese diplomat and general named Chang K'ien. He had been sent by the emperor on a mission to enlist the aid of the Sacas against the Hsiung-Nu, the yet more powerful tribe which had driven the Sacas southward to Bactria. Chang K'ien reports the reply of the Sacas to his mission 'that they were tired of wandering and of fighting and wished to settle down in peace'. He also visited Bactria, which he called Ta Hia, and described it as a country of small walled townships without a central government. Apparently what Greeks had not been killed in the fighting of twenty years earlier had by now merged with and become lost in the native Iranian population.

INDIA

Demetrius I of Bactria and his son or nephew Menander were the founders of the Greek kingdoms of India. But the story begins more than a century and a half before when, in the spring of the year 326 BC, the cavalry vanguard of the army of Alexander the Great, 'a glitter of strange spears, a line of mailed men' rode over the passes of the Hindu Kush into the Punjab, the Land of the Five Rivers.

Alexander had spent the previous winter in quelling the hill tribes to the north of Bactria and, having meanwhile received reinforcements from Macedonia, he was now ready for the conquest of India. He crossed the upper Indus by a bridge of boats and marched down to Taxila, the capital of King Ambhi or Taxiles, whose kingdom included Gandhara and who earlier had sent emissaries offering submission and tribute to the great conqueror from the west. At Taxila the army rested for a time, marvelling at this strange people and their civilization; the university, where the eighteen accomplishments were studied, the 'Towers of Silence' where the dead were exposed to be eaten by vultures, the merchants and the market places.

The army now continued across the Punjab to the river Jhelum, there to meet in battle array the formidable King Porus, rival and enemy of Ambhi. His force included a large number of armoured war elephants and only after heavy losses to both sides was Porus wounded, defeated and captured. It is a measure of Alexander's generosity and statesmanship that, admiring Porus' courage and person, he reinstated him in his kingdom, making of him a warm friend and ally. And to commemorate the battle, Alexander built on its site a city which he named Alexandria Bucephala, in memory of his famous war-horse which had died on the march.

Alexander had now equalled the conquests of Cyrus the Great but his energy and ambition were as fierce as ever. At Taxila he had learned of the kingdom of Maghada and its great city of Pataliputra on the Ganges, an even mightier river than the Indus. That it was hundreds of miles farther east with an eleven days' march across intervening desert did not deter him. He wanted to explore to the world's end as well as conquer it.

Leaving the Jhelum he continued across the Punjab, his forces enlarged by contingents from those of Ambhi and Porus. But it was the time of the monsoon, with heavy rains and the rivers in flood. The army crossed the Chenab and then the Ravi, but with difficulty; there were losses by drowning and Alexander's men became discontented and apprehensive. Ever more battles to fight, more fearsome war elephants to face, no knowledge of what might lie ahead. And at the river Beas, a tributary of the most westerly of the five main rivers of the Punjab, the Macedonian veterans at last mutinied. They were tired of years of fighting and marching, they would go no farther.

It was Alexander's first real defeat, and a bitter one which he had no choice but to accept with as good grace as possible. A sacrifice to the gods was made and, of course, the omens were against a further advance. Alexander and his army turned back on the long road to Babylon, and there in the month of June in the year 323 BC he died, in the thirty-third year of his age and in the full tide of his fame and glory.

Before leaving India, Alexander founded several new cities, all Alexandrias, one of them on the Indus delta near Patala. He divided his conquests into three provinces. Gandhara and the western Punjab were put under the rule of King Ambhi with two Macedonian generals, Philip and Eudamus, as satraps or military governors. The remainder of the Punjab as far as the Jhelum river was left to the government of King Porus. Another Macedonian general, Peithon son of Agenor, was made satrap of Arachosia Seistan and the lower Indus territory. All this was in 326 BC.

The news of Alexander's death three years later brought confusion to the Greeks in India. The soldiers he had left to garrison his new cities and military posts became restive, they wanted to go home. Within a short time Peithon disappears and Eudamus, after killing King Porus to secure his corps of elephants, left India and lost his life fighting in Media. Before long this first period of Greek rule in India had come to an end.

Its close was hastened by Chandragupta Maurya, the ambitious young man who was to be the founder of the Mauryan empire and the grandfather of the great Asoka. At the time of Alexander's invasion one of the two principal states of India was the kingdom of Maghada, ruled by the Nanda dynasty whose capital was Pataliputra on the Ganges, the city Alexander

CHANDRAGUPTA
MAURYA

had been prevented from reaching by the revolt of his men at the Beas. By one account Chandragupta was said to be the illegitimate son of the reigning king; or he may have been a man of no special importance. The story goes that after an unsuccessful palace revolt Chandragupta fled to the Punjab, and there he met with Alexander and urged him to advance on Pataliputra, claiming that it was a plum ripe for the picking; instead Alexander had been compelled to turn westward.

Following the news of Alexander's death, and realizing that Greek rule in India must now weaken, Chandragupta proceeded to raise a revolt in the Punjab, calling on the people to 'cast off the yoke of servitude from their necks and slay their masters'. As the revolt proceeded and succeeded, Chandragupta raised an army and marched eastward. He reached Maghada with his force increased by the discontented he found on his way there, defeated the Nanda king and installed himself in the palace at Pataliputra as the new ruler.

Seventeen years later, in 302 BC, a second Greek army appeared in India. Seleucus Nicator came, proclaiming himself heir to the conquests of Alexander the Great. But in the western Punjab he was confronted by Chandragupta with a great army, said to have included 6000 war elephants. There was no fighting; instead a treaty of friendship between the two monarchs was signed, under the terms of which Seleucus ceded to Chandragupta the territory in India and the Kabul valley to which by now he had only nominal claim (the Paropamisadae, Aria and Arachosia, the capitals of which were respectively Kabul, Herat and Kandahar, also Gedrosia, the modern Baluchistan). In exchange he received 500 of Chandragupta's war elephants. It was a small return for his pretensions to dominion in India, but these walking tanks were a most useful tool of war. With them in the following year he joined the army of Lysimachus (p. 186) to fight the battle of Ipsus against Antigonus the One-eyed. Antigonus was defeated and killed, and Seleucus at last was secure. Also, a marriage was arranged between a daughter of Seleucus and Chandragupta, though whether this ever took place is not known. It is interesting to conjecture that Chandragupta's grandson, the great Asoka, the most revered of all Indian monarchs, may have been a descendant of such a union.

Seleucus continued his friendship with Chandragupta, maintaining a correspondence with him and for many years keeping an ambassador named Megasthenes (who had served as an officer at Kandahar) at Pataliputra. Megasthenes employed his leisure in compiling an account of India, its geography, products and political institutions, part of which survives in the form of extracts made by other authors. Seleucus' son, Antiochus I, later replaced Megasthenes with his own ambassador, Deimachos. Meanwhile Megasthenes' 'Journal' continued to be the prime authority on ancient India until the nineteenth century. He was credulous as to what he merely heard, but is to be trusted on matters which came under his own observation.

In 206 BC Antiochus the Great of Syria mounted the third Greek invasion of India. After his failure to subdue Euthydemus at Bactra (p. 235) Antiochus continued eastward into India, determined that there, unlike his great-grandfather, Seleucus Nicator, he would succeed. And in Gandhara he too was met by an Indian army, under the command of a King Sophagasenus; Tarn claims that he was a Mauryan, others that he was merely a local king. Whatever may be, he faced Antiochus with little of the power with which Chandragupta had halted that earlier invasion. For the Mauryan empire was now in decline and its western boundaries, more than a thousand miles from Pataliputra, could get little help from there. So this time also there was no fighting. Sophagasenus promised substantial tribute and meanwhile gave Antiochus provisions for his army and 50 war elephants. With these and the 200 he had received from Euthydemus, Antiochus turned south and west. He had been on campaign for three years.

DEMETRIUS I 200–185 BC

We come now to the advent in India of the Bactrian Greek king, Demetrius I and his son – or nephew, Menander. Against all imagining, almost entirely cut off from the Greek world, for more than a hundred and fifty years they and their descendants ruled in western India. They lived, spoke and thought as independent Greek kings long after Greece itself had fallen wholly under the power of Rome.

According to Megasthenes the Mauryan empire was composed of a vast number of lesser kingdoms and principalities, which could be held together only by a strong central government, firmly controlling its provincial governors. Asoka was the last strong man of that dynasty. He was succeeded by his grandsons, Dasaratha in the eastern provinces and Samprati in the western, and from then to the death of the last Mauryan king the succession is clouded. It ended in 185 BC when Brindharatha was killed by his commander-in-chief, Pushyamitra, founder of the Sunga dynasty.

Long before this the Bactrian Greeks would have known that India's western provinces were weakly held; perhaps they had broken away into independent states before Euthydemus and Demetrius had felt secure enough from Seleucid pressure to begin probing eastward. For not only would Bactria have official representatives at Pataliputra, Bactria itself was on the main trade route, 'the silk road', from India to the west and there would be a constant flow of merchants and travellers bringing news of affairs in the distant capital as well as of the intervening territories.

152, 155

In preparation for the advance into India proper Demetrius proceeded to secure the lands on his eastern boundary. There is no record of resistance as he pushed over into the Paropamisadae and down the Kabul valley by way of Ghazni to Kandahar – an Alexandria founded by that earlier invader. South of Ghazni, Demetrius too founded a city which he named Demetrias for himself; by this time Euthydemus was dead, otherwise the new city would have been named for him. Demetrius also took the province of Arachosia, though whether he went down into Sind is not known.

Turning northward – all this is a matter of years rather than any single campaign – he conquered Gandhara and the western Punjab as far as Taxila. Demetrius was now master of a great sweep of territory. However, as shown by the difficulties of the Seleucids, it is one thing to conquer and quite another to rule. But to this problem Euthydemus had found an answer. Himself a usurper and knowing how unreliable the Persian system of satraps could be, he instituted a practice of setting up sons and brothers as sub-kings in the various provinces of his kingdom. Each sub-king or joint-king was semi-independent and had the right to strike his own coinage. In the event, with the one exception of Eucratides' son Plato (p. 238), family loyalty did indeed prove strong and tenacious among the Indo-Greek kings. Demetrius' eldest son, Euthydemus II, was made joint-king of Bactria; his second son he set up as Demetrius II in Badakshan, to hold there against the Saca nomads. The two younger sons, Pantaleon and Agathocles, also as sub-kings, were given Arachosia and Seistan in the south. They would have been trained in border warfare and, possessed of adequate military forces, could be expected to hold their own there.

EUTHYDEMUS II

The coin portaits of Euthydemus II of Bactria show a gentle, un-Greek face, there is none of his father's burly aggressiveness. It may be that his mother was a daughter of the Iranian nobility rather than the Seleucid princess promised by Antiochus the Great (p. 236). In the event, like his father he proved no match for Eucratides. Demetrius II in Badakshan also vanishes before long, probably another of Eucratides' victims.

137, 142

PANTALEON *c.* 185–175 BC
AGATHOCLES *c.* 180–165 BC

Of Demetrius' two younger sons Pantaleon appears to have been the lesser; of him little but his coins remain and he probably died while still young. Agathocles was the energetic fighting man; after the death of Demetrius he moved up the Kabul valley into Gandhara, until he controlled the entire north-south reach of territory to the east of Bactria, so that Eucratides was safely contained.

156, 160

158, 161

This last triumphant survivor of Demetrius' four sons set up his capital at Taxila and to celebrate his achievements he struck a number of commemorative coins or medals of the Greek monarchs who had preceded him in Bactria and India, from Alexander the Great to Demetrius I. He also issued coins of Indian weight with his name and titles in Greek on the obverse and in Kharoshti on the reverse.

Agathocles ruled for about fifteen years and his reign appears to have been prosperous and secure. The evidence of the coins now indicates that the next ruler at Taxila was King Menander.

MENANDER *c.* 165–130 BC

Menander was far and away the most important of the Greek kings of India. A great warrior, a philosopher-king, to his Indian subjects he became a saint. When he died his ashes were shared among the principal cities of his kingdom so that each might erect a sacred monument to his honour.

Alone of the Greek kings who ruled there, Menander survives in the literature of India. The *Melinda-panha* (Tales of Melinda, meaning Menander) records a debate between the king and a Buddhist sage, Nagasena. The discussion ends with the conversion of Menander to Buddhism. His origins are in doubt. In the *Melinda-panha* he says that he was born in a hill village not far from Sakala in the eastern Punjab. He looks very like Euthydemus II, especially on his earlier coins. The dates of his rule are given as some time between 160 and 130 BC and judging from the progression from youth to middle age on his portrait coins he ruled for about thirty-five years. Like the other Greek rulers of India, Menander was a king *in* India, *not* an Indian king. Composed as it was of a vast number of petty kingships and principalities, the India of the time had little or no concept of nationhood. As to the Greeks, they were a military caste in the service of the royal family, living in amity with, but separately from, the native peoples.

Menander's empire was large, especially considering that communications were limited to the speed of a horse. He ruled the Punjab directly, with the outer provinces in the hands of sub-kings. The backbone of his power was of course the army, units of which were posted at centres of government.

164, 165, 167
162, 166
163

With the exception of a unique Attic-weight tetradrachm Menander's coinage was bi-lingual, with his name and titles in Greek on the obverse around his portrait, and in Kharoshti on the reverse around a standing Athena. The very quantity of these coins and the wide range of their find-spots reflect a busy and prosperous commerce within the empire. There was an active coastal trade and merchant vessels from India sailed to the Tigris and to Aden on the south Arabian coast. Overland there was the famous trade route from Taxila to Bactra and thence by way of the Oxus river to the Caspian, the Black Sea and Byzantium, or south-west to Antioch and the Mediterranean.

Having consolidated his conquests to the east of Bactria, Menander turned to the prize which Alexander and Demetrius had been unable to grasp, the great city of Pataliputra on the Ganges, more than seven hundred miles to the south-east. It had been the capital of Chandragupta's empire and of Asoka, but their dynasty had been ended by Pushyamatra the Nanda, himself now in old age or dead.

Megasthenes describes Pataliputra in the time of Chandragupta as a beautiful city on the river bank, nine miles long and two miles wide. In the centre was the palace of the king, within a walled garden in which peacocks flaunted beneath ornamental trees. The palace was of the grandeur of Persepolis, and its gilded columns were decorated with golden vines and silver birds. The city was protected by a massive timber wall with many towers and pierced by gates which were approached by drawbridges across a wide moat. Pataliputra was prosperous, with two and three storied houses on well laid out and clean streets, with inns and theatres and meeting houses for its guilds and religious sects. In the markets was produce of every kind, for the soil was rich and well irrigated, producing two or three crops a year.

The *Yuga Purana* (part of the *Gargi Samhita*, an astrological work) tells of Menander's advance. The 'Yavanas', as the Indians called the Greeks, appear at Mathura. Then, having conquered or made an alliance with its king, whose army joins that of Menander, the combined force continues eastward, swelled on the way by contingents of other principalities, eager for plunder. When Menander finally appears before the walls of Pataliputra, and when its inhabitants see the full glittering panoply of his great army with its war elephants, chariots and cavalry, all thought of resistance is abandoned and the city is surrendered.

With the capture of Pataliputra, Menander was master of north-east India, and despite the weakness and disunity into which the empire of Chandragupta had fallen it was an enormous triumph. But he was unable to control the troops of his Indian allies, who sacked and burned the city and then took to fighting among themselves. Menander was a wise man and a shrewd general. It is one thing to conquer, another to hold. Here he was, weeks away from his base, with a long and fragile line of communication. He turned away from the now empty prize of his conquest, to take the long road back to the Punjab.

AGATHOCLEA, STRATO I *c.* 130–75 BC AND STRATO II *c.* 90–75 BC

Menander died in about 130 BC. His heir, Strato I, was but a boy at the time, and for some years his mother, Menander's queen Agathoclea, ruled as regent. She appears to have been a strong and capable woman, for she held much of this large kingdom or empire during what must have been a difficult time. Her coinage begins with an Athena head on the obverse and an owl on the reverse. Then there is a bust of Agathoclea and a warrior, perhaps to represent the growing Strato, on the reverse. Finally there are jugate busts of Agathoclea and Strato, showing their joint rule.

168, 172

After the death of Agathoclea, Strato's coins show a stern and helmeted warrior. But it would appear that he did not inherit the quality of his parents, for his later coins show a face that sags as it ages. Then for some fifteen years in place of Strato's there appear the coins of his younger brother Apollodotus, who had ousted him. When, after the death of Apollodotus, the coins of

Strato again appear, he is shown as an old man, with his grandson, Strato II, as joint ruler.

The reader is again reminded that the coins, and the places where they have been found, are almost the sole evidence for the existence of the Indo-Greek kings and for the location of their kingdoms. None of the coins are dated and the very locale of some of the lesser kingdoms is often a matter for conjecture. Sequence of reign, who followed whom, must often depend on the analysis of hoards which turn up from time to time and on overstrikes where, through shortage of metal or a desire to obliterate a predecessor's memory, one king will restrike the coins of the king he has succeeded without entirely obliterating the original type.

APOLLODOTUS II *c.* 115–100 BC

170, 173

Apollodotus was a son of Menander and Strato's younger brother. In about 115 BC he revolted and seized the throne; there would have been ready support from the army and the native aristocracy for during Strato's first reign much of the empire had been lost or fallen away. His portrait coins show a man of strength and dignity.

Narain gives him a ten-year reign, but it may have been five or even ten years longer. He regained the Paropamisadae and Arachosia, Gandhara and parts of the eastern Punjab, also moving into Sind, well earning his title of Soter – 'Saviour'. His coins have been found plentifully in the Indus country.

It is after the death of Apollodotus that Greek rule in India can be seen coming to an end. A primary cause was that the Parthians had long ago cut off the flow of Greek mercenaries and settlers. Inevitably there had been much intermarriage with the native peoples and the Indianization of the 'Yavanas' was speeded by conversion to Buddhism, as in the case of Menander himself. Another weakness was the hazard of the succession. With the later kings especially, unless the heir designate was to the army's liking he would be promptly replaced, and thus loyalty to the dynasty greatly declined. Thus it would have been against little opposition that the Eucratids crossed over from Bactria to take the Paropamisadae, and before long Apollodotus' empire was broken up into its component parts, each ruled by one or another descendant of Diodotus, Euthydemus or Eucratides.

HERMAEUS AND CALLIOPE *c.* 75–55 BC

Some fifteen Greek kings reigned in western India during the half century following the death of Apollodotus, but they left little or no record of their rule or of the confused times in which they lived. Almost all that is known of them is gleaned from the coins they issued and their find spots. Therefore since this book is addressed to the general reader we forbear to present here what can be little more than a catalogue of hitherto almost unknown monarchs. Instead we go directly to the last of them all, Hermaeus and his queen Calliope.

Hermaeus was of the house of Eucratides, some of whose members had escaped to the mountains when the nomads had overrun Bactria about seventy years before. He was a son of Amyntas – the name is Macedonian – and came to the throne in about 75 BC; to judge by the quantity and spread of his coinage, his kingdom was substantial and prosperous. His queen Calliope who appears with him on the coin illustrated here is presumed to have been a daughter of Hippostratus, who ruled in the region of Taxila between 85 and 70 BC. She is shown wearing the royal diadem, an affirmation of her own independent royalty.

174, 178

176, 179

Shut off from the outer world, his Greek inheritance almost a legend, this last of the Greek kings of India would have kept his fortress state like some medieval baron in later Europe. All we know of the end of Hermaeus' kingdom is that his coinage ceases, and in its place appears that of the invading Saca king, Azes I.

CHAPTER SIX

The Kingdoms of Pergamum, Bithynia and Pontus

THE ATTALIDS OF PERGAMUM
PHILETAERUS 282–263 BC

The fortress city of Pergamum in Asia Minor stood on a rocky hill rising some thirteen hundred feet between two tributary streams of the Caicus river, about sixty miles north of Smyrna and twenty from the sea. It was guarded on three sides by steep slopes and on the fourth by an easily defended winding roadway and crowned by a strongly walled acropolis.

Nothing is known of early Pergamum. It was not a Greek foundation and it first comes to notice in the *Anabasis* of Xenophon – the March of the Ten Thousand. In 399 BC the remaining six thousand tired and hungry Greek mercenaries reached Pergamum, and there Gongylus, the then tyrant of Pergamum, advised his friend Xenophon to replenish his stores by raiding a neighbouring city; he himself was in short supply. Pergamum again comes into history almost a century later. After the battle of Ipsus in 301 BC (p. 147), Lysimachus of Thrace secured the Macedonian war chest, loot of Alexander's conquest of the Persian Empire, amounting to 25,000 talents, far too much to be kept in any one place. Pergamum (the name appears to mean stronghold or citadel) was in Lysimachus' territory and he placed 9000 talents of the treasure there under guard of a garrison commanded by an officer named Philetaerus, son of Attalus. And there, in this hitherto almost unknown city, Philetaerus and his successors were to rule for the next hundred and seventy years. Under them Pergamum became for a time the strongest power in Asia Minor, a rich and beautiful city standing worthily beside Antioch and Alexandria as a centre of culture in the Hellenistic world.

180, 184

Philetaerus came from the Greek city of Tius in Paphlagonia, on the south-west corner of the Propontis. It was said that he was a eunuch, having been injured in infancy, but his career as a mercenary officer in the army of Antigonus the One-eyed and the burly, aggressive head on his portrait coins bespeak a most masculine man. Perhaps the story was invented to account for his not having married or left known children – or out of malice. Lysimachus was a good judge of men. Philetaerus was dependable, a competent administrator. Despite the temptation of the vast sum in his keeping he remained firmly loyal to his master for the next almost twenty years, changing his allegiance only when his own life was endangered by the follies and intrigues of Lysimachus' old age.

At court in Lysimachia, the city in Thrace which Lysimachus had built as his capital, Philetaerus came to be known as a supporter of Agathocles, eldest son of Lysimachus and heir to the throne. Meanwhile Lysimachus' third wife, young Arsinoe of Egypt, had borne him three sons and being the woman she was there were palace intrigues. But Agathocles was an able and popular man, and as the governor of Pergamum approached his sixtieth year he would have felt secure in the indefinite continuance of his position and authority. Then in 283 BC tragedy overtook Lysimachus and his family. Agathocles and many of his friends were executed on suspicion of treason, the work of Queen Arsinoe, who was determined that *her* son should succeed to the throne. Because of his friendship with Agathocles, Philetaerus' own position was endangered, exposed to the enmity of Arsinoe and her party. Despite his almost two decades of faithful service, he could expect little support from the embittered old king.

Thus it was that he decided to change masters when, two years later, Seleucus Nicator of Syria came marching north against Lysimachus. He sent messages to Seleucus offering his support and the nine thousand talents in his keeping. The offer was welcomed, and after the defeat and death of Lysimachus in 281 BC Seleucus retained Philetaerus as governor of Pergamum and left the treasure there in his care.

A few months later all was again confusion. While on the march to Macedon, Seleucus was assassinated by Ptolemy Keraunos, brother of Lysimachus' queen, Arsinoe (p. 189). The heir to the Seleucid empire was Seleucus' son Antiochus, and he was in distant Babylonia. At a loss for a leader the army at last was prevailed on to accept Ptolemy Keraunos as king but meanwhile Asia Minor was masterless, with local rulers and the independent cities looking about for conquest, or for allies for defence.

Philetaerus was cautious. In his fortress city he was secure against immediate enemies, and Keraunos was fully occupied in Macedonia. For a sizeable payment Philetaerus secured the body of the murdered Seleucus and with due ceremony gave it to the funeral pyre, sending the ashes to Antiochus. With them went his own assurance of loyalty to the Seleucid cause and in return he was confirmed in his post. The treasure was not offered. Who now had more right to the nine thousand talents than the governor of Pergamum himself?

During the rule of Lysimachus the Pergamene mint had produced his regular silver tetradrachms with a head of Alexander on the obverse and a seated Athena reverse, but when Philetaerus went over to Seleucus the types were changed. A vivid portrait of the new overlord Seleucus now occupies the obverse, while on the reverse the name of Philetaerus accompanies the Athena of Lysimachus, tantamount almost to a declaration of independence.

50, 53

EUMENES I 263–241 BC

Philetaerus was succeeded by his nephew Eumenes, son of Eumenes of Tius. A capable and quiet man, free of the vain ambitions of many Hellenistic monarchs, he was to rule Pergamum for twenty-one years.

He moved to shed Seleucid suzerainty, to which end he made an alliance with Egypt and in response Antiochus I came up from Syria in 262 BC. There was a battle at Sardis with Eumenes the victor, and henceforth Pergamum was free and independent. Though neither he nor his uncle had assumed the title, Eumenes is reckoned the first king of Pergamum. His policy was simply to consolidate Pergamene territory and to cultivate the friendship of the neighbouring cities with help in time of famine or attack. The main danger was from the Gauls and as protection Eumenes built, or enlarged, two fortress cities peopled with his mercenaries, Philetaeria near Mount Ida to the north and Attalia on the Hermus river to the south. Meanwhile he made no bones about making payment to the Gauls to avoid their punishing raids.

The coastal town of Elea near the mouth of the Caicus river was developed as a port – Pergamum was twenty miles from the sea – and agriculture and manufacture encouraged. Slowly and quietly Eumenes continued Philetaerus' work, laying the foundations of the Pergamene state that was to become a political and cultural force in the Hellenistic world. He died in 241 BC.

ATTALUS I 241–197 BC

Like Philetaerus, Eumenes had no son to succeed him. He was
followed by a nephew or cousin named Attalus, who also was a
capable fighting man and shrewd politician. As was said of
Philip of Macedon, the Attalids bought allies and bought off
enemies when they could, and fought when they had to. They
were very good at the game.

The first third of Attalus' forty-four year reign was preoccupied with war against the Gauls and Antiochus Hierax, both
separately and together. It was a long struggle, with battles in
Lydia, Phrygia and Caria, but by 226 BC the barbarians and
Hierax had been driven out of western Asia Minor and Attalus
was hailed by the Greek cities of the coast as Soter – Saviour.
Two years later in celebration of the victory Attalus formally
assumed the diadem, proclaiming himself Attalus I, King of
Pergamum.

Pergamum was the smallest of the great Hellenistic kingdoms
though its compactness was a strength. At this time its territory
was roughly that of the satrapy of Orontes under Artaxerxes II.
Inland it covered most of ancient Mysia and along the coast
it ran from Myrina to the south of the Troad. On the north
it included the southern slopes of the range of hills called Mount
Ida, the scene of the Judgment of Paris, whose pine forests
supplied timber and pitch for shipbuilding. The core of Pergamene prosperity was the Caicus valley, agriculturally rich and
with substantial deposits of silver, some copper and a little
gold.

We cannot here attempt to describe the politics, the alliances
and intrigues of the Aegean world, torn between the Ptolemies,
the Antigonids, the Seleucids and the Greek states, with Rome,
surly and jealous, determined that no one power should become
strong enough to threaten her interests in the area.

In 202 BC Philip V of Macedon set out to take what had been
the kingdom of Lysimachus (p. 227). He put garrisons in
Lysimachia and Chalcedon and besieged and took Cius on the
Propontis. This was a direct threat to the Black Sea trade route,
vital to the corn supplies of Greece and menacing to Pergamum
and the Greek cities which were its neighbours. In the following year, despite a considerable victory over Philip's fleet by the
combined forces of Pergamum, Byzantium and Rhodes,
Attalus appealed to Rome for help. This was the forerunner of
an alliance which in the short run would bring great wealth
and power to Pergamum. But the Roman connection was to

end for Pergamum as for the lady from Niger in the limerick, 'With the smile on the face of the tiger'.

Meanwhile Attalus busied himself making alliances in Greece against Philip, and it was during a speech on the matter at Thebes that he suffered the stroke from which he died in the year 197 BC.

EUMENES II 197–160 BC

Attalus was succeeded by the eldest of his four sons, Eumenes II, an able and energetic man. Throughout his long and prosperous reign he followed his father in making and in maintaining alliances with the neighbouring Greek cities, with Rhodes, in Greece, and especially with Rome. He proved to be a good ally.

182, 185

Eumenes came to the throne in a turbulent time, with Pergamum and north-west Asia Minor beset by the ambitions of Philip V of Macedon to the west, and by Antiochus the Great from the south. It was the firm policy of Rome to oppose the aggrandisement of Macedon, Syria or Egypt, and when in 192 BC Antiochus landed an army in Greece, Eumenes gave help in driving him out. Two years later when Rome sent an army to Asia Minor against the Syrian king, Eumenes prepared its unopposed crossing of the Hellespont. At the battle of Magnesia in 190 BC, Pergamene forces helped to swing the balance against Antiochus, who was overwhelmingly defeated (p. 203).

Rome, who wanted no territory or responsibilities in Asia, evidenced her gratitude. The settlement with Antiochus required him to retire permanently beyond the Taurus mountains, and Pergamum received large areas of Seleucid territory. Thus almost overnight she was transformed from a city-state into a large and strong kingdom with a population estimated at five and a half million and an area of more than sixty-five thousand square miles. In further token of Rome's regard for him Eumenes got all the loser's war elephants and four hundred talents of cash indemnity to boot.

Thus Pergamum became quite the strongest power in Asia Minor; it was also the richest. The dynasty had been born with a silver spoon in its mouth, the treasure which Lysimachus had entrusted to Philetaerus. It did not shrink, for the Attalids loved money and were industrious in its acquisition.

Pergamum belonged to the king, who also owned large areas outside the city, and the Attalids were keenly interested in agriculture, viticulture, stockbreeding and the like. Pergamum was a fortress city, a capital city and a manufacturing city. Using much slave labour it produced all manner of woven and dyed fabrics, pottery, metalwork and perfume, and there was profitable silver mining nearby.

Before printing, the hand-copying of manuscripts was an important area of library activity. The library of Pergamum was second only to that at Alexandria, but Egypt kept a jealous monopoly of papyrus – paper. Pergamum developed the making of parchment – pergamentum – as an industry; the paged book, or codex, is said to have originated there.

The Attalids needed money, a great deal of money, to pay for mercenaries and warships, to help friends at home and to buy allies and prestige abroad, of which last the Stoa of Attalus at Athens is but one example. Above all it was spent, lavished, on Pergamum itself, which Eumenes rebuilt and beautified to be his personal immortality.

By terracing on a grand scale the old city was extended down the slope and enclosed with a new wall – at that its area was only about 225 acres. Eumenes built a gymnasium, a second agora, a beautiful theatre which is still to be seen, the famous library and, to crown all, his great Altar of Zeus. Its four-hundred-foot-long frieze is in East Berlin, though the foundations remain *in situ* at Pergamum. Sculptured in high relief, most of it is devoted to the battle of the Gods and the Giants, symbolising the victories of the Attalids over the Gauls.

Throughout his thirty-eight year reign, Eumenes was an active force for Hellenism, providing strength and protection for the Greeks of Asia Minor against the Gauls and other 'barbarians'. Also he was constant in his efforts to retain Rome's friendship, for she had come to dominate in the Aegean world. But his growing strength and his success as leader of the Greek cities fed Rome's jealousies and suspicions and once the Senate even refused him a hearing. Nevertheless, when in 172 BC Eumenes came to warn Rome against the ambitions of Perseus of Macedon he did get a warm welcome, and Pergamene troops fought with the Romans against Perseus in the war which ended at Pydna in 168 BC (p. 228).

Of the Hellenistic kings only a handful can be described in complimentary terms and few can be said to have served the cause of civilization, to have left their kingdoms the better for their reigns. Perhaps Ptolemy Soter and his son Philadelphus, Seleucus Nicator, Antigonus Gonatas, Menander in distant India; at best it is a short list. Eumenes was one of them and like

183

these others, appears to have been a most likeable man. When he died in 160 BC many would have mourned his passing.

ATTALUS II 160–138 BC

The Attalids were a loyal and affectionate family, in pleasing contrast to the Ptolemies and Seleucids who made it a practice on accession to put away any possible rival to the throne. Eumenes had three brothers, Attalus who succeeded him, Philetaerus and Athenaeus. All worked actively in his support, in the field and as his representatives abroad.

Attalus was sixty years old when he came to the throne and during his twenty-one year reign he ably maintained Pergamene strength and prestige. He was especially well-liked in Rome, though at the very beginning of his reign he risked the displeasure of the Senate through his Cappadocian policy. The Romans had permitted the division of Cappadocia between two brothers, Ariarathes V and Orophernes, but Attalus assisted his brother-in-law, Ariarathes, to drive out Orophernes and reunite his kingdom. He also tried to compel the people of Priene to restore to Ariarathes a large sum of money which Orophernes had deposited in the local temple of Athena. The people of Priene stood by their obligations to Orophernes, and were eventually rescued only by Roman intervention.

210, 211, 212

As a base and port of entry into Pamphylia on the south coast of Asia Minor he founded Attalia (modern Antalya). But there could be no thought of expansion and he was careful to do nothing without Rome's approval, where there were many who looked with greedy eyes on the wealth of Asia Minor. But the Senate remained firm in its policy not to acquire territorial responsibilities there. Attalus died in his eighty-first year, to be succeeded by his nephew of the same name.

ATTALUS III 138–133 BC

Attalus III, also a middle-aged man when he succeeded to the throne of Pergamum, was quite unlike his outgoing uncles. He appears to have been unkindly, mistrustful and aloof, and his interests were not of the state but in zoology, husbandry, metalworking and the like and he wrote a book on agriculture which was much quoted. Certainly he appears to have disliked his subjects, and they him.

After five years of otherwise unremarkable reign he died childless, and then came the astonishing news that his will bequeathed the Pergamene kingdom to Rome.

The reason for the extraordinary legacy? Perhaps it was that Attalus realized that Rome, dominant now in the Aegean as in the Mediterranean, was the only power able to enforce peace in Asia Minor when he was gone. Or perhaps he was just a little 'queer' in his admiration for her.

Certainly Rome was not prepared for the legacy. In the ensuing confusion there was a revolt by one Aristonicus, who claimed to be a son of Eumenes II by a concubine. He won support from the peasants and native tribesmen, the dispossessed of the Pergamene social order, and it was several years before he was defeated and captured by a Roman army. He was put to death and the kingdom of Pergamum became the nucleus of the Roman province of Asia.

The summer visitor to the hill of Pergamum is jostled by troops of tourists, each with its guide recounting the catalogue of the buildings that once climbed in terraces to the acropolis above. Sections of the walls of Eumenes II still stand and the theatre seating ten thousand. Of the great Altar of Zeus only the foundations remain.

Thinking of other ruins, in Italy, Sicily, Greece and Asia Minor, one marvels at the feeling for grandeur that possessed the builders of these cities. Termessus to the south soars higher in the sky, but from what history and archaeology have to tell no city in its time ever stood more beautiful than Pergamum.

THE KINGS OF BITHYNIA

The Bithynians told Herodotus that they had come from the Strymon valley in Thrace, whence they had been driven out by invading tribesmen from the north. Wandering eastward, they had crossed the Bosphorus to find at last this country of fertile valleys, forests and mountains. It was sparsely populated and against little opposition they settled there permanently. Herodotus describes the 'Bithyni' as a wild and savage people, who in battle wore fox skins on their heads and whose weapons were the javelin and the dirk.

The several petty chieftains of Bithynia were under Persian suzerainty until the invasion of Asia Minor by Alexander the Great in 334 BC. With Alexander's overthrow of the Persian Empire the country became more or less independent for he had by-passed this area; but not until about forty years later did a Bithynian chief named Zipoetes emerge strong enough to be recognized as king. He had fended off several Macedonian incursions including one by Alexander's satrap of Hellespontine

Phrygia whom he defeated and killed. Zipoetes did not strike coins and there is little other record of his reign.

NICOMEDES I c. 279–255 BC AND ZIAELAS c. 255–228 BC

186, 190

His son and successor, Nicomedes I, was the first of the dynasty to issue a coinage: the one illustrated here is characterful. On his father's death he followed the almost customary practice of killing off his several brothers, of whom only one escaped. Nicomedes was responsible for bringing into Asia Minor the dreaded Galatians or Gauls. They were of much help in his struggles to extend his territory, but a calamity for the peoples of the neighbouring states.

With the help of the Galatians and his own driving ambition Nicomedes was able to break Bithynia out of its hitherto land-locked state to the eastern coast of the Propontis, where he built a new capital for himself called Nicomedia. It was planned as a Greek city and when later it became the capital of the Roman province of Bithynia, Nicomedia was described as 'comparing in greatness to Rome, Alexandria and Antioch'. It survives as Izmid at the head of the Gulf of that name. Nicomedes was a philhellene and he and his successor Ziaelas let it be known that Greek settlers, mariners and merchants were welcome in Bithynia and assured of safety there.

Little is known of Ziaelas. He had been disinherited in favour of a half-brother, but secured the throne with the help of the king of Armenia and of Galatians, who in the end murdered him. He did not strike silver coins.

PRUSIAS I 228–185 BC

188, 191

Nicomedes' grandson Prusias had a long reign. His portrait coins show a man of intelligence and sensibility, who like his grandfather worked unceasingly to extend and to strengthen his kingdom. But whatever the ambitions of her kings, politi-cally and geographically Bithynia was hemmed in between the stronger powers of Pergamum to the west, Pontus on the east and the Seleucids to the south. Only in alliance with one or the other could she hope to survive, while after the battle of Magnesia (p. 203) all three were in fact client states of Rome, jealous and overbearing.

Prusias sided with Philip V of Macedon in the First Mace-donian War, aiding him with ships so as to prevent Rome and her ally Pergamum from carrying on war at sea against Philip. In return Philip later presented Prusias with two cities on the

Propontis, Cius and Myrleia, but first he sacked them and sold their inhabitants into slavery.

Prusias did expand by taking the Greek coastal cities along the Propontis from the Bosphorus east to the Rhyndacus river, which was his western boundary, and along the Black Sea to Heraclea, which strong city he failed to take only because of the accident of a broken leg, though he did secure possession of Heraclea's important territories around the city. And when after Magnesia Rome declared the freedom of all the Greek cities, Prusias yet held on to his gains.

Bithynia was now a rich and prosperous country, with an area of about 18,000 square miles. There was much fertile agricultural land and forests which provided timber and pitch for shipping. The coastal towns harvested the rich tunny fishing, especially of the Black Sea, salting and packing the catch for export. There was also a considerable transit trade, especially at Nicomedia which was at the head of the main land route from Pontus and Armenia. Next in importance to Nicomedia was Nicaea at the end of Lake Ascania, noted chiefly at this time for the fertility of its surrounding plain and its silk production. Later the city became famous for the Council of Nicaea convoked by Constantine the Great in 325 BC.

The Hellenistic kings busily founded and refounded cities, especially capital cities bearing their own names; this was immortality. Prusias was no exception, and the foundation walls of the citadel of his city of Prusa may still be seen on a height above the large modern city of Bursa. A collection of several hundred ancient coins is displayed in a small museum on the site but, oddly enough, at the time of writing there were none to be seen of Prusias, the founder of the city, or indeed of any of the Bithynian kings.

It was said that the great Carthaginian general Hannibal selected the site of Prusa. Despite his services to Carthage, of which he was then Suffete (head of state), in 202 BC Hannibal had been driven to flight; his enemies had spread tales in Rome that he was plotting with Antiochus III of Syria to mount an invasion of Italy, and Rome demanded his extradition. Hannibal made his way to Antiochus' headquarters at Ephesus where he was welcomed and, during his war with Rome, given a sea command. One of the terms of the peace imposed by Rome on Antiochus after his defeat at Magnesia (p. 203) was that Hannibal be handed over to her. But he again escaped and after some years of wandering came to Prusias in Bithynia, who warmly received him and during his war with Eumenes II of Pergamum gave him command of his fleet. Prusias lost his land battles, but Hannibal evened the score with a decisive victory at sea.

At last, in his sixty-fourth year, worn out by a lifetime of war and wandering, Hannibal retired to a country house near a village called Libyssa, on the north coast of the Gulf of Izmid a few miles from Nicomedia. But Rome would not permit 'the one man she had ever feared' to end his days in peace. In 183 BC T. Quinctius Flamininus, the victor over Philip V of Macedon at Cynoscephalae (p. 227) came to demand that Hannibal be handed over to Rome's vengeance, and Prusias prepared to comply. The story goes that hearing a noise in the night Hannibal sent a slave to enquire the cause, who returned to report that the house was surrounded with soldiers. Rather than be taken Hannibal drank the poison which he habitually had by him for some such eventuality. 'Let us ease' he said 'the Romans of their continual dread and care, who think it long and tedious to await the death of a hated old man' – thus reported Plutarch.

There is question as to dates and which Prusias was involved in this episode. Prusias I was an honourable and courageous man who would surely have helped Hannibal to escape, rather than send soldiers in the night to seize him, while the accession date of the pusillanimous Prusias II is sometimes given as 185 BC, two years before Hannibal's suicide. Prusias II, sycophant of Rome as he was, might well have done this.

About fifty kilometres from Istanbul on the road to Izmid a sign on the right, in English and Turkish, points to 'Hannibal's Grave', and the track to it winds uphill past a brickyard to a grassy field on a bluff overlooking the Sea of Marmora. It is a lovely open space of about four acres, dotted with gorse and fringed in part with tall cypress trees. The only evidence of a grave or memorial is a single shaft of marble (in September 1970) about six feet long, perhaps the lintel of a doorway or window of a temple or tomb. It lies tilted, half buried, as if left behind when the stones of the rest of the structure were carted away.

It is all a lovely open space, 'under the wide and starry sky' and, whether or not Hannibal's bones do lie there, a fit resting place for a great man.

PRUSIAS II 185–149 BC

The portrait coins of Prusias II appear to confirm his reputation. *192, 196*
Polybius describes him as a poor creature, alien alike to war and
the arts. It says much for the belief in the divinity of kings that
this one survived on the throne for more than three decades.

Prusias married his cousin, the sister of Perseus of Macedon,
but when it came to war between Macedonia and Rome family
loyalty gave way to policy and Prusias sent five warships to aid
the Roman fleet in harassing the cities of the Macedonian coast.
When Perseus had been defeated Prusias journeyed to Rome
to present in person his congratulations to the Senate, humbly,
'as a freedman of Rome'.

Bithynia's nearest enemy and her rival for favour at Rome
was Pergamum, and Prusias continually intrigued against her.
Soon after the accession of Attalus II (p. 256) Prusias, with the
aid of the Galatians, invaded Pergamene territory, ravaging
the countryside and destroying the temples. Attalus withdrew
within his fortress walls and appealed to Rome for help, who
sent commissioners to enforce a peace. Prusias was compelled
to withdraw, to hand over twenty warships to Pergamum, to
pay one hundred talents for the damage he had done and also
to pay a war indemnity of five hundred talents in twenty annual
instalments.

He followed the policy of most Hellenistic kings in putting
himself forward as a warm friend of Greek culture, and there
is note of his gifts to the temple of Apollo at Didyma and that
in gratitude for his help the Aetolians had erected a statue in his
honour at Delphi. But he was disliked and hated by his subjects,
both for his person and his fawning subservience to Rome,
and in 149 BC he came to a bad end.

NICOMEDES II EPIPHANES 149–128 BC

Nicomedes, the elder son of Prusias, and by now a man in his *194, 197*
forties stationed in Rome as his father's representative became
impatient of his father's longevity. Perhaps it was at the instigation of Attalus II, Prusias' old enemy, that he decided to seize
the throne. Attalus supplied the troops and accompanied the
expedition. At the news of Nicomedes' arrival the army and the
people rose in revolt and the old king fled for sanctuary to the
temple of Zeus at Nicomedia. There, at the very altar of the
god, he was struck down and killed.

Despite his parricide and sacrilege Nicomedes took to himself
the title of Epiphanes (the god manifest), but, unlike his father,

he came to enjoy a good reputation among his subjects and with the Romans whom he was always ready to serve, as for instance in giving prompt help in quelling the revolt of Aristonicus (p. 257). He was honoured by the Ionian Federation, and the city of Priene in gratitude for his aid founded a cult for his worship, complete with priest and sacrifice. He loved art, or at least the repute which the possession of outstanding works of art gives.

In all, his reign which had begun so badly proved to be peaceful and prosperous.

NICOMEDES III EUERGETES 128–94 BC

At the time of the accession of Nicomedes III, Bithynia was no longer an independent state; in foreign affairs certainly she was no more than a client of Rome. Her kings rather were magnates, riding on the backs of a largely serf population and making great profits from the agriculture, commerce and industry of the country, which was a property rather than a kingdom. They were wealthy, as illustrated by the incident of Nicomedes sending off his son Socrates, born of a concubine named Hagne, to the mother's native town of Cyzicus, giving her 500 talents to set her up there. This of course to ensure the boy's safety when in due time his elder brother came to the throne.

The Bithynian kings were also large scale moneylenders, one instance being the loan to the city of Cnidus, which Nicomedes III offered to cancel in exchange for the famous statue of Aphrodite by Praxiteles – an offer that was declined. Nicomedia achieved a reputation as a city of great luxury and vice, so great that one of the aspersions cast on the character of Julius Caesar was that as a young man he had spent some months there. They were slave traders, supplying the market from among their own subjects, but in this field of endeavour there was competition. The defeat of Aristonicus' revolt (p. 257) in neighbouring Pergamum had produced large numbers of slaves for Rome and later the 'publicani' (the tax farmers) of the new Roman province of Asia, into which Pergamum was incorporated, entered into the slave trade of the area. They were so active and ruthless that when during the war against the Cimbri in southern France the Roman general Marius asked Nicomedes for aid with troops, he answered bitterly that he had none to send 'since the majority of his subjects had been carried off by the publicani and sold into slavery'. Rostovtzeff, however, is of the opinion that it was Bithynia's hostile neighbours, Galatia and Pontus, who slave raided into Bithynia 'under the benevolent eye of the Roman governor of Asia and with the co-operation of the publicani'.

By this time slaving was almost an industry. The supply was mostly in the hands of pirates, based on the Cilician coast. Because neither the Seleucids, the Ptolemies or Rhodes were strong enough to keep them down they raided from Cyrene to Cyprus, from the Peloponnese to the coasts of Asia Minor and the islands of the Aegean almost with impunity. The main market was on the island of Delos and often thousands of slaves were auctioned off in a day. There was a frequent glut, dealers and suppliers complaining of the low prices these goods brought. At last the Senate acted. A decree was passed that all enslaved allies of free birth should be set free, and the Roman governors were enjoined to carry it out in their provinces.

Nicomedes died in 94 BC.

NICOMEDES IV 94–74 BC

Nicomedes IV was the last king of Bithynia. His character held none of the iron of the early Bithynian kings and he was quite unable to stand up to his eastern neighbour, Mithradates VI of Pontus, and certainly not to Rome, whose Province of Asia was his western boundary. He was reputed to be self indulgent and vicious.

Soon after Nicomedes' accession, and probably at the instigation of Mithradates, his half-brother Socrates presented himself at Rome asserting that he and not Nicomedes should be king of Bithynia. The Senate rejected him and reconfirmed Nicomedes, and Socrates went off to Pontus. There Mithradates supplied him with the troops for a successful invasion of Bithynia and Nicomedes fled for his life. Whereupon Rome intervened, ordering the Pontic troops out of Bithynia and Nicomedes back on his throne. Mithradates had little option but to comply, withdrawing his troops and, for good measure, killing off Socrates.

Some years later, under Roman orders, Nicomedes mounted an invasion of Pontus but was disastrously defeated and driven out of that country and his own. He escaped to Italy, to be restored to his dignities in about 85 BC by Sulla.

During the later years of his reign Nicomedes was no more than a cringing vassal of Rome, his country impoverished and himself deeply in debt. He had no legitimate male heir and came to realize that there could be no prospect ever of an independent

Bithynia, and that only Roman power could save his people from the savagery of Mithradates. And so, following the precedent set by Attalus III of Pergamum in 133 BC and Ptolemy Apion of Cyrene in 96 BC, at his death he willed his country to Rome. The Senate accepted the bequest and Marcus Aurelius Cotta, the consul of 74 BC, was sent out to organize Bithynia as another Roman province,. with Nicomedia as its capital.

THE KINGDOM OF PONTUS

Most of Asia Minor is a high plateau, hot and dry in summer and bitterly cold in winter. To the north where the plateau descends to the Pontic or Black Sea coast there are ranges of mountains and wooded hills, between which are fertile valleys and plains, rivers and lakes. It is a peculiarity of these mountain ranges and thus of their rivers and valleys that most of them run parallel to the coast and that the rivers are navigable for only a short distance from the sea. The principal rivers are the Halys to the west, the Lycus, the Iris and the Thermodon, the river of the Amazons. This is the country which became the kingdom of Pontus or, more correctly, Cappadocia-on-the-Pontus.

During the second millennium BC this territory had been the western heartland of the Hittite empire. It then fell to the Phrygians, and with the rise to power of Cyrus the Great (559–529 BC) became a Persian satrapy. When Alexander the Great invaded Asia Minor in 334 BC Pontus was governed by a Persian satrap named Ariarathes, whose palace and garrison were at Gaziura on the Iris river. Alexander's line of march bypassed this northern territory which, with the downfall of the Persian empire, became in some measure independent.

The native inhabitants were mainly of Hittite stock; the Greeks called them Leucosyri, white Syrians. They were agriculturists, living in villages and firmly retaining their ancient culture and religion. They worked the land in the service of their Persian overlords, who lived as feudal barons in fortress castles strategically placed about the country. In eastern Pontus these were tribes of non-Hittite origin, including the metalworking Chalybes, said to descend from the Chaldeans. Pontus was landlocked for more than a century after its founding as an independent kingdom, cut off from the Black Sea coast by the Greek cities which had been established there during the eighth and seventh centuries BC.

Amasia on the Iris river was the capital of the early Pontic kings. The Roman historian Strabo was born there, and here is his almost lyrical description of the plain of Themiscyra at the mouth of the same river:

> 'The plain in question is always moist and covered with grass and can support herds of cattle and horses alike and admits of the sowing of millet seed and sorghum seeds in great, or rather unlimited quantities. Indeed their plenty of water off-sets any drought, so that no famine comes down on these people, never once, and the country along the mountain yields so much fruit, apples and nuts, that those who go out to the forest at any time in the year get an abundant supply, and numerous also are the catches of wild animals, because of the good yield of food.'

The mineral wealth of Pontus was as important as its agriculture. In the eastern part of the country there were deposits of copper, silver and especially of easily worked iron ore. The very invention of iron and steel was ascribed to the Chalybes tribe of the region. In remote antiquity these people had taken to hammering with stones the lumps of native copper lying about on the plateau, first into sheets and then into weapons and utensils. When this supply ran out they took to melting the copper out of the rocks in which they found it, also above ground. Later tin was added to make the much harder bronze. Then came the unknown genius who experimented with the melting of other and darker ores, to find iron. For hundreds of years caravans carried these metals east and south, to Assyria and Babylonia, to Phoenicia and Egypt and westward to the Aegean. The city of Sinope on the south coast of the Black Sea was founded from Miletus around the mid-eighth century BC to handle this trade in metals, the export of tunny fish and Pontic grain. A century later Sinope herself founded the city of Trapezus further east along the coast to deal with the traffic of the mining country itself. It was at at Trapezus that Xenophon and the remainder of the Ten Thousand at last reached *thalatta*, the sea.

Religion was strong. The temples of Ma at Comana, of Men Pharnaku at Cabeira and of Anaitis at Zela owned large areas of land and many slaves. At Comana, which was a centre for trade with Armenia, the temple was said to own six thousand slaves who worked the land and serviced the temple. The priesthoods were hereditary and powerful, the high priest at Comana being second only to the king.

The history of the Mithradatic kings of Pontus begins with a David and Jonathan story. The father of Mithradates I was a Persian nobleman, dynast of the city of Cius on the Propontis,

who together with his son was in the service of or allied to
Antigonus the One-eyed, the then lord and master of Asia
Minor (p. 138). Antigonus, who was not a trusting soul, came to
suspect both father and son of treachery and decided to put
them to death. But meanwhile Antigonus' son Demetrius and
the young Mithradates, who were of an age, had become warm
friends and Demetrius gave warning of his father's purpose.
Both fled, in different directions; the father was caught and
killed but the young Mithradates escaped to Paphlagonia where
at the fortress city of Kimiata he succeeded in establishing himself over the years as the leading chieftain of the area.

In 301 BC Antigonus was defeated and killed by Seleucus and
Lysimachus (p. 186) and with this threat gone Mithradates united
under his rule the several petty chieftains of the country, which
now became the independent kingdom of Pontus.

Asia Minor west of the Taurus went to Lysimachus of Thrace
as his share of the spoils of the victory of Ipsus, but he continued
to be preoccupied with matters nearer home and left Mithradates undisturbed. After the battle of Corupedion twenty years
later (p. 188) Seleucus Nicator sent his general Diodorus with
an army against Mithradates, who defeated and killed him.
Later, with the aid of the Galatians, he fended off an attack by
Antiochus I, Seleucus' son and successor. Mithradates did not
strike coins and he died about 265 BC.

MITHRADATES III *c.* 220–185 BC AND PHARNACES I 185–169 BC

Little is known of the early kings of Pontus and their dates are
uncertain. Mithradates I was followed by his son Ariobarzanes,
who after a ten-year reign was succeeded by his son Mithradates
II (255–220). The fourth of the line, Mithradates III, was the
first to strike portrait coins. The head is strikingly different
from the Macedonian Ptolemies and Seleucids. The kings of
Pontus claimed to be of the highest Persian nobility, descended
from Perses, the eldest of the six sons of the hero Perseus and
Andromeda. Though the reverse of the coin bears the seated
Zeus of Alexander's silver tetradrachms, it also carries the star
and crescent, the sun and moon of the Persian Ahura Mazda.

The story is that Pharnaces I 'arranged' his father's death; his
portrait does shown an ungracious and impatient face. Always
aggressive, his capture of the city of Sinope, situated about the
centre of the southern Black Sea coast, at last gave Pontus her
outlet to the sea. Sinope became the capital of the Pontic kings

198, 202

119

200, 203

(it survives today as Sinop) and they enlarged and beautified it. Pharnaces also built a new coastal city to the east, which he called Pharnacia and peopled with the inhabitants of the nearby towns of Cerasus (whence cherries) and Cotyra. He invaded Bithynia but was later driven out by a coalition of Pergamum, Cyzicus and Heraclea.

In middle age Pharnaces married Nysa, daughter of Antiochus the Great. When he died in 169 the son of this marriage was too young to rule and the throne was taken by Pharnaces' brother, who as Mithradates IV continued Pharnaces' aggressive policies. After his death in 150 Pharnaces' son succeeded him as Mithradates V. Pontus was now a rich Hellenistic state, a formal 'ally and friend' of Rome, whom she aided against Carthage in 149–146 BC.

204, 206

MITHRADATES VI EUPATOR DIONYSUS (THE GREAT) 120–63 BC

Few men have led a fuller life than Mithradates VI, the last king of Pontus. At the age of eleven his father's death left him heir to the throne, but his mother Laodice took power as regent and friends who feared for the boy's life took him to hide in the mountains. There he became a man of great hardihood, with all of his parent's passion for dominance. Seven years later and with the help of friends, or better put perhaps, of his mother's enemies, he took Sinope and imprisoned his mother, killed his younger brother and mounted the throne. He next married his full sister Laodice.

Mithradates built himself an enormous reputation for courage and athletic prowess. He was a gargantuan eater and drinker, fluent in several languages and a warm friend to Greek men of letters. Yet, despite his Philhellenism, he lived and ruled as an oriental monarch, generous to his friends and intimates but suspicious, cruel and murderous. Towards the end of his career he ordered the killing of the five hundred women of his harem to prevent them falling into the hands of his enemies. He was clever, tireless and infinitely resourceful but it was fear, not loyalty, that held his subjects to him.

207, 209

Once firmly on the throne Mithradates proceeded to the conquest of what is now the Crimea of South Russia on the north coast of the Black Sea. There were several Greek cities in the area of which Panticapaeum was made the capital and where later one of Mithradates' sons ruled as viceroy. This conquest was followed by that of Colchis on the east coast of of the Black Sea. The expeditions against the Crimea and Colchis were made under the command of Mithradates' general Diophantos, and they brought back substantial amounts of revenue and a good supply of native soldiery.

Meanwhile Mithradates was in field command of operations against his neighbours within Asia Minor, and he so encroached on the territories of Cappadocia, Galatia, Paphlagonia and Bithynia that he became altogether too strong for Rome's liking. Though all these countries of Asia Minor, including Pontus, were nominally 'allies and friends of Rome', actually they were her vassals, and when in 92 BC she ordered Mithradates to relinquish his gains he obeyed, promptly if resentfully. He was permitted to retain his conquests on the north and east of the Black Sea.

Here it must be noted that at the height of his career Mithradates fielded an army of more than 125,000 foot, several thousand horse and many scythed chariots, and his fleet was said to total four hundred men of war.

Illustrating his independence of mind, some years earlier Mithradates had set out to see for himself the state of affairs in the various parts of Asia Minor. It was a long journey and he travelled incognito, returning convinced that he would be fully able to hold his own should there come a clash with Rome.

The First Mithradatic war with Rome began in 88 BC. Mithradates easily defeated the Roman and allied forces brought against him and proceeded to take all Rome's possessions in Asia Minor. In order to commit the Greek cities of Asia Minor irrevocably against Rome he ordered a general massacre of all their Italian residents, said to number more than eighty thousand, and few cities disobeyed the order.

Then, as liberator of the Greeks, he called on mainland Greece to rise against its Roman master and in the same year, having command of the Aegean, he landed a large expeditionary force at Athens under his general Archelaus. But the Romans were better soldiers, Mithradates' generals were not good enough. With a far smaller force Sulla defeated Archelaus at Chaeronea in 86 BC and at Orchomenus a year later. He then crossed the Hellespont and Mithradates sued for peace.

Sulla's terms were not over harsh; Mithradates must evacuate Pergamum, which was now his headquarters and all his gains in Bithynia, Paphlagonia and Cappadocia. He must also pay Rome 2000 talents indemnity and hand over seventy fully equipped warships. Rome would then confirm him in his other possessions and declare him her confederate. In the following year Mithradates and Sulla met at Dardanus in the Troad. According to Plutarch, Mithradates was escorted by 20,000 foot soldiers and 6000 cavalry together with a large train of scythed chariots; Sulla had with him only four cohorts and two hundred horsemen. After long and heated discussion the terms were agreed, Mithradates handed over seventy ships of his fleet and returned to Pontus.

The Second Mithradatic war, which commenced only a year later, arose out of raids into Pontus by the Roman propraetor Murena. In 81 BC peace was re-established on the basis of the settlement at Dardanus.

The Third Mithradatic war began in 74 BC. Nicomedes IV of Bithynia (p. 263) had died childless, bequeathing his kingdom to Rome and Mithradates moved to seize Bithynia for himself. He easily defeated the first Roman force sent against him under the command of Aurelius Cotta, but Cotta's successor Lucullus drove him from Pontus to shelter with his son-in-law Tigranes of Armenia. Lucullus defeated Tigranes in 69 BC but his troops then mutinied, allowing Mithradates to reconquer Pontus and to lay about him in Bithynia and Cappadocia.

Lucullus was superseded by Pompey the Great, who three years later at Nicopolis in Pontus defeated Mithradates and compelled the surrender of Tigranes. Mithradates fled to Panticapaeum and was preparing for a new attack when his troops, led by his son Pharnaces, revolted against him. There had been too many defeats. He tried to poison himself but this failing, he ordered one of his mercenaries to run him through.

Plutarch tells how the news of the death of 'Rome's ancient and inveterate enemy' was received by Pompey's army. 'Pompey . . . told them the news of Mithradates' death, how he had put an end to his life upon the revolt of his son Pharnaces and that Pharnaces had taken all things there into his hands and possession, which he did, his letters said, in right of himself and the Romans. Upon this news the whole army, expressing their joy, as was to be expected, fell to sacrificing to the gods, and feasting as if in the person of Mithradates alone there had died many thousands of their enemies.'

CHAPTER SEVEN

The Coins of the Hellenistic Kingdoms

The royal portrait coins with which this book has been illustrated are important contemporary documents for a period from which contemporary evidence is scanty. They are our only source for the physical appearance of most of the rulers of the time; and, apart from the usually stylized features of Egyptian Pharaohs, their portraits are the first series of portraits in human history. For some rulers their coins provide the only surviving evidence that they ever existed. From the titles and from the designs which they chose for their coins we are given a glimpse of their characters and policies and of the guise in which they presented themselves to their subjects. In time these coins became the model for the coins of Imperial Rome, and through Rome for all subsequent regal coinage right up to modern times.

Hellenistic coinage itself had a long ancestry in earlier Greek coinages. The first coins of the Greek world had been minted in Asia Minor towards the end of the seventh century BC, and for long the designs stamped on them were strictly impersonal; they symbolized the continuing public authority which had issued the coins rather than the changing individuals who represented the authority from time to time. Even so mighty a potentate as the Great King of Persia himself appeared reign after reign only as a stylized royal figure carrying the weapons with which he chastised his enemies, but otherwise devoid of any individuality.

From the late sixth century, however, references to individuals begin to be included in the designs of Greek coins. Such references were at first inconspicuous – tiny changing symbols or initials which enabled the officials responsible for successive issues to be identified. As time passed such differentiating marks became more prominent and were used more regularly, but they still retained their practical function of distinguishing between successive issues and of identifying the officials responsible for their production. Indeed, the typical Greek system of government by bodies of citizens elected to office for short periods gave little scope for the glorification of individuals. In consequence it was in the peripheral areas of the Greek world, where kingship was the normal form of government, that there developed the practice of recording on coins the names and titles of individual rulers.

The governors of the western provinces of the Persian Empire also often enjoyed the status of independent monarchs, remote from the Great King at Susa, and untroubled by him so long as tribute was regularly remitted. Their security rested upon the loyalty of their armed forces, and the portrait and name of the ruler upon the coins with which the soldiers were paid reminded them where their duty lay. At first such 'portraits' were little more than idealized heads, on which a beard might indicate authority and a helmet military leadership; identity was provided by the accompanying name. Such heads differed little from the heads of gods identified by a trident or a thunderbolt. But soon these heads were given the recognizable features of individuals and true portraiture on coins was born. During the fourth century such satrapal portraits occur at a number of mints in western and southern Asia Minor; and even the Greek city of Cyzicus occasionally honoured distinguished citizens by displaying their portraits on the civic electrum coinage.

There was thus ample precedent for Alexander's use of his name and the title Basileus, 'king', upon his coinage. Whether he also followed satrapal precedent by ordering his own head to be shown on the obverse in the guise of Heracles has been much disputed. But, irrespective of Alexander's intention, there is little doubt that from soon after his death the head of Heracles upon his coinage was regarded as a portrait of Alexander himself. His silver coinage thus forms the link between the sporadic portraits of the fourth century and the regular use of portraits by the Hellenistic kings. It also established the formula of Hellenistic royal coinage: on the obverse, the king's portrait with the attributes of kingship or divinity; on the reverse, the royal name and titles framing his protecting deity.

When Alexander died in 323 BC his empire was divided among his principal officers, who at first continued to mint unaltered Alexander's imperial coinage, and so maintained for a while the fiction that they were satraps in a unified empire. In the upshot none proved strong enough to subdue the

14
49, 5, 118

6

remainder, and each in turn declared their independence – and their rivalry – by adopting the title King: Ptolemy in Egypt, Seleucus in Syria, Lysimachus in Thrace, and Demetrius in Macedon. All, except Lysimachus, replaced the head of Heracles-Alexander with their own heads wearing the royal diadem; Lysimachus alone used the posthumous portrait of Alexander to legitimize his kingship.

Though the formula of Hellenistic coinage was thus derived directly from the coinage of Alexander himself, its application varied in detail according to the needs and policies of different dynasties. In Macedonia alone the tradition of the divine head on the obverse died hard, for the Heracles of Alexander was succeeded by the Pan head of Antigonus Gonatas, the Poseidon head of Doson, and the Perseus head of Philip V – though some or all of these may have been recognized by contemporaries as bearing the features of the monarchs who issued them. Philip

127

V was the first king of Macedon to exhibit his portrait in human form unequivocally upon his coins, a step which perhaps resulted from his friendly relations with Antiochus the Great of Syria, where the numismatic portraiture of successive rulers was a long established practice. Philip's initiative in Macedonia was

128

followed by his son Perseus, who invariably placed his distinctive features upon his coinage.

Elsewhere portraiture was used in two different ways: either the constant repetition over long periods of the head of the dynasty's founder (accompanied by occasional special issues bearing the head of the current ruler), or the regular portrayal of each successive king upon his own coins. The Ptolemies and the Attalids are the principal examples of the first practice, the Seleucids and the Kings of Bactria and India of the second.

Just as Lysimachus had used the head of Alexander to legitimize his position, so his Attalid successors regularly repeated

184

the unadorned head of Philetaerus, the dynasty's founder, from reign to reign. This royal reticence is characteristic of the well-conducted Attalid family, with its regular and peaceful transference of power from one generation to the next, and an absence of usurpers and internecine feuds. But one consequence is that today, apart from Philetaerus, and a unique numismatic

185

portrait of Eumenes II, we possess no certain likenesses of Lysimachus or of most of the members of the Attalid dynasty.

Likewise in Egypt the coinage regularly displayed on the obverse increasingly unfaithful repetitions of the head of the

17

dynasty's founder, Ptolemy I, which he himself had placed on his own coinage. The deliberate monotony was accentuated by the adoption of the same name Ptolemy by every ruler in turn. Only on a few special issues, sometimes minted outside Egypt, was the portrait of the contemporary ruler used. A distinctive feature, however, of the Ptolemaic coinage is the importance accorded to the portraits and names of queens. The portrayal of queens in the other major dynasties is uncommon, and when it does occur, can often be traced to Egyptian influence; this is true of Philistis at Syracuse, and of Cleopatra Thea, almost the only woman to appear on the Syrian coinage, who was a daughter of Ptolemy VI.

20, 28, 34
46, 47

114, 115

In contrast to the Attalid and Ptolemaic dynasties, the Seleucids rejected the posthumous portrait in favour of the changing heads of each successive ruler. Their features were realistically presented with all the effects of age or changing fashion. From most of these portraits the king himself could be recognized on his public appearances, though sometimes on coins from mints remote from the capital, the features may be less distinctive because no official portrait was available for the die-sinkers to copy. The plain band of the royal diadem is usually the only adornment of these heads, but occasionally a further attribute was added. Seleucus I sprouts a discreet bull's horn, as his defeated enemy Demetrius Poliorcetes had done; the young Antiochus VI carries the rays of the sun; but such additions are rare, and for the most part the portraits speak for themselves, alone and unadorned on the obverses of the coins.

52
121
105

The Greek kingdom of Bactria had been originally a province of the Seleucid empire, and for geographical reasons its relations remained closer with the Seleucids than with the other Hellenistic kingdoms. Its coinage thus naturally followed the Seleucid model, and the long succession of portraits of rulers, many of whom are known only from their surviving coins, is its most remarkable and informative aspect. In one respect, however, the portraits of the Bactrian kings differed from those of the Seleucids. Though the latter had their wars, and some even took such titles as Nicator and Nicephorus, their world and the Greek civilization which they represented ran no risk of being submerged beneath waves of alien invaders. But the Bactrian kings were on a remote frontier, where their imported Greek civilization was maintained only precariously. Their subject populations and neighbours were not Greek, and some of them had strong and ancient cultural traditions of their own. In these conditions both individual rulers and the culture they

155
148, 149, 178
154

stood for could survive only by constant fighting, and it is for this reason that they are portrayed so often in military guise, either wearing the elephant's scalp as conqueror of India, like Demetrius I, or helmeted like Eucratides and many others, or thrusting with spear in actual battle.

The reverses contain two elements which must be treated separately – the inscription or legend, and the figured type. The legend gives the name of the ruler portrayed on the obverse, normally accompanied by the title 'King', but its message is more than a simple caption to the head on the obverse, otherwise it would more naturally accompany that head, as has been normal practice in more recent times. Moreover the use of the genitive ('of King') rather than the nominative case implies that the coin was not only issued by the authority of the king, but remained in some sense his property. This separation between head on obverse and legend on reverse remained invariable on Hellenistic coins until the Greek kings of India in the second century BC decided that it was politic to announce 151,169
169, 171, 177 their names and titles not only in Greek but in Kharoshti as well for the benefit of their predominantly Indian subjects. The need for two legends required the use of both sides of the coin, the Greek encircling the head on the obverse, leaving the reverse free for the Kharoshti text. It is worth noting that Roman practice was from the start different from the Greek, for the imperial head was surrounded by its caption, normally in the nominative case.

Hellenistic kings were usually given honorary titles such as 'Saviour' or 'Benefactor' which served to distinguish between rulers of the same name; the modern practice of distinguishing by number was not employed in the ancient world. At first these honorary titles were recorded by the coinage only on occasional special issues, but Antiochus IV of Syria (175–164 81 BC) established the fashion for including them regularly on the Syrian coinage; thereafter every king publicizes at least one honorific title on his coins. This fashion had a mixed reception in the rest of the Hellenistic world. Egypt maintained her custom of referring to each successive Ptolemy by the undifferentiated formula 'of King Ptolemy'. Elsewhere, however, in Bithynia, Pontus, Cappadocia and Bactria epithets were proclaimed and multiplied: rulers asserted their distinction (Epiphanes), their divinity (Theos), their justice (Dikaios), their piety (Eusebes), their military prowess (Nicator), their ideal family relationships (Philopator, Philometor, Philadelphos), and a number of other desirable regal qualities. The practice was eventually carried to excess by the Parthian kings (not dealt with in this book), some of whom crowded as many as five or six honorific titles onto their coins.

Before leaving this brief review of coin legends one other observation is worth making. In the whole geographical range of the Hellenistic monarchies, from Sicily to the Indus and from the Black Sea to Egypt, Greek speakers were vastly outnumbered by non-Greek; yet, with the sole exception of the Kharoshti legends of the Greek kings of India, no Hellenistic king ever addressed his coins directly to his non-Greek subjects; to name only the most obvious, Hebrew, Aramaic, Persian or Egyptian could all have been alternatives to Greek in appropriate areas. Greek language, script and iconography was universally adopted not only by dynasties of genuine Macedonian descent like the Seleucids and the Ptolemies, but also by the Pontic, the Cappadocian and the Parthian.

Finally we come to the second element of the reverses – the pictorial types, and here a word of warning is necessary. While both the portraits and the legends illustrated in this book are reasonably representative, the same is not true of the reverse types. Because of the quality of preservation and of the portraits themselves, single tetradrachms only have usually been chosen for illustration, and these can give little idea of the total iconographic range on all denominations. Nevertheless the tetradrachm was the principal standard coin of each state, and the design of its reverse, though often unchanged over long periods, can never have been pointless or left to chance; and even more obviously any departure from an established type must have been made with a purpose. Almost invariably the reverse types represented deities, or alluded to deities, but as with the other elements of the coinage, usage varied, so that each of the principal kingdoms had best be examined separately.

In Macedonia the reverse types changed from reign to reign, and each type was more or less closely connected with the ruler of the day. The naval successes of Demetrius Poliorcetes made Poseidon an obvious choice as patron. The fighting Athena, tutelary goddess of the Macedonian capital, Pella, was chosen by Antigonus Gonatas and Philip V, but Philip also had another and more personal type – the club of Heracles within the oak wreath of Zeus. The wreath alludes to the alleged descent of the Macedonian kings from Heracles. Philip's son, Perseus, modified this design by replacing the club of Heracles with an

118
120, 124

126

eagle carrying a thunderbolt, so that the whole type now re-
ferred to Zeus.

Both the Attalid and the Ptolemaic dynasties rejected the
Macedonian practice of varying the reverse type. Just as both
dynasties retained as their standard obverse types the posthumous portraits of their founders, Philetaerus and Ptolemy Soter,
so they also retained the reverse types originally associated with
those portraits. At Pergamum the type was the graceful seated
5
Athena, originated by Lysimachus, for whom Philetaerus had
181
governed Pergamum; this Athena became the prototype of
innumerable later Minervas, Romas and Britannias.

In Egypt Ptolemy I had presented himself to his subjects
17
wearing the aegis of Zeus, and on the reverses of his coins this
theme is developed by the use as his personal device of the
14
eagle of Zeus carrying a thunderbolt. This design became the
dynastic badge of the whole Ptolemaic dynasty, used both by
kings and queens ruling in their own right; it conveyed in
Greek symbolism the absolute power which the ruler of Egypt
traditionally wielded. Another equally expressive type was
22, 26, 32, 42
normally associated with Ptolemaic queens – a single or double
cornucopiae, filled with the fruits of the earth and bound with
a diadem. The message is that the fertility of Egypt is dependent
upon the fertility of the royal couple, as is made explicit in the
109
inscription accompanying a cornucopiae on a Syrian coin of
the Egyptian-born Cleopatra Thea – 'of Queen Cleopatra [who
is] divine fertility'.

Seleucid usage of reverse types was not essentially different
from that of the kingdoms already considered, though the long
history of the dynasty produced a number of variations. Apollo
was the divine protector of the dynasty, and Apollo, whether
55, 59
seated on the omphalos or standing, is the normal reverse type
for tetradrachms from Antiochus I until the first years of the
reign of Antiochus IV (175–164 BC). The only noteable devia-
tion was due to Achaeus who, though related to the Seleucid
house, was in revolt against Antiochus III; his opposition was
expressed by supplanting the traditional Apollo with a fighting
68
Athena. The precise significance of the choice is not clear, but
it may be a declaration that he favoured Macedonian rather
than native interests in the Seleucid empire. As with titulature,
so the first major change of reverse type by a legitimate
Seleucid king was due to Antiochus IV, who after his early
81
years replaced Apollo with a seated Zeus; a type which thereafter remained associated with the Seleucid dynasty and with

their capital city Antioch. The reason for the change may be two-fold. First the type recalled the reverse of Alexander the Great's tetradrachms which had continued to be minted and to circulate long after his death; and, second, an association with Zeus was perhaps intended to put Antiochus on an equal footing with his great enemy Ptolemy VI of Egypt, whose dynasty also had Zeus as its protector.

After Antiochus IV Seleucid reverse types became somewhat more varied, a change which reflects the confused politics of the day; rival branches of the royal family constantly fought for power with each other and with usurpers, and each faction claimed divine protection; mints were sometimes established at provincial centres such as Side or Mallus, where coins bore the cult-statue of the local divinity. In the fragmentary state of our knowledge the precise significance of some types, such as the Dioscuri of the young and short-lived Antiochus VI, must escape us, but all such variations from the standard dynastic types of Apollo or Zeus are evidence of a period of turmoil and conflicting interests.

104

100

Last of all we come to the reverses of the Greek kings of Bactria and India; here the historical record is so deficient that we can usually only guess at the factors which determined the choice of one deity or the other. Nevertheless it is clear that in principle each ruler chose a different reverse type from his predecessor; cases of the repetition of the same type by different rulers, either in succession or after an interval, must be attributed to kinship, genuine or assumed, or to an attempt at political association with a prestigious predecessor. Once again, and even more remarkably in this remote area, the iconography is purely Greek; native traits are almost wholly lacking, until a late date, when elements of the imported Greek culture became fused with native traditions.

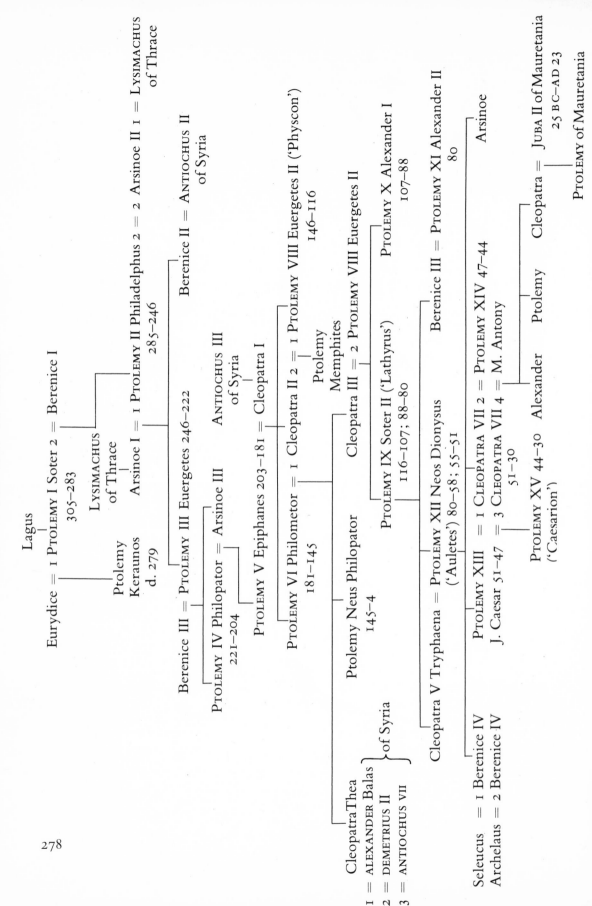

THE PTOLEMIES OF EGYPT

THE SELEUCIDS OF SYRIA

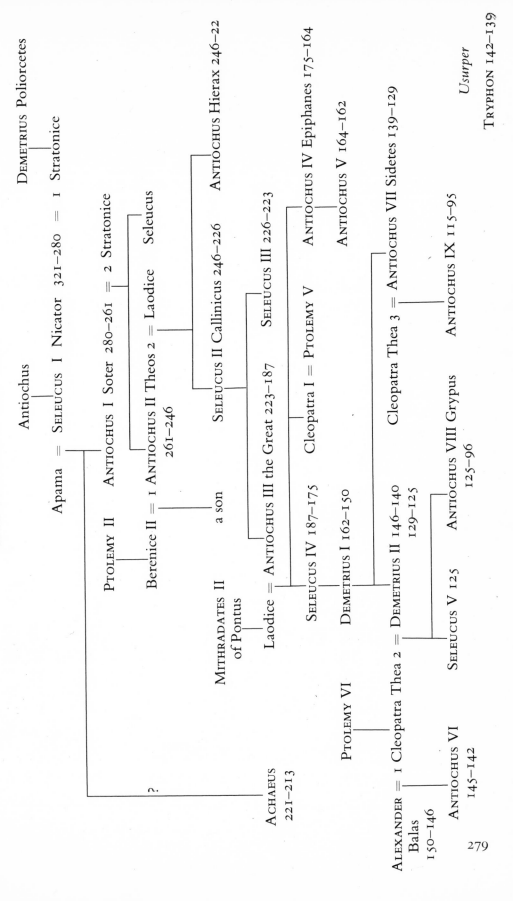

KINGS OF MACEDON

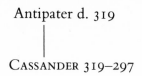

Antipater d. 319
|
CASSANDER 319–297

THE ANTIGONIDS of Macedon

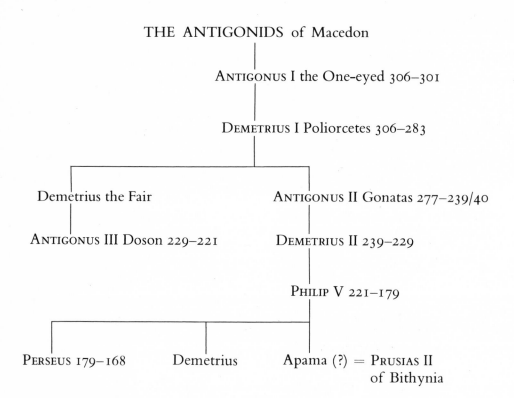

ANTIGONUS I the One-eyed 306–301
|
DEMETRIUS I Poliorcetes 306–283

Demetrius the Fair   ANTIGONUS II Gonatas 277–239/40

ANTIGONUS III Doson 229–221   DEMETRIUS II 239–229

PHILIP V 221–179

PERSEUS 179–168   Demetrius   Apama (?) = PRUSIAS II
                                                           of Bithynia

THE GREEK KINGS OF BACTRIA

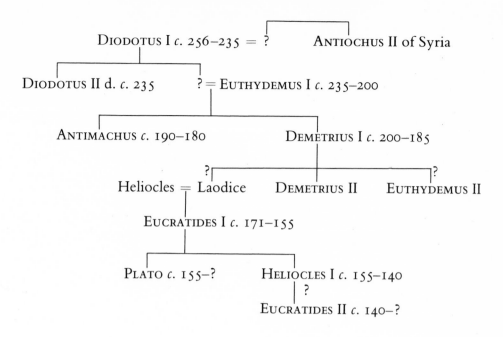

DIODOTUS I *c.* 256–235 = ?   ANTIOCHUS II of Syria

DIODOTUS II d. *c.* 235   ? = EUTHYDEMUS I *c.* 235–200

ANTIMACHUS *c.* 190–180   DEMETRIUS I *c.* 200–185

? Heliocles = Laodice   DEMETRIUS II   EUTHYDEMUS II ?

EUCRATIDES I *c.* 171–155

PLATO *c.* 155–?   HELIOCLES I *c.* 155–140
?
EUCRATIDES II *c.* 140–?

THE GREEK KINGS OF INDIA

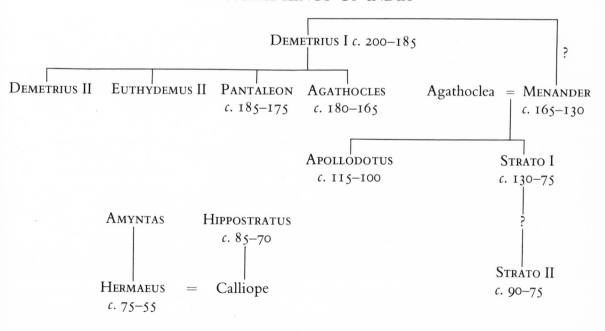

DEMETRIUS I *c.* 200–185   ?

DEMETRIUS II   EUTHYDEMUS II   PANTALEON   AGATHOCLES   Agathoclea = MENANDER
c. 185–175   *c.* 180–165   *c.* 165–130

APOLLODOTUS   STRATO I
c. 115–100   *c.* 130–75

AMYNTAS   HIPPOSTRATUS   ?
c. 85–70

HERMAEUS   =   Calliope   STRATO II
c. 75–55   *c.* 90–75

THE ATTALIDS OF PERGAMUM

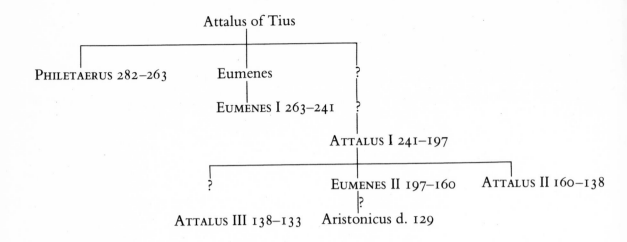

Attalus of Tius

PHILETAERUS 282–263　　Eumenes　　　　　?

EUMENES I 263–241　　?

ATTALUS I 241–197

?　　　　EUMENES II 197–160　　ATTALUS II 160–138

ATTALUS III 138–133　Aristonicus d. 129

THE KINGS OF BITHYNIA

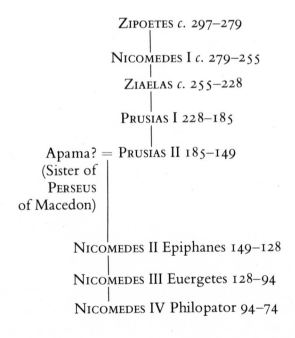

ZIPOETES c. 297–279

NICOMEDES I c. 279–255

ZIAELAS c. 255–228

PRUSIAS I 228–185

Apama? = PRUSIAS II 185–149
(Sister of
PERSEUS
of Macedon)

NICOMEDES II Epiphanes 149–128

NICOMEDES III Euergetes 128–94

NICOMEDES IV Philopator 94–74

THE KINGS OF PONTUS

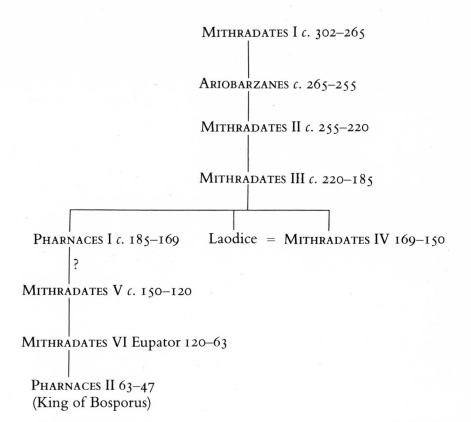

MITHRADATES I *c.* 302–265

ARIOBARZANES *c.* 265–255

MITHRADATES II *c.* 255–220

MITHRADATES III *c.* 220–185

PHARNACES I *c.* 185–169   Laodice = MITHRADATES IV 169–150

?

MITHRADATES V *c.* 150–120

MITHRADATES VI Eupator 120–63

PHARNACES II 63–47
(King of Bosporus)

Sources of Coins Illustrated

BM = British Museum (not published in *BMC*).
BMC = Catalogue of Greek Coins in the British Museum (followed by subtitle).
ND = Mr Norman Davis, Seattle, U.S.A.
ND followed by a number = H. A. Troxwell, *The Norman Davis Collection*, American Numismatic Society, New York, 1969.
PCG = A Guide to the Principal Coins of the Greeks, British Museum, 1932 and 1959 (all coins are in the British Museum).
All photographs are from the original coins and are by P. Frank Purvey unless otherwise stated.
All coins are silver tetradrachms unless noted otherwise.

On the cover, Lysimachus, AV stater, ND.		43	Ashmolean Museum, Oxford; AR denarius.
2–3	*PCG* pl. 29, 5.	44–5	ND.
4–5	ND 119.	48–9	*PCG* pl. 27, 11.
8–9	ND 326.	50–51	*BMC, Mysia* p. 114, no. 27.
11–12	*PCG* pl. 27, 4; AR decadrachm, Babylon (?).	54–5	*BMC, Seleucid Kings*, p. 9, no. 15?.
13–14	ND 328.		
15–16	ND 329; AV octadrachm.	56–7	*PCG* pl. 33, 12.
		58–9	ND 259.
21–2	ND 330; AV decadrachm.	63–4	ND.
		65–6	*BMC, Seleucid Kings*, p. 22, no. 3.
23–4	*PCG* pl. 34, 24; AV octadrachm.	67–8	Photo by courtesy of Professor M. Hirmer.
25–6	*BMC, The Ptolemies*, pl. XIII, 6; AR decadrachm.	72–3	ND 260.
29–30	ND 332.	74–5	*PCG* pl. 33, 13.
31–2	ND; AV octadrachm.	78–9	ND.
35–6	*PCG* pl. 34, 29; AV octadrachm.	80–81	*PCG* pl. 40, 20; AV stater, Antioch.
37–8	ND.	82–3	ND.
41–2	ND 336; AE.	87–8	ND 269.

89–90 ND 271.

93–4 ND.

95–6 Courtesy of Dr Albert A. Davis.

99–100 ND.

101–2 *PCG* pl. 41, 26.

103–4 ND 272.

108–9 *PCG* pl. 41, 29.

110–11 *PCG* pl. 41, 30.

112–13 ND 276.

117–18 ND 94.

119–20 Berlin; photo by Münz-kabinett, Staatliche Museen; courtesy of Dr H.-D. Schultz.

123–4 *PCG* pl. 35, 6.

125–6 ND 99.

129–30 ND 258.

131–2 ND 299.

135–6 ND 300.

137–8 BM.

139–40 *PCG* pl. 33, 20.

144–5 *PCG* pl. 41, 32.

146–7 BM.

150–51 ND 307.

152–3 *PCG* pl. 33, 17.

156–7 BM.

158–9 BM.

162–3 ND 315.

164–5 BM.

168–9 BM.

170–71 BM.

174–5 Khabul Museum; photo Josephine Powell; AR 20 drachma piece.

176–7 ND 322.

180–1 ND 199.

182–3 *BMC, Mysia*, pl. XXIV, 5.

186–7 Paris, de Luynes 2421; photo by Cabinet des Médailles.

188–9 ND 190.

192–3 ND 191.

194–5 ND 192.

198–9 *PCG* pl. 32, 1.

200–1 *PCG* pl. 39, 2.

204–5 Paris; photo by courtesy of Professor M. Hirmer.

207–8 *PCG* pl. 44, 2; photo from electrotype.

210–11 *PCG* pl. 40, 19.

Glossary

Aegis   An attribute of Zeus and Athena; usually worn by Athena as a short cloak, fringed with snakes, and supporting at the centre the head of the Gorgon, Medusa, which turned beholders to stone.

Agora   The civic centre of a Greek town; usually a four-sided area flanked by public buildings (= Roman *forum*).

Anabasis   An ascent, as from the coast to the interior of a country. Used by Xenophon as the title of his account of the march of the Greek mercenaries into the interior of Asia in 401–399 BC.

Chiliarch   Vizier; literally 'commander of 1000 men' because the Persian vizier commanded the royal guard of one thousand horsemen.

Cistophori   Large silver coins minted at a number of cities in western Asia Minor (including Pergamum and Ephesus) from the early second century BC until the reign of Hadrian. The name ('basket-bearers') is derived from their normal obverse type of a sacred snake emerging from a basket. They were valued at three Roman denarii.

Coele Syria   'Hollow Syria'; the territory to the east and south-east of the Anti-Lebanon range, in which the principal city was Damascus.

Consul   Two consuls, elected annually, were the civil and military heads of the Roman Republic; years were described officially by the names of the consuls in office.

Decadrachm   A coin weighing ten drachmae *(q.v.)*.

Diadem   A blue band with white spots worn by the King of Persia round the royal tiara; adopted by Alexander and his successors as an emblem of royal power.

Diadochi   'Successors'; applied especially to the associates of Alexander the Great who partitioned his empire.

286

Drachm(a) A unit of weight, varying from place to place; thence a silver coin weighing a drachma.

Gymnasium A sports ground with appropriate buildings; often the centre of associations formed to promote athletic or military training.

Kausia A broad-brimmed sun-hat, especially popular in northern Greece.

Kharoshti A North-west Indian script used on the reverses of Indo-Greek coins.

Legend The inscription on a coin.

Legion A Roman regiment numbering from 4000 to 6000 men.

Museum Originally a haunt of the Muses; then a place where the arts over which they presided were practised or studied. The Museum at Alexandria could be described as an institute of advanced study.

Nomes Administrative districts in Ptolemaic and later Egypt.

Pharos An island in the bay of Alexandria, on which the lighthouse was built; hence a lighthouse. (*cf.* French, phare.)

Pillars of Hercules Straits of Gibraltar. According to legend Hercules erected two pillars, one on each side of the Straits, at the extremities of Africa and Europe.

Polybius Born at Megalopolis in Arcadia, *c.* 203 BC. He had a political career in the Achaean League before being deported to Rome in 167 BC. There he gained the patronage of the Scipios and composed his history of the years 220–144 BC, the surviving books and excerpts of which form a primary source for the period. He died *c.* 120 BC.

Proconsul The Roman governor of a province or provinces; originally provinces were governed by consuls after their year of office in Rome, but with the increase in the number of provinces during the later Republic, proconsular power was extended to governors holding military commands who had never actually been consuls.

Propontis The Sea of Marmara, which precedes (Pro-) the Black Sea (Pontus).

Propraetor After holding office in Rome for a year, praetors took charge of minor provinces which usually had no military garrison; *cf.* Proconsul.

Publicani Usually tax-collectors, organized in a company which had bought the right to collect a particular

	tax. Drawn from the Roman equestrian order the publicani undertook other contract work such as the provisioning of armies or the working of mines.
Sacas	A Scythian people from Central Asia who over-ran Bactria and North-west India early in the first century BC.
Satrap	The governor of a province in the Persian Empire.
Soter	'Saviour'; an honorary title given to several Hellenistic rulers, especially to Ptolemy I by the Rhodians for help received during the seige of Rhodes by Demetrius Poliorcetes (p. 146).
Talent	A weight containing 6000 drachmae *(q.v.)*, but varying according to the weight of the basic drachma; one of the commonest was the talent on the Attic system, which weighed about 56 lbs.
Tetradrachm	A coin weighing four drachmae *(q.v.)*.
Triumph	A Roman victory parade involving much ancient ritual; the right to hold a triumph had to be granted by the Senate.
Type	The design on either face of a coin (obverse or reverse).
Yavanas	'Greeks'; an oriental term apparently derived from 'Ionian'.
Yuga Purana	A section, containing historical information, of a larger Indian work on astrology.
Zebina	'The bought one'; the nick-name of the Seleucid usurper, Alexander II (128–3 BC), implying a servile origin.
Zoroastrianism	The religion of the ancient Persians in which Ahuramazda, the god of light, opposes Ahriman, the god of darkness; it was based on the teaching of Zoroaster (= Persian Zarathustra), seventh to sixth centuries BC.

Bibliography

THE ANCIENT SOURCES

Of the works of some 1100 writers of the Hellenistic Age whose names are known, very few indeed survive in more than the briefest excerpts or quotations. Of contemporary historians only Polybius (*see* Glossary) survives in any quantity in his original form, and what does survive relates mainly to the affairs of Greece and Macedon. Many writers, however, of the Roman or the Byzantine periods prepared extensive summaries of works which have since perished, or used them as sources for their own compositions; the works of some of these later writers have survived until today. The most important among them are the following:

Arrian (second century AD) wrote a surviving history of Alexander based mainly on the narrative of Ptolemy Soter; of his other works only fragments have come down to us.

Diodorus (first century BC) wrote a history of the world up to his own day; his books on Alexander are preserved complete, but those on the Hellenistic Age are fragmentary.

Plutarch (*c.* AD 45–125), among many other works, wrote a surviving series of biographies of famous men; those of Alexander, Eumenes of Cardia, Demetrius Poliorcetes, Pyrrhus and T. Quinctius Flamininus, Julius Caesar and Mark Antony are particularly relevant to the period.

Pompeius Trogus (first century BC – first century AD) wrote a history of the world which survives only in an epitome by Justin (third century AD).

Quintus Curtius Rufus (first century AD) composed a surviving history of Alexander.

In the surviving sources the latter part of the period, when the Roman Republic was heavily involved, is far more fully recorded from the Roman side than is the earlier from the Greek side. Many hints and stray references have to be gathered from writings of all kinds such as the *Geography* of Strabo (*c.* 64 BC–AD 21).

Much strictly contemporary, though often fragmentary, evidence has been yielded by archaeology in the form of inscriptions on stone or bronze, papyrus documents (especially from Egypt), and coins.

GENERAL HISTORIES

CAMBRIDGE ANCIENT HISTORY
    Vol. VI: Macedon 401–301 BC. Cambridge 1927.
    Vol. VII: Hellenistic monarchies and the rise of Rome. Cambridge, 1928.
    Vol. VIII: Rome and the Mediterranean, 218–133 BC. Cambridge, 1930.
    Vol. IX: The Roman Republic, 133–44 BC. Cambridge, 1932.
    Vol. X: The Augustan Empire, 44 BC–AD 70. Cambridge, 1934.
Cary, M. *History of the Greek World, 323–146 BC*, London, 1963.
Grimal, P. (and others). *Hellenism and the Rise of Rome*. London, 1968.
Toynbee, A. J. *Hellenism. History of a Civilization*. Oxford, 1959.
Will, E. *Histoire politique du monde hellénistique* (2 vols). Nancy, 1966–7.

SPECIAL SUBJECTS

Bieber, M. *Alexander the Great in Greek and Roman Art*. Chicago, 1964.
— *The Sculpture of the Hellenistic Age*. New York, 1961.
Charbonneaux, J. (and others). *Hellenistic Art*. London, 1972.
Cook, J. M. *The Greeks in Ionia and the East*. London, 1962.
Griffith, G. T. *The Mercenaries of the Hellenistic World*. Cambridge, 1933.
Havelock, C. M. *Hellenistic Art*. London, 1971.
Levi, M. A. *Political power in the Ancient World*. New York, 1968.
Magie, D. *Roman Rule in Asia Minor*. Princeton, 1950.
Rostovtzeff, M. *The Social and Economic History of the Hellenistic World* (3 vols). Oxford, 1967.
Tarn, W. W. and Griffith, G. T. *Hellenistic Civilization*. 3rd ed. London, 1958.

CHAPTER ONE Alexander the Great.
Bamm, P. *Alexander the Great*. London, 1968.
Bury, J. B. *A History of Greece to the Death of Alexander the Great* (Ch. XVI–XVIII). 3rd ed. London, 1951.
Fuller, J. F. C. *The Generalship of Alexander the Great*. London, 1958.
Green, P. *Alexander the Great*. London, 1970.
Griffith, G. T. (ed.). *Alexander the Great: the main problems*. Cambridge, 1966. Studies reprinted from various sources.
Hammond, N. G. L. *A History of Greece to 322 BC* (Bk VI), Oxford, 1967.
Tarn, W. W. *Alexander the Great* (2 vols). Cambridge, 1948.
Wilcken, U. *Alexander the Great*. London, 1932.

CHAPTER TWO The Ptolemies.
Bevan, E. R. *History of Egypt under the Ptolemaic Dynasty*. London, 1927.

Mahaffy, J. P. *A History of Egypt, vol. IV: Ptolemaic Dynasty*. London, 1899.
— *The Empire of the Ptolemies*. London, 1895.

CHAPTER THREE Seleucids of Syria.
Bevan, E. R. *The House of Seleucus*. London, 1902.
Mørkholm, O. *Antiochus IV of Syria*. Copenhagen, 1966.

CHAPTER FOUR The Antigonids of Macedon.
Tarn, W. W. *Antigonus Gonatas*. Cambridge, 1913.
Walbank, F. W. *Philip V of Macedon*. Cambridge, 1940.

CHAPTER FIVE The Greek Kings of Bactria and India.
Narain, A. K. *The Indo-Greeks*. Oxford, 1957.
Tarn, W. W. *The Greeks in Bactria and India*, 2nd ed. Cambridge, 1951.
Wheeler, Sir Mortimer. *Flames over Persepolis*. London, 1968.

CHAPTER SIX The Kingdoms of Pergamum, Bithynia and Pontus.
Hansen, E. V. *The Attalids of Pergamum*. Ithaca, New York, 1947.
McShane, R. B. *The Foreign Policy of the Attalids of Pergamum*. Urbana, 1964.

CHAPTER SEVEN The Coins of the Hellenistic Kingdoms.
Mørkholm, O. *Studies in the Coinage of Antiochus IV of Syria*. Copenhagen, 1963.
Newell, E. T. *The Coinage of Demetrius Poliorcetes*. Oxford, 1927.
— *The Coinage of the Eastern Seleucid mints: Seleucus I–Antiochus III*. New York, 1939.
— *The Coinage of the Western Seleucid mints: Seleucus I–Antiochus III*. New York, 1941.
— *Royal Greek Portrait Coins*. New York, 1937.
Seltman, C. T. *Greek Coins* (Ch. XII–XV). London, 1955.

Index

Principal references in heavy type; references to illustrations in italics.
P = enlarged portrait f. = father k. = king m. = mother s. = son w. = wife.

Lysimachus, k. of Thrace 138 f., **144** ff., 156, 186 ff., 223, 250 f., 272 f.

Maccabees, Book of 164, 210 f.
Macedonia 19, 28, **221** ff.
Magas, brother of Ptolemy IV 161 f.
Magas, k. of Cyrene 151, 158 f.
Magnesia, Battle of **202** f., 254
Mark Antony *see* Antony
Masson, C. 231
Mazaeus 23 ff.
Media 140, 145, 160, 194, 196 f., 213
Megasthenes 186, 243, 246
Meleager 139
Melinda-panha 231, 245
Memphis 22, 141 ff., 166 f., 207
Menander, king 231, **245** ff.; *162–3, 164–5, 166 (P), 167 (P)*
Menander, satrap 139
Menelaus, brother of Ptolemy I 145 f.
Menelaus, High Priest 210
Miletus 19, 157
Mithradates I, of Parthia 216, 238
Mithradates I, of Pontus 265 f.
Mithradates II, k. of Pontus 192, 195
Mithradates III, k. of Pontus **266**; *198–9, 202 (P)*
Mithradates IV, k. of Pontus 267; *204–5, 206 (P)*
Mithradates VI, k. of Pontus 170, 220, 263, **267** ff.; *207–8, 209 (P)*
Molon 194 ff.
Myriandrus 27

Naucratis 23, 140 f., 206
Nearchus 29
Nicaea 259
Nicomedes I 190, **258**; *186–7, 190 (P)*
Nicomedes II, Epiphanes **261** f.; *194–5, 197 (P)*
Nicomedes III, Euergetes **262** f.
Nicomedes IV, Epiphanes Philopator **263** f.
Nicomedia 258, 260 ff., 264
Nomes of Egypt 149

Octavia 175, 177, 180
Octavian 14, **174** ff.
Olympias, 146, 221
Ophellas 143
Orophernes 256; *210–1, 212 (P)*

Palestine 160, 162, 164, 176, 191, 194
Pamphylia 139

Panion, Battle of 165
Pantaleon **244** f.; *156–7, 160 (P)*
Paphlagonia 140
Parchment 255
Parium 147
Parmenio 16, 21 f., 26, 28
Paropamisadae 236, 238, 248
Parthia 31, 160, 176, 184, 194, **196** f., 216 ff., 234, 239
Pataliputra 231, 242 f., 246 f.
Peithon, satrap of India 241
Peithon, satrap of Media 140, 143, 184
Pella 26, 140, 275
Pelusium 146, 162, 165, 172 f., 206 f., 218
Perdiccas **137** ff., 181 f.
Pergamentum *see* Parchment
Pergamum 11 ff., 31, 147, 188, 190, 200, 205, **250** ff.; Library of 255
Persepolis 26 f.
Perseus **227** ff., 255, 261, 272, 275; *125–6, 128 (P)*
Phalanx 16 f., 201 f.
Pharnaces I. k. of Pontus **266** f.; *200–1, 203 (P)*
Pharsalus, Battle of 173, 178
Philetaerus 147, 188, **250** ff., 272; *180–1, 184 (P)*
Philip II of Macedon 10, 16, 27, 141
Philip III, Arrhidaeus 139, 146, 221
Philip V 165, 199 ff., **226** f., 253 f., 258 f., 271, 275; *123–4, 127 (P)*
Philippi, Battle of 174, 178
Philotas 28, 139
Phoenicia 18, 20 ff., 145, 147, 157, 162
Phrastes II 217
Phrygia, Hellespontine 139
Phrygia, Major 138 f., 147 f., 193
Physcon *see* Ptolemy VIII
Piraeus 145
Plato, s. of Eucratides 238 f.
Polybius 165, 167, 195, 213, 235 f., 261
Polycrates of Argos 166
Polyxenidas 202
Pompeii, House of Faun at 21
Pompey, Sextus 14
Pompey, the Great 173, 176, 220, 269
Pontus **264** ff.
Popilius Laenas, C. 207 f.
Porus 29, 181, 240 f.
Pothinus 172 f.
Priene 256, 262
Prinsep, J. 231